Vietnam at a Crossroads

DIRECTIONS IN DEVELOPMENT
Trade

Vietnam at a Crossroads

Engaging in the Next Generation of Global Value Chains

Claire H. Hollweg, Tanya Smith, and Daria Taglioni, Editors

WORLD BANK GROUP

Contents

Boxes

Figures

Tables

Preface

Vietnam is at a crossroads. Fragmentation of production across increasingly complex global value chains (GVCs) will continue to create both opportunities and challenges. The domestic policies that Vietnam enacts in the near future will determine whether it will be pushed further toward its current specialization of low value-added assembly functions—or whether it will manage to leverage the current wave of growth to diversify and capture higher value-added functions in GVCs. This upper development path will require Vietnam to address a large and complex supply-side agenda by sequencing carefully the next wave of reforms.

So we ask the question: Which economic policies and investment priorities will allow Vietnam to situate itself firmly on the path toward higher income status, as the economy matures toward 2035? And can further integration in networks of global production—GVCs—support such a goal?

Purpose, Genesis, and Structure of This Volume

With this in mind, the purpose of this volume is to support Vietnam's path to economic prosperity by identifying policies and targeted interventions that will drive development through leveraging GVC participation and that will take major shifts in trade policy and rapid technological advances in ICT into account. Vietnam is, itself, experiencing an unprecedented wave of structural change and industrialization, and is entering a phase of compressed development. Young people are moving from the countryside to urban areas, out of agriculture and into industry and services, with foreign investment driving employment in manufacturing. Readers will gain a strong understanding of Vietnam's current and potential engagement with GVCs—and will learn about strategic GVC policy tools that can help developing countries achieve economic prosperity in the context of compressed development.

The volume is based on a compilation of studies completed by World Bank staff and external consultants in 2015 supporting the "Enabling Economic Modernization and Private Sector Development" chapter of the *Vietnam 2035* report. The objective of these studies was to diagnose Vietnam's current participation in GVCs, visualize where Vietnam could be by 2035 in the context of a changing global environment, and identify the policy actions needed to get there. The studies also supported topics related more broadly to export competitiveness, including firm-level productivity, services, and connectivity. The findings touch on many of the transformations identified within *Vietnam 2035*.

These studies produced a depth of background material and new knowledge across a range of areas related to GVC participation in Vietnam and offer key insights relevant to other countries as well. In this volume, we distill key take-aways from each study, deploy a unified framework to assess challenges confronted, solutions proposed, lessons learned, and the potential for replication in other countries. We also focus on key required outcomes, drivers, and enablers, along with barriers, threats, and challenges.

How This Volume Informs Vietnam's Policy Options

The chapters in this volume concur that Vietnam is involved in GVCs but at the lower end of value-added activities. In an environment of compressed development where high growth is associated with rapid structural transformation and industrialization of the domestic economy, this position in the value chain presents major challenges for the country in transforming economic growth into sustained economic prosperity. Given that Vietnam is experiencing a wave of structural change and industrialization unprecedented in its history, and due to the extensive and deep network of trade agreements that it is negotiating with international trade heavyweights, it has opportunities that may support its ambitions to put itself on the path toward higher-income status. Yet the current era—characterized by fast, digital-technology changes and internationally fragmented production—poses risks that Vietnam needs to address, urgently.

Overview

Chapter 1 explores Vietnam's export competitiveness and the role played by integration into GVCs. It shows that Vietnam's gains in export competitiveness were entirely driven by supply-side improvements in export performance. Its exports remain highly regionalized in Asia and its export performance is constrained by the export product mix, which remains at the low value-added end. Vietnam's challenge is to make GVCs more inclusive by moving up the value chain into higher value-added functions. But the policies that have enabled it to grow as an export platform may also challenge further diversification, while cross-cutting bottlenecks on the supply side could inhibit this shift. Targeted actions should prioritize the following areas: low-productivity growth, inadequate skills, few backward linkages to domestic suppliers, infrastructure gaps, and other sector-specific constraints.

Part 1: Cross-Cutting Determinants of GVC Participation

This part delves deeper into the analysis of the priority targeted actions identified in the Overview.

Chapter 2 looks at the determinants of firm dynamics, jobs flows, and productivity growth. Productivity growth, which has been on a broad-based, long-term declining trend, requires greater attention, as productivity and innovation eventually will have to become the main drivers of growth. The government will need to prioritize reforms with more immediate payoffs, such as strengthening the microeconomic foundations of the market economy. The main challenge is to level the playing field for domestic, foreign, and state-owned firms.

Chapter 3 considers the role of services in upgrading in GVCs. Indeed, services sector provision inevitably will form a large part of building a competitive private sector in Vietnam as inputs into manufacturing, agriculture, and other services. In relative terms, Vietnam's exports in GVC-intensive sectors rely less on domestic services inputs for their exports than in comparator countries and in the economy at large. Enhancing the competitiveness of the services sector involves creating an enabling regulatory environment for service providers; targeting supply-side factors including human capital, technical skills, and infrastructure; and leveraging trade agreements to enable the economy to become a regional supplier of modern services such as ICT, while ensuring greater access to low-cost services from abroad.

Chapters 4 and 5 move on to look at Vietnam's connectivity to global markets—for goods, services, capital, and people, and the role of logistics and the related institutional environment. Chapter 4 considers Vietnam's performance in connectivity metrics, and argues for rapid and comprehensive upgrading as Vietnam transitions to higher per capita income levels. It suggests the following steps be taken: closing the infrastructure gap; developing competitive services markets in backbone sectors; streamlining border procedures and making them more transparent and predictable; and leveraging existing trade initiatives.

Chapter 5 measures and analyzes Vietnam's connectivity logistics from a macro perspective. It presents possible scenarios stemming from the impact of the Association of Southeast Asian Nations (ASEAN) Economic Community and the impact of national logistics infrastructure and facilitation projects by 2030. Current logistics, particularly those facilitating connectivity, must be improved if economic growth is to be sustained. The supporting institutional environment establishing rules and logistics regulations must also be updated.

Chapter 6 discusses how preferential trade agreements (PTAs) both drive market access for domestic firms and present challenges to GVC participation and upgrading. Complex standards and rules of origin make it difficult for many domestic firms to take advantage of preferential market access. Moreover, it is unclear whether the agreements lock in the status quo—that is, foster Vietnam's current comparative advantage in production stages associated with low value added—or promote a dynamic transition to more sophisticated tasks. The chapter calls for leveraging available policy instruments in support of upgrading, and for raising awareness of PTAs in Vietnam and of the associated capacity for engagement.

Part 2: In-Depth Studies of GVC-Intensive Sectors

This part presents six sector-specific chapters. Each identifies key features of the GVCs, examines Vietnam's current and potential roles, and provides policy recommendations for each sector (and major subsector, where appropriate) to facilitate greater integration and upgrading.

The main thrust of chapter 7 is that Vietnam specializes in low-value, labor-intensive assembly in textiles and apparel. Policymakers should prioritize sectoral upgrading by leveraging the combination of low labor costs, access to backward linkages, and preferential access to large and wealthy consumer markets in Japan, the EU, and North America. Simultaneously, Vietnam should reduce workforce gaps.

Chapter 8 argues that land reform, mechanization of operations, better logistics, and moves to higher value-added products and processing are policy priorities if agriculture and agribusiness are to realize their full potential in the next 20 years. Advances will require investment in skills and capital to help agribusiness overcome constraints in the domestic market and stimulate increases in productivity and value-added growth.

The ICT sector—a key services input for the whole economy—is discussed in chapters 9 and 10. Chapter 9 makes the case that, while emphasis in Vietnam's policymaking primarily is on the information and communication technology (ICT) hardware industry, the software sector holds more promise and warrants more attention. Policy focus should be on developing a domestic supplier base and in supporting an accelerated shift from ICT manufacturing towards software and services. In addition, state investments in telecommunications infrastructure are needed to ensure high-speed bandwidth and uninterrupted ICT connectivity. Finally, the chapter suggests that the government should move to better use the skills, experience, and connections of overseas Vietnamese and returnees.

Chapter 10 looks at the quality of regulation and institutions as one of the main components for developing the services sector, reviewing those services with the greatest potential for helping upgrade the ICT industry. It points to horizontal and vertical regulatory and institutional measures that can support expansion of the services sector. The main policy recommendations focus on mandatory procedures for domestic and foreign firms, such as company registration and licensing; greater capacity and transparency, and removal of caps to foreign participation in the telecoms sector; implementation of the ASEAN Mutual Recognition Arrangements for professional services; and the government's promotion of removing the remaining formal restrictions to trade and investment in services between ASEAN partners.

The automotive sector is reviewed in chapters 11 and 12. The two chapters are complementary. The auto industry in Vietnam is small and underdeveloped by regional standards and dominated by motorcycle production and by the car assembly segment of imported parts and components. On the demand side, a shift in thinking is needed, from mobility of vehicles to mobility of people. The government should consider investing more heavily in road infrastructure and public transport to create a networked, multimodal system of mobility. On the supply side, Vietnam faces severe fragmentation and chronic overcapacity. Automakers should be encouraged to share suppliers whenever possible, to achieve minimum efficient scale and cost competitiveness that can begin to boost export growth, as is already happening in motorcycles.

Part 3: Operationalizing the GVC Agenda for Vietnam

Drawn from the preceding material, part 3 identifies the following interrelated priorities for Vietnam's GVC agenda: foster the domestic private sector in GVCs by improving the drivers of investment and by leveling the playing field; strengthen Vietnam's GVC integration and economic upgrading by promoting servicification, and by shifting the goals of industrial policy toward focusing on higher-value specialization within GVCs; facilitate GVC participation in sustainable development by promoting social upgrading and cohesion through skills development; focus on building domestic capacity, supported by quality regulations and institutions, particularly in the higher value-added sectors of ICT and services; and close the connectivity gap with peer countries in hard and soft infrastructure.

These responses are urged on the understanding that Vietnam is a compressed developer, where rapid structural changes and industrialization can swiftly undermine the sustainability of economic growth. The World Bank and the government of Vietnam should jointly pursue strategies for economic upgrading, supported by regulatory and connectivity improvements. This ambitious agenda requires a solid package of horizontal reforms as well as vertical initiatives in specific sectors. Moreover, actions are not to be implemented in isolation. Success can be achieved only by a comprehensive agenda that cuts across the many dimensions discussed. These strategies will require focused commitment by both parties over many years to refine, operationalize, and monitor Vietnam's GVC development, as they reinforce the national sustainable development agenda articulated in Vietnam 2035.

Acknowledgments

Vietnam at a Crossroads: Engaging in the Next Generation of Global Value Chains is a product of the World Bank Group's Trade and Competition Unit of the Trade and Competitiveness Global Practice. Edited by Claire H. Hollweg, Tanya Smith, and Daria Taglioni, it is based on a compilation of background studies completed by World Bank staff and external consultants in 2015 supporting the "Enabling Economic Modernization and Private Sector Development" chapter of the World Bank report, *Vietnam 2035: Toward Prosperity, Creativity, Equity, and Democracy.*

The editors would like to thank Mona Haddad and Sandeep Mahajan for continual guidance throughout the development of the background studies, and in particular for helping to pinpoint the most pressing topics around global value chains in Vietnam. We would also like to thank Viet Anh Nguyen, Duc Minh Pham, Lien Anh Pham, Van Hoang Pham, and Linh Anh Thi Vu for supporting the contributing authors during field visits in Vietnam. We are grateful to Communications Development Incorporated, led by Bruce Ross-Larson and Mike Crumplar, for editing the book, and to Cindy Fisher and Jewel McFadden from the World Bank's Publishing Program for overseeing publication and dissemination. The background studies and the book would not have been possible without the financial support of the Vietnam 2035 project as well as the Multi-Donor Trust Fund for Trade and Development. Finally, we acknowledge the collaborative effort of a large team of people who supported and helped deliver the background studies, but we leave these acknowledgements to the contributing authors' respective chapters.

About the Editors

Claire H. Hollweg is an economist with the Trade and Competitiveness Global Practice of the World Bank Group. She holds a PhD and an MA in economics from the University of Adelaide. Prior to studying economics, she worked as a journalist in newspaper and radio, and she holds a BS in journalism from the University of Colorado at Boulder. She also has work experience with the government of South Australia and the Pacific Economic Cooperation Council in Singapore. Her research interests include development economics with a recent focus on the nexus between trade, labor markets, servicification of manufacturing, and upgrading in global value chains.

Tanya Smith is a consultant with the Trade and Competitiveness Global Practice of the World Bank Group. She holds a MSc in development studies from the London School of Economics and a BAH in international development from the University of Guelph. She has work experience with the United Nations Development Program, Aboriginal and federal governments, and the private sector. She specializes in development economics with a focus on disaster/climate risk management and social protection.

Daria Taglioni is a lead economist with the Trade and Competitiveness Global Practice of the World Bank Group and the Global Solutions Lead for Global Value Chains. Her experience in economic policy analysis covers issues of trade, international competitiveness, globalization, and the links between financial markets and trade. Prior to joining the World Bank Group, Daria worked at the European Central Bank and the Organisation for Economic Cooperation and Development. She holds a PhD in International Economics from the Graduate Institute, Geneva.

Contributing Authors

Guillermo Carlos Arenas, Economist, World Bank Group

Reyes Aterido, Economist, World Bank Group

Ruth Banomyong, Associate Professor, Thammasat Business School

Axel Berger, Political Scientist, German Development Institute/Deutsches Institut für Entwicklungspolitik (DIE)

Dominique Bruhn, Economist, German Development Institute/Deutsches Institut für Entwicklungspolitik (DIE)

Stacey Frederick, Research Scientist, Duke University Center on Globalization, Governance and Competitiveness

Mary Hallward-Driemeier, Senior Economic Advisor, World Bank Group

Miles McKenna, Analyst, World Bank Group

Martín Molinuevo, Senior Private Sector Specialist, World Bank Group

Richard Record, Senior Economist, World Bank Group

Ben Shepherd, Principal of Developing Trade Consultants Ltd.

Tim Sturgeon, Senior Research Affiliate, MIT Industrial Performance Center

Ezequiel Zylberberg, Doctoral Candidate, University of Oxford

Abbreviations

AFTA	ASEAN Free Trade Area
APEC	Asia-Pacific Economic Cooperation
ARP	Agricultural Restructuring Plan
ASEAN	Association of Southeast Asian Nations
BPO	business process outsourcing
CAGR	compound annual growth rate
CGE	computable general equilibrium
CMT	cut-make-trim
DIE	German Development Institute/Deutsches Institut für Entwicklungspolitik
DWT	deadweight tonnage
EU	European Union
EVFTA	European Union–Vietnam Free Trade Agreement
FDI	foreign direct investment
FOB	free on board
FPT	Financing and Promoting Technology Corporation
FTA	free trade agreement
GAP	good agricultural practice
GDP	gross domestic product
GHG	greenhouse gas
GVC	global value chain
ICD	inland clearance depot
ICT	information and communications technology
IPR	intellectual property right
ISIC	International Standard Industrial Classification
IT	information technology
ITS	intelligent transportation system
LPI	Logistics Performance Index
MARD	Ministry of Agriculture and Rural Development

MIC	Ministry of Information Communication
MNC	multinational corporation
MRA	mutual recognition agreement
NAFTA	North American Free Trade Agreement
ODM	original design manufacturing
PTA	preferential trade agreement
R&D	research and development
RCEP	Regional Comprehensive Economic Partnership
RTPI	real-time passenger information
SME	small and medium enterprise
SOE	state-owned enterprise
SPS	sanitary and phytosanitary standards
STRI	Services Trade Restrictiveness Index
SVMC	Samsung Vietnam Mobile R&D Center
TiVA	Trade in Value Added
TPP	Trans-Pacific Partnership
TTIP	Transatlantic Trade and Investment Partnership
VAT	value-added tax
VICT	Vietnam International Container Terminal
VINASA	Vietnam Software Association
VNPT	Vietnam Posts and Telecommunications Group
WTO	World Trade Organization

CHAPTER 1

Overview

Claire H. Hollweg, Tim Sturgeon, and Daria Taglioni

Key Takeaways

Vietnam's consistent policy of openness to trade and investment paved the way for significant gains in export competitiveness. Trade grew on the backbone of global value chains (GVCs), and Vietnam has emerged as an Asian manufacturing powerhouse (Nakamura 2016) specializing in assembly functions by primarily foreign firms. Exporting—and importing inputs for exporting—has enabled Vietnam to grow its own domestic value added embodied in gross exports, by 16.6 percent annually between 1995 and 2011, just below what had been achieved by China. A closer look at sectoral heterogeneity reveals the remarkable performance in automotive, electronics, agribusiness, and textiles and apparel. The economy has benefited from its export-oriented development strategy, where export opportunities created jobs and propelled economic growth and poverty reduction.

Current and future trends of the global economy will shape the evolution of Vietnam's export competitiveness. The system of preferential trade agreements (PTAs) signed by Vietnam promises a surge in exports due to preferential access to major markets and their consumers. Trade agreements with the EU and Japan and other megaregional trade agreements could either allow Vietnam to continue its growth as an export platform, pushing it further toward its specialization of low value-added assembly functions, or such agreements will enable Vietnam to leverage the current wave of growth to climb the value chain into higher value-added functions. However, additional diversification and capture of higher value-added products and activities will require Vietnam to address a large supply-side agenda by sequencing the next wave of reforms for productivity growth, greater competition, and enhanced efficiency.

Challenges Confronted

Vietnam's gains in export competitiveness were entirely driven by supply-side improvements in export performance that included capital deepening through foreign direct investment (FDI) flows and structural transformation from agriculture to manufacturing. The economy remains constrained by the geographic structure of its trading partners and its product mix. Sourcing and selling patterns in GVCs are highly concentrated among regional trading partners. Where connected to GVCs, Vietnam is generally carrying out the lowest technology step of production. It has become an assembly platform, specializing in final production stages, including information and communications technology (ICT) hardware and textiles and apparel; inputs that Vietnam creates and sells to other countries tend to be low value-added.

Vietnam's challenge is to make GVCs more inclusive by moving up the value chain into higher value-added functions. Yet it faces challenges and bottlenecks in the domestic economy that could block this transformation, such as declining productivity growth, for example. The policies that have allowed Vietnam to grow as an export platform may also challenge diversification. For example strong investment promotion in a domestic competition environment where foreign-owned private firms have distinct advantages over other ownership groups may make it difficult for the domestic private sector to participate in GVCs. Additional challenges include cross-cutting issues—such as low productivity growth, inadequate skills, few backward linkages to domestic suppliers, and infrastructure gaps—as well as other sector-specific constraints.

Solutions Proposed

Vietnam is at a crossroads. It can grow as an export platform for GVCs, specializing in low value-added assembly functions with industrialization occurring in enclaves with little connection to the broader economy or society; or it can leverage the current wave of growth, enabled and accelerated by its successful participation in GVCs, to diversify and move up the chain into higher value-added functions. Even more ambitious—and more challenging—is to grasp the opportunity to nurture a nascent set of dynamic, innovative, and autonomous domestic firms that can drive the country toward long-term success in local, regional, and global markets with their own "invented in Vietnam" products. Success in both these areas will require Vietnam's policymakers to view the processes of development differently, and to take new realities of the global economy more fully into account.

There is urgency to these interventions for three reasons. First, Vietnam likely will undergo structural change regardless of which path its policymakers choose. Second, the window of opportunity for Vietnam in labor-intensive manufacturing could be brief. A scenario where waves of low-cost assembly jobs flow into and then out of Vietnam, leaving masses of newly urbanized workers without employment, could be a very dark one for the country. Third, the rapid pace of global technological change poses challenges to countries unprepared to adapt quickly. Perhaps 70–80 percent of the productivity gap between developed and emerging economies can be explained by the lag in transitioning to technology-led changes from previous economic restructuring processes (Comin and Mestieri 2013).

Thousands of new manufacturing jobs are created each week as the country emerges as the first sourcing alternative to China—sometimes referred to in GVCs as the China+1 strategy—especially for the assembly of smartphones, apparel, and footwear for export. While the country is poised to grow rapidly in this manner, it faces challenges and bottlenecks to sustainable growth that require both general improvement in Vietnam's infrastructure and other cross-cutting (horizontal) policies and some sector-specific (vertical) measures.

Vietnam needs a new approach to competitiveness, which must reflect the realities of current and future trends of the global economy, most notably the continuing proliferation of GVCs; deeper international economic integration, primarily through megaregional trade agreements; and fast technological change, particularly in ICT.

Institutions and policies that successful countries have used to encourage this upgrading are identified through econometric analysis to find key priority areas for Vietnam. The objective is to facilitate domestic firms' entry into GVCs; stimulate economic upgrading and diversification; strengthen domestic firms' absorptive capacity; and promote social upgrading and cohesion.

Commitments under major international trade agreements, the Trans-Pacific Partnership (TPP) in particular, offer an opportunity to carry out many demanding and politically sensitive reforms. Although the TPP will not enter into force in its current form due to the withdrawal of the United States from the agreement in January 2017, much of the reform agenda set out in the TPP will still need to be implemented by Vietnam. Ultimately, Vietnam can leverage these commitments to operationalize its GVC agenda.

Current Conditions and Challenges

Vietnam's consistent policy of openness and export-led growth has paid off. Economic reforms undertaken since the 1990s and culminating in its 2007 accession to the World Trade Organization (WTO) enabled the country to follow the path of other East Asian economies and to leverage trade and FDI for economic growth and poverty reduction. Vietnam experienced large inflows of FDI, and as a share of gross domestic product (GDP), exports are more than twice the predicted potential for the country's income level. At nearly 180 percent, Vietnam has among the highest trade-to-GDP ratios and has become one of the most open economies in the world.

Vietnam's export performance has outperformed world export growth consistently over the past decade, demonstrating increased export competitiveness. The economy has made gains in global export market shares (a commonly accepted measure of competitiveness), as indicated by the blue bars (or the area between the orange and green lines) in figure 1.1, except for limited periods after the global trade collapse and later liquidity crisis. Between 2006 and 2014, Vietnam's global export market share grew at an annual rate of 9.8 percent, exemplifying the country's dynamism.

Trade developed on the backbone of GVCs, allowing Vietnam to grow its own domestic value added through exports. Vietnam has shown higher integration in GVCs as a buyer and seller since 1995. This is best exemplified by the concept of importing to export, where one country exports goods or services that are incorporated in the exports of another country. Measures of importing to export consider that much of a country's exports consist of value that was added in

Figure 1.1 Export Growth and Export Market Shares, Vietnam, 2005–14

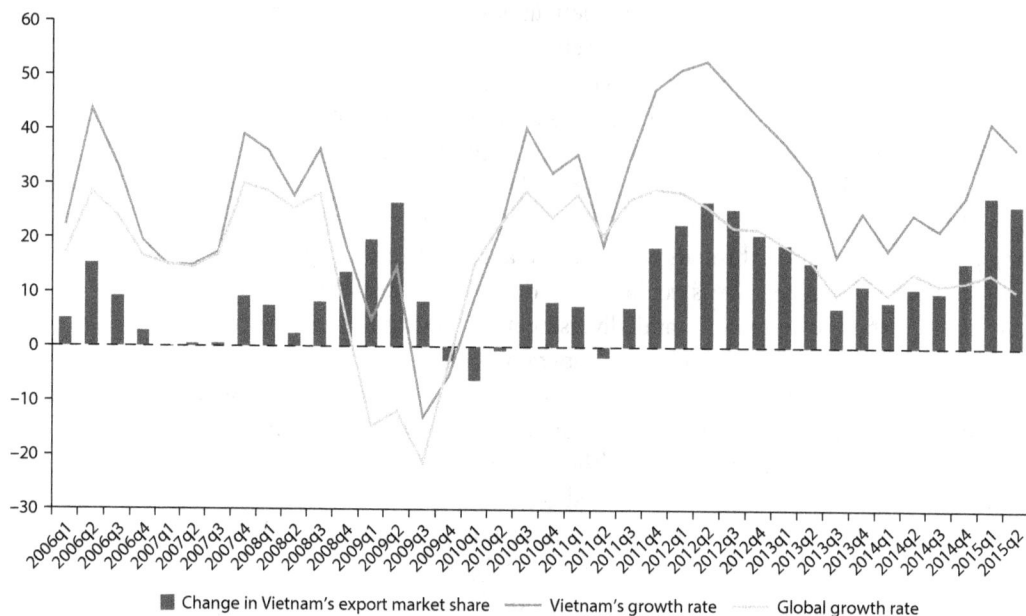

■ Change in Vietnam's export market share ——— Vietnam's growth rate ········ Global growth rate

Source: World Bank Measuring Export Competitiveness database.

another country—from a buyer or seller perspective. Foreign value added embodied in Vietnam's gross exports as a share of gross exports increased from 20.9 percent to 36.3 percent between 1995 and 2011, while Vietnam's domestic value added embodied in gross exports of third countries increased from 13.1 percent to 16.0 percent between 1995 and 2011.

Though expansion has been smaller as a seller, this has allowed Vietnam to rapidly grow its own domestic value added. Growth in domestic value added embodied in gross exports increased annually by 16.6 percent between 1995 and 2011. Put in perspective, this was slightly below China (17.9 percent) and significantly above that in other East and Southeast Asian economies such as the Republic of Korea; Malaysia; Singapore; Taiwan, China; and Thailand.

Pull factors, which include geographic structure and product/sector specialization of Vietnam's exports, have contributed negatively to the country's export growth. Figure 1.2 illustrates the channels through which export growth is stimulated. It decomposes the source of Vietnam's export growth (measured as changes in global export market shares) into geography, product mix, and the supply side to understand the role of demand-side pull factors versus push factors. The slowdown in demand from Vietnam's trading partners and changes in world prices of its export products, which grew less than the world average, have exerted negative pull effects on Vietnam's exports. Vietnam's gain in export market shares would have been equal to more than 11.6 percent annually, on average, if the country had a geographic and sectoral specialization equal to the world average.

Figure 1.2 Decomposing Export Market Shares, Vietnam, 2005–14

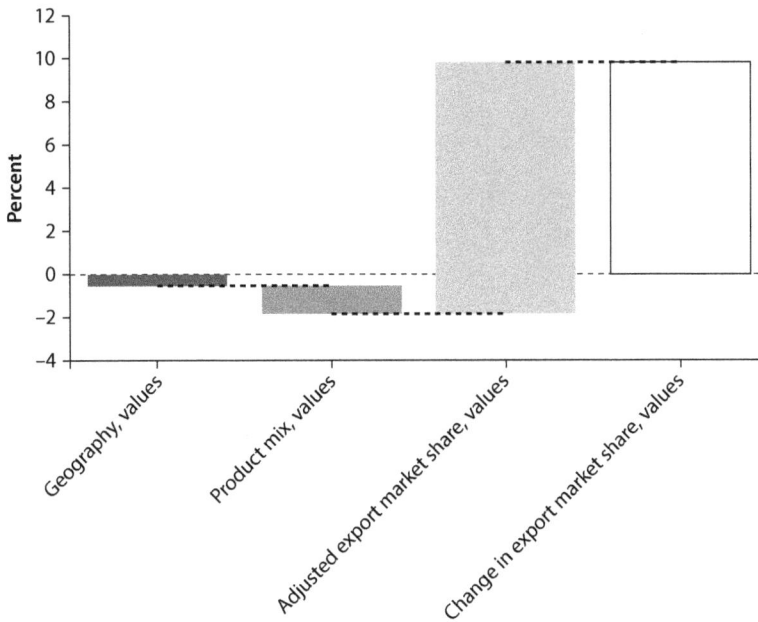

Source: Kummritz et al. 2016.

These gains have been entirely driven by push factors, which include improvements in productivity and accumulation of factors of production.

Vietnam's supply-side performance was driven by accumulated factors of production, including capital and labor. As highlighted in chapter 2, growth was driven by structural transformation out of agriculture and into services and manufactruing, and by capital deepening, including foreign investments, rather than by total factor productivity. Exports created jobs, directly and indirectly, and the labor value added contained in Vietnam's exports increased after 1995 (figure 1.3). This includes the wages paid to directly produce exports, as well as wages paid for domestic inputs of exports. In 2004 (latest data available), 45 percent of jobs were supported by exports. Yet thousands of new manufacturing jobs are being created each week as Vietnam continues to grow as a manufacturing powerhouse.

Markets

Current and future trends of the global economy will have an important role in shaping the evolution of Vietnam's economic growth and its ability to leverage GVCs for economic development. Vietnam has gained much from external trade, even though the pull effect that Vietnam's trading partners exerted on its exports has been small and negative, offsetting gains in world market shares by 0.5 percent (see figure 1.2). Market access however is expected to become more important in Vietnam's export competitiveness, with growth prospects of GVC exports by geographic pull underpinned in part by the ongoing shift toward deep,

Figure 1.3 Direct and Total Labor Value Added of Exports, 1995–2011

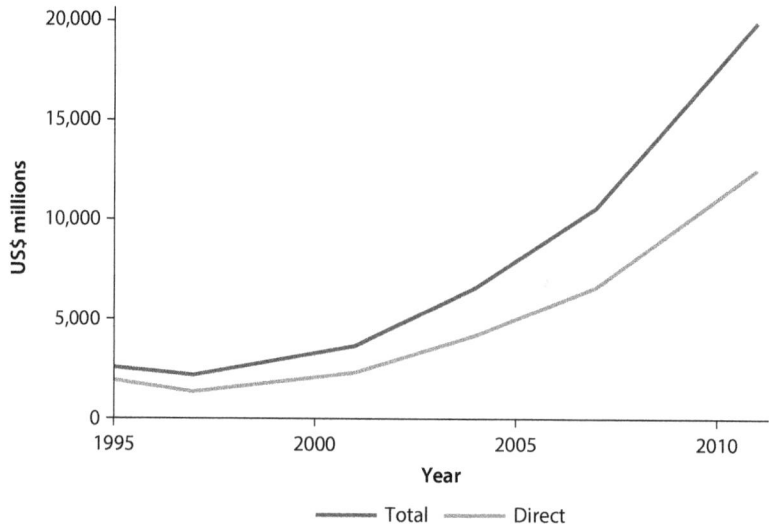

Source: World Bank Labor Content of Exports database.

megaregional trade agreements. The extent and depth of the country's PTAs mean that it will undergo substantial structural transformation in the coming years and decades.

Sourcing and selling patterns in GVCs are highly concentrated among regional trading partners. In 1995, Vietnam's international sourcing and selling linkages for import to export showed a strong degree of regionalization, with sourcing primarily from Japan, Korea, and Taiwan, China, and selling primarily to Japan and Singapore. By 2011, regional sourcing and selling ties had become more binding, confirming global trends toward a polarization of value chain linkages in regional blocks. A significant share of the foreign value added in Vietnam is sourced from regional anchor countries, while two-thirds of the country's outflow of domestic value added is absorbed regionally, most notably by China and Japan. And while the majority of Vietnam's exported value added is consumed by Association of Southeast Asian Nations (ASEAN) and East Asian economies, final demand for Vietnamese goods increasingly comes from North American Free Trade Agreement (NAFTA) countries.

These trends reflect the fact that Vietnam is part of various PTAs (see figure 6.2 in chapter 6), but the few that are considered deep, that is, going beyond market access issues, are regionally focused. The Japan–Vietnam Economic Partnership Agreement, Korea–Vietnam free trade agreement (FTA), and the ASEAN–Australia–New Zealand FTA are the only deep agreements in which Vietnam participates.

The global landscape of trade agreements is changing, however, to become megaregional and deep(er), acknowledging the realities of a trade landscape in which GVCs increasingly are important. Market access across multiple countries is important in the context of GVC trade where countries import to export because it secures access to inputs that can qualify for rules-of-origin provisions. The coverage of PTAs by policy areas also has widened, going beyond traditional market access issues. Importing to export creates new forms of crossborder policy effects compared with a situation where goods are produced in a single location. Thus, in order for crossborder production to operate efficiently, national policies (including policy to promote competition and efficiency in domestic markets), investment, infrastructure, and institutions should be harmonized across countries (Antràs and Staiger 2012; Lawrence 1996). Analysis based on the new World Bank dataset on PTA content shows that agreements signed before 1991 averaged nine provisions, against 15 for agreements signed between 2005 and 2015.[1]

Vietnam has embraced this wave of megaregional trade agreements and is well positioned to gain from them. Notable opportunities are the TPP and European Union–Vietnam Free Trade Agreement (EVFTA). In both, Vietnam is the lowest-income member, a position that signals both advantages and challenges. Thus, it is essential that Vietnam's development goals and strategies be considered in perspective of its major international agreements. The ASEAN Economic Community, which in 2016 moved ASEAN from an FTA to an economic community, is projected to bring considerable economic benefits. Especially noteworthy is the TPP. Although the TPP will not enter into force in its current form, Vietnam was projected to draw the greatest domestic gains, at upwards of 8 percent of GDP (Minor, Walmsley, and Strutt 2016). As argued in chapter 6, the EVFTA is as big as the TPP and will have similar effects for Vietnam. Also significant are the Free Trade Area of the Asia-Pacific and the Regional Comprehensive Economic Partnership, though neither is in negotiations as advanced as other megaregional trade agreements.

All of these trade agreements will create opportunities and challenges for Vietnam. For example, Vietnam's recent PTAs likely will boost its participation in GVCs. EVFTA will unlock the entire GVC system of Europe, and enhanced market access from these trade agreements is expected to lower trade costs. However, challenges for Vietnam to take advantage of these opportunities for upgrading remain, as chapter 6 suggests. For example, while rules of origin in textiles and apparel offer opportunities to grow a domestic supply network, the extensive coverage of behind-the-border regulations in deep PTAs makes it hard for firms to take advantage of these opportunities.

Although China is left out of most of the deeper agreements that Vietnam will become party to, producers can continue to benefit from the combination of domestic low wages and close proximity to the Chinese supply chain. Vietnam's nearness to China—a central hub to many of these production networks—gives it a meaningful competitive edge. As real wages in China continue their sharp rise, many of its production bases will continue to look southward in search of lower wages, attracting what has become known in the electronics GVC as the China+1 strategy. Trade with China accounts for 20 percent of Vietnam's total, up from 10 percent in 2000. The significant flow of FDI into Vietnam is also linked, in part, to a shift in low-wage production from China (World Bank 2016a).

Notably, these new agreements involve economies at the center of technology, which could offer additional spillovers. As noted in chapter 4, it is fundamental to keep in mind who the main sources of technology and main sources of demand are, as it matters where value added is sold to and sourced from, as well as the final consumers of that value added. Connecting to centers of technology, such as the European Union, Korea, Japan, and the United States, is very important for productivity spillovers, and can drive upgrading through high-income consumer preferences.

These agreements also place Vietnam at a crossroads: Should it continue to grow as an export platform, or diversify and move up the value chain into higher value-added functions? The PTAs entering into effect may have an important role in shaping the evolution of Vietnam's comparative advantage in years to come. Despite providing market access to further integrate into GVCs, it is not clear if these agreements will lock in the status quo, that is, foster Vietnam's comparative advantage in production stages associated with low value added, or promote a dynamic transition to more sophisticated products or tasks.

Product Mix

To increase value added, Vietnam must continue diversifying and moving toward more sophisticated products.[2] Its export basket already is more diversified than a decade ago, reflecting a transition from exporting primary commodities to exporting low- and medium-tech manufactured goods (apparel, furniture, and footwear) and then to more sophisticated products (machinery and electronics). At the sectoral level, Vietnam's domestic value added in gross exports grew at two-digit rates in most sectors, exhibiting the highest growth rates among its peers (figure 1.4). Nevertheless, the product mix—the production specialization—exerted a dampening effect, offsetting gains in world market shares by 1.4 percent (see figure 1.2).

A closer look at sectoral heterogeneity reveals the remarkable performance in automotive, electronics, agribusiness, and textiles and apparel—four sectors in particular that currently are important sources of exports and employment, and appear to be new emerging engines of growth (figure 1.4). Vietnam's growth of domestic value added in the automotive industry was as high as 44 percent annually between 1995 and 2011 (moving from $0.9 million to over $309 million). The country's average compound annual growth rate was around 16 points higher than China's in that sector, and more than double that of Thailand and Korea. However, Vietnam's aggregate domestic value added in the automotive sector is marginal relative to that in other economies, ranking below the 35th percentile of the sample distribution.

In electronics, only two countries of the full sample outperformed the 21.2 percent annual increase recorded by Vietnam, notably China (28.7 percent) and Romania (28 percent—not shown). Vietnam also showed impressive 16–17 percent annual growth rates in agribusiness and textiles and apparel.

Vietnam has become an assembly platform, or a GVC factory, that specializes in final production stages, although it also creates and sells inputs to

Figure 1.4 Growth of Domestic Value Added Embodied in Gross Exports, Selected Economies, 1995–2011

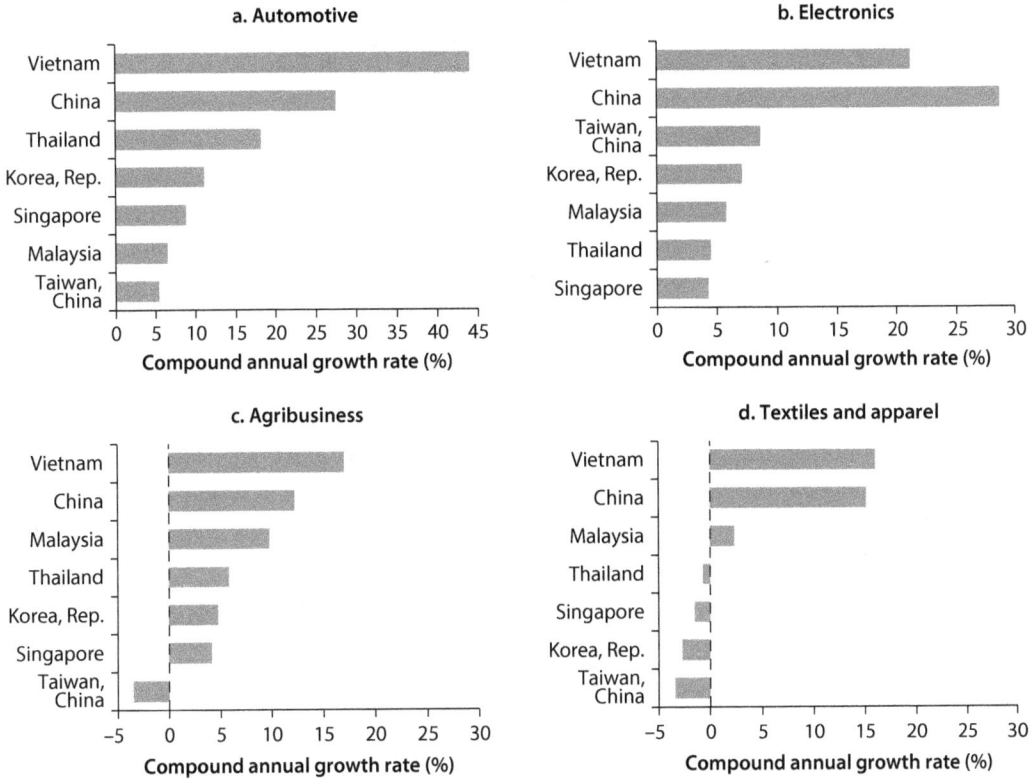

a. Automotive

Vietnam
China
Thailand
Korea, Rep.
Singapore
Malaysia
Taiwan, China

Compound annual growth rate (%)

b. Electronics

Vietnam
China
Taiwan, China
Korea, Rep.
Malaysia
Thailand
Singapore

Compound annual growth rate (%)

c. Agribusiness

Vietnam
China
Malaysia
Thailand
Korea, Rep.
Singapore
Taiwan, China

Compound annual growth rate (%)

d. Textiles and apparel

Vietnam
China
Malaysia
Thailand
Singapore
Korea, Rep.
Taiwan, China

Compound annual growth rate (%)

Source: Kummritz et al. 2016.

other countries that tend to be of low value-added. This includes the GVCs of agribusiness and ICT that are considered strategic by the government, as well as the automotive and the textiles and apparel GVCs, where global competition is fierce and the country is locked at the low end of the value chain. Where connected to GVCs, Vietnam generally performs the lowest technology step of production, consistent with Vietnam's GVC integration and expansion as a seller being smaller than as a buyer (as noted).

While the creation of tens or even hundreds of thousands of new assembly jobs will be a welcome facilitator of Vietnam's structural transformation, the benefits of this mode of growth can be short lived as incomes and wages rise. While the economy is poised for rapid development in its current activities, the remaining window of opportunity for Vietnam in labor-intensive manufacturing could be relatively brief as lower cost countries such as Myanmar enter into regional trade and investment flows. The challenge will be to create, through domestic structural transformation and domestic and trade policy, an ecosystem that supports a nascent set of dynamic, innovative, and autonomous domestic firms to grow, move up the value chain into higher value-added functions in these GVCs by leveraging external demand, and eventually become lead firms themselves. But such success requires a strong supply-side agenda to overcome bottlenecks to creating a more sophisticated and diversified export basket.

The Supply Side

Vietnam's gains in export competitiveness since 2005 were driven entirely by supply-side improvements in export performance, such as efficiency gains and the accumulation of factors of production (see figure 1.2). Analysis of export and import upstream positions suggests ample opportunities to continue increasing value creation by expanding the scope of activity in the production stages where Vietnam already is active and enjoys a comparative advantage. While Vietnam's imports typically are upstream, its export basket is closer to final demand. This gap implies that several production steps are carried out domestically, and that opportunities to increase domestic value added along the chain exist. These opportunities will be reinforced if Vietnam also can engage in product, process, and functional upgrading, which will help it take over more sophisticated stages in GVCs.

Yet Vietnam faces horizontal and vertical (sector-specific) constraints to innovating its export basket to allow for the capture of more value added and to move up the value chain into higher value-added functions. (This topic absorbs much of the rest of this volume.)

Most export jobs remain in the unskilled worker range, where the unskilled component of labor value added is much larger in Vietnam than in other Asian economies. This pattern is seen across most sectors, including processed foods, machinery and equipment, and textiles and apparel.

Backward linkages with the domestic economy are weak. Most of the growth in domestic value added exported came directly from export activities rather than indirectly through domestic inputs. In 2011, the contribution of direct value added from exports was 62 percent of the total, while the value added generated by the domestic pipeline supplying exports was 37 percent.

The services share in value added is low by international standards, where forward linkages to manufacturing export sectors from the backbone services sectors necessary for competitive industry are weak (chapter 3). Because the high value-added segments of GVCs are often rich in services content, enhancing the competitiveness of the services sector to enable servicification—the role of services, not only as inputs into the economy, but as a means to change the way value is created—is a priority for upgrading in GVCs. And once the domestic services sector is competitive enough by international standards, services exports themselves can enhance Vietnam's export diversification.

Weak backward linkages is largely the result of weak linkages from FDI firms, which do much of the exporting, to a domestic private sector. While institutions usually play a positive role in linking FDI with the domestic economy, in Vietnam none of the key institutional variables matter.

Overall economic growth should be driven by fundamentals, not merely by transformation, but firms' capacity to absorb productivity spillovers appears weaker in Vietnam than in other low- and middle-income countries. Productivity growth, which has been on a long-term declining trend, requires greater attention (chapter 2).

International and domestic connectivity also will require upgrading. Relative to its income level, Vietnam typically performs quite well on connectivity metrics. But as highlighted in chapters 4 and 5, as Vietnam's export structure and markets evolve, the necessary transport and logistics supply chains will need to expand to support this transformation. Vietnam will need to keep investing in transport and logistics to be competitive, particularly against East and Southeast Asian peers.

Other sector-specific bottlenecks exist, including outdated curriculum, low input quality, and preferential procurement and tax incentives. In-depth studies of GVC-intensive sectors identify other policy interventions (chapters 7–12), based on key features of these GVCs and Vietnam's current and potential roles within them.

Although GVCs can create new opportunities on the demand side, and lead to faster economic upgrading, supply cannot meet demand if these constraints remain. This serves to illustrate the importance for Vietnam of embedding national policies for attracting GVCs and of upgrading across a broad portfolio of policies to improve competitiveness (chapter 13).

Drivers and Enablers

What does it take for a country to move up the value chain? The strategic policy framework developed by Taglioni and Winkler (2016) combines GVC performance with indicators of the regulatory and institutional framework using cross-country econometric techniques to provide a set of policy recommendations for greater integration and upgrading. The GVC performance indicator used is growth in domestic value added exported. Applying the strategic policy framework to Vietnam reveals that progress needs to be made across the board.

In particular, econometric analysis suggests that Vietnam's market institutions, factor markets, and learning and innovation may require policy intervention to support further alignment with a GVC strategy aimed at maximizing the benefits of domestic value-added creation from participating in international production networks (GVCs). Targeted action should prioritize the following areas (figure 1.5):

- Facilitating domestic firms' entry into GVCs by improving the drivers of investment, in particular the functioning of market institutions (such as asset protection) and by improving the functioning and quality of the domestic segment of value chains and the quality of services inputs.
- Promoting economic upgrading, including by strengthening linkages between buyers and sellers in GVCs.

Figure 1.5 Strategic Policy Framework Applied to Vietnam

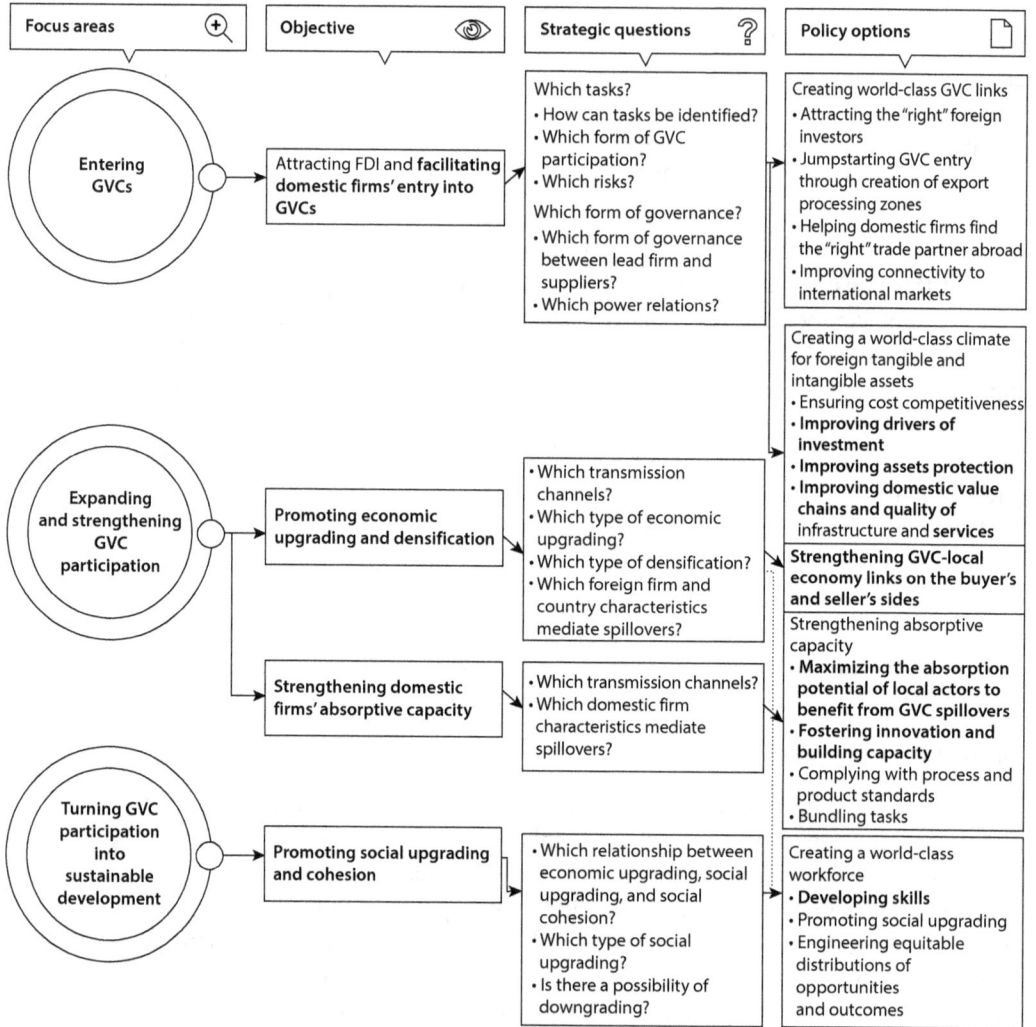

Focus areas ⊕	Objective 👁	Strategic questions ?	Policy options 📄
Entering GVCs	Attracting FDI and **facilitating domestic firms' entry into GVCs**	Which tasks? • How can tasks be identified? • Which form of GVC participation? • Which risks? Which form of governance? • Which form of governance between lead firm and suppliers? • Which power relations?	Creating world-class GVC links • Attracting the "right" foreign investors • Jumpstarting GVC entry through creation of export processing zones • Helping domestic firms find the "right" trade partner abroad • Improving connectivity to international markets
Expanding and strengthening GVC participation	Promoting economic upgrading and densification	• Which transmission channels? • Which type of economic upgrading? • Which type of densification? • Which foreign firm and country characteristics mediate spillovers?	Creating a world-class climate for foreign tangible and intangible assets • Ensuring cost competitiveness • **Improving drivers of investment** • Improving assets protection • **Improving domestic value chains and quality of infrastructure and services** **Strengthening GVC-local economy links on the buyer's and seller's sides**
	Strengthening domestic firms' absorptive capacity	• Which transmission channels? • Which domestic firm characteristics mediate spillovers?	Strengthening absorptive capacity • **Maximizing the absorption potential of local actors to benefit from GVC spillovers** • **Fostering innovation and building capacity** • Complying with process and product standards • Bundling tasks
Turning GVC participation into sustainable development	Promoting social upgrading and cohesion	• Which relationship between economic upgrading, social upgrading, and social cohesion? • Which type of social upgrading? • Is there a possibility of downgrading?	Creating a world-class workforce • **Developing skills** • Promoting social upgrading • Engineering equitable distributions of opportunities and outcomes

Source: Kummritz et al. 2016.
Note: FDI = foreign direct investment; GVC = global value chain. The actions in bold were identified as significant when applying the strategic policy framework to Vietnam.

• Maximizing the absorption potential of local actors (especially their innovation capacity) to benefit from GVC spillovers and to seize opportunities for upgrading.
• Focusing on skills development, which helps promote economic upgrading and densification of the GVC space with more domestic suppliers and maximizes the benefits of GVC participation by promoting social upgrading and cohesion.

Vietnam can use PTAs to push a domestic reform agenda. The extent of harnessing these opportunities for growth will depend on whether the country can engineer a new round of bold institutional and policy reforms. Trade agreements offer Vietnam more than the opportunity to leverage the current wave of growth to move up the value chain: commitments under them offer an opportunity to carry out many demanding and politically sensitive reforms.

Barriers, Threats, and Challenges

Observers of structural transformations (Gershenkron 1962) suggest that national policymakers must adopt strategies that fit the prevailing conditions of the contemporary industrial era. This is particularly true for countries in an initial phase of high growth, or growth associated with a major transformation of the domestic economy. Business systems formed during this initial high-growth phase have a powerful and long-lasting influence on that country's economic institutions, including innovation systems, business culture, corporate governance, and industrial organization (Stinchcombe 1965). In other words, rapid growth leaves a lasting imprint (Whittaker et al. 2010).

Digital ICTs are having a profound effect on nearly every country and sector, blurring the boundaries between traditional industries and changing the nature of production, consumption, distribution, and work. This creates a dual effect, with somewhat competing policy requirements. ICT is the propulsive sector of the era, driving productivity improvements in traditional sectors and enabling the development of innovative products and services with no real precedent. Thus a strong argument can be made for policy measures that encourage the deployment and adoption of leading-edge ICT technologies across all sectors. These leading-edge products, built largely from imported technologies and products, enable productivity improvements and innovation economy wide, even if domestic ICT infrastructure is lagging.

But innovation in ICT is so rapid and pervasive that new products and services are constantly created. While this pattern is disruptive to longtime incumbents, ICT creates a fertile environment for investment in, and development of, new (domestically embedded) firms and industries, and also drives a stream of investment (domestic and foreign) that can be harnessed to drive development, technological learning, innovation, and knowledge-intensive employment within the domestic ICT sector. Effectively balancing policies that improve connectivity through the deployment of leading edge ICT technologies with those that support the development of a domestic ICT sector undoubtedly represents a challenge for Vietnam's policymakers.

If Vietnam's future economy and society are to be imprinted with the main characteristics of the current industrial era, the focus must be on the key feature of the 21st-century economy: the interplay of technological change and globalization, which is driving cross-border integration and connectivity in the context of GVCs. National input-output structures are being overlain with global input-output structures, and this means that policymakers must deal with a wider range of actors than ever before.

Vietnam at a Crossroads • http://dx.doi.org/10.1596/978-1-4648-0996-5

The instruments that Vietnam has put in place to integrate into GVCs in the past may have created bottlenecks for the next stage of GVC upgrading. For example, strong investment promotion without the right domestic competition policy risks creating a dual economy with little domestic transformation and even less improvement in forward and backward linkages. Trade policies often contain many investment provisions, particularly toward services provided as well as mobility of skilled workers. Trade, investment, and competition policies must therefore be viewed together. So, the sequencing of the reform agenda is important. Enhancing market access without developing the supply side might lock Vietnam into its current activities. For example, the removal of barriers to trade will not have the expected effect on the domestic economy unless the right competition framework is in place that promotes increased competition rather than the capture of rents by foreign firms. It is important for Vietnam to overcome bottlenecks on the supply side by prioritizing and sequencing reforms that boost domestic and foreign competitiveness.

Such an ambitious endeavor requires a solid package of horizontal reforms and vertical initiatives in specific sectors. Moreover, actions are not to be implemented in isolation. Success can be achieved only by a comprehensive agenda that cuts across the many dimensions discussed in figure 1.6.

Figure 1.6 Eleven Action Agendas

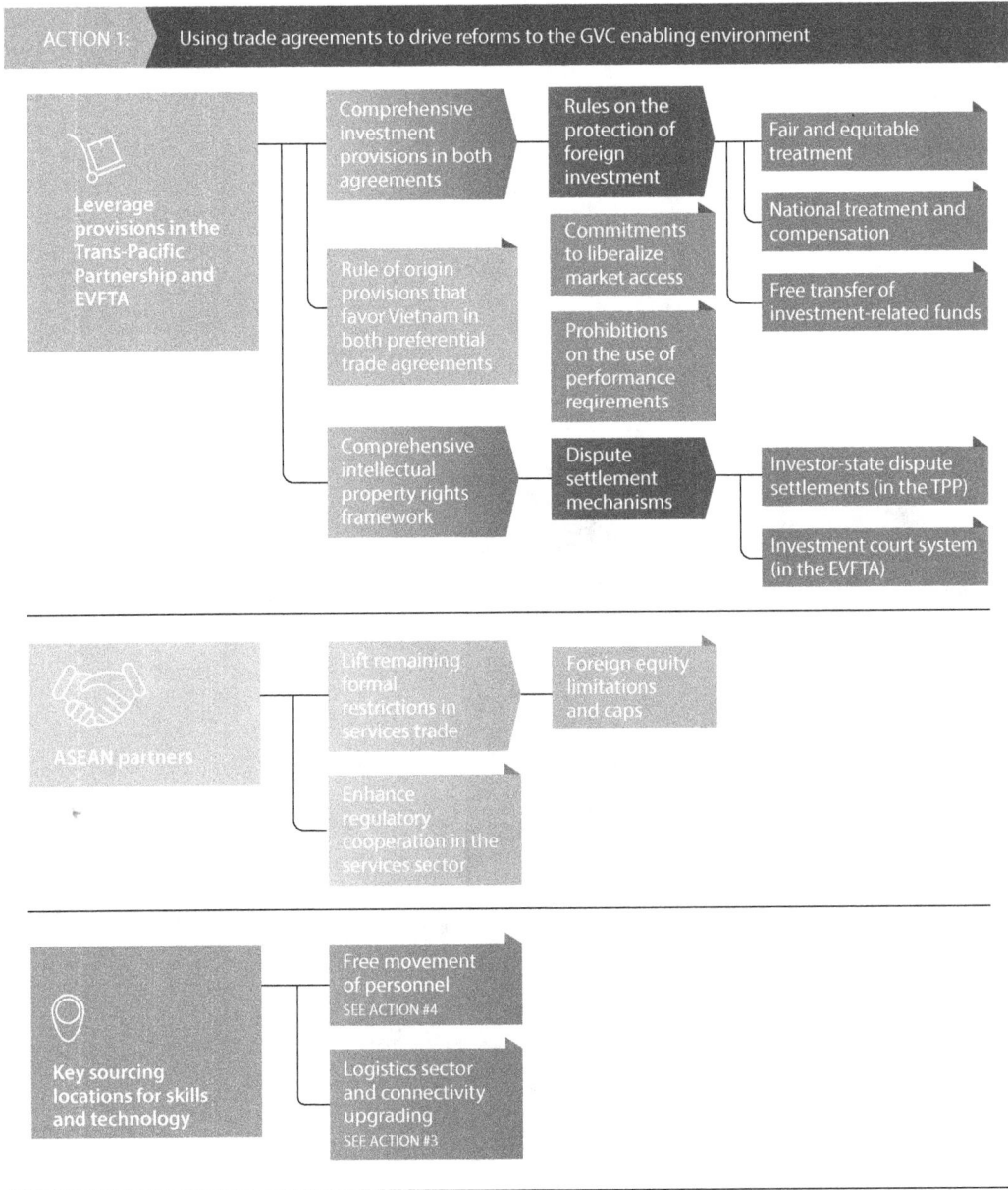

ACTION 1:   Using trade agreements to drive reforms to the GVC enabling environment

Leverage provisions in the Trans-Pacific Partnership and EVFTA

- Comprehensive investment provisions in both agreements
  - Rules on the protection of foreign investment
    - Fair and equitable treatment
    - National treatment and compensation
    - Free transfer of investment-related funds
  - Commitments to liberalize market access
  - Prohibitions on the use of performance requirements
- Rule of origin provisions that favor Vietnam in both preferential trade agreements
- Comprehensive intellectual property rights framework
  - Dispute settlement mechanisms
    - Investor-state dispute settlements (in the TPP)
    - Investment court system (in the EVFTA)

ASEAN partners

- Lift remaining formal restrictions in services trade
  - Foreign equity limitations and caps
- Enhance regulatory cooperation in the services sector

Key sourcing locations for skills and technology

- Free movement of personnel
  SEE ACTION #4
- Logistics sector and connectivity upgrading
  SEE ACTION #3

figure continues next page

Figure 1.6 Eleven Action Agendas *(continued)*

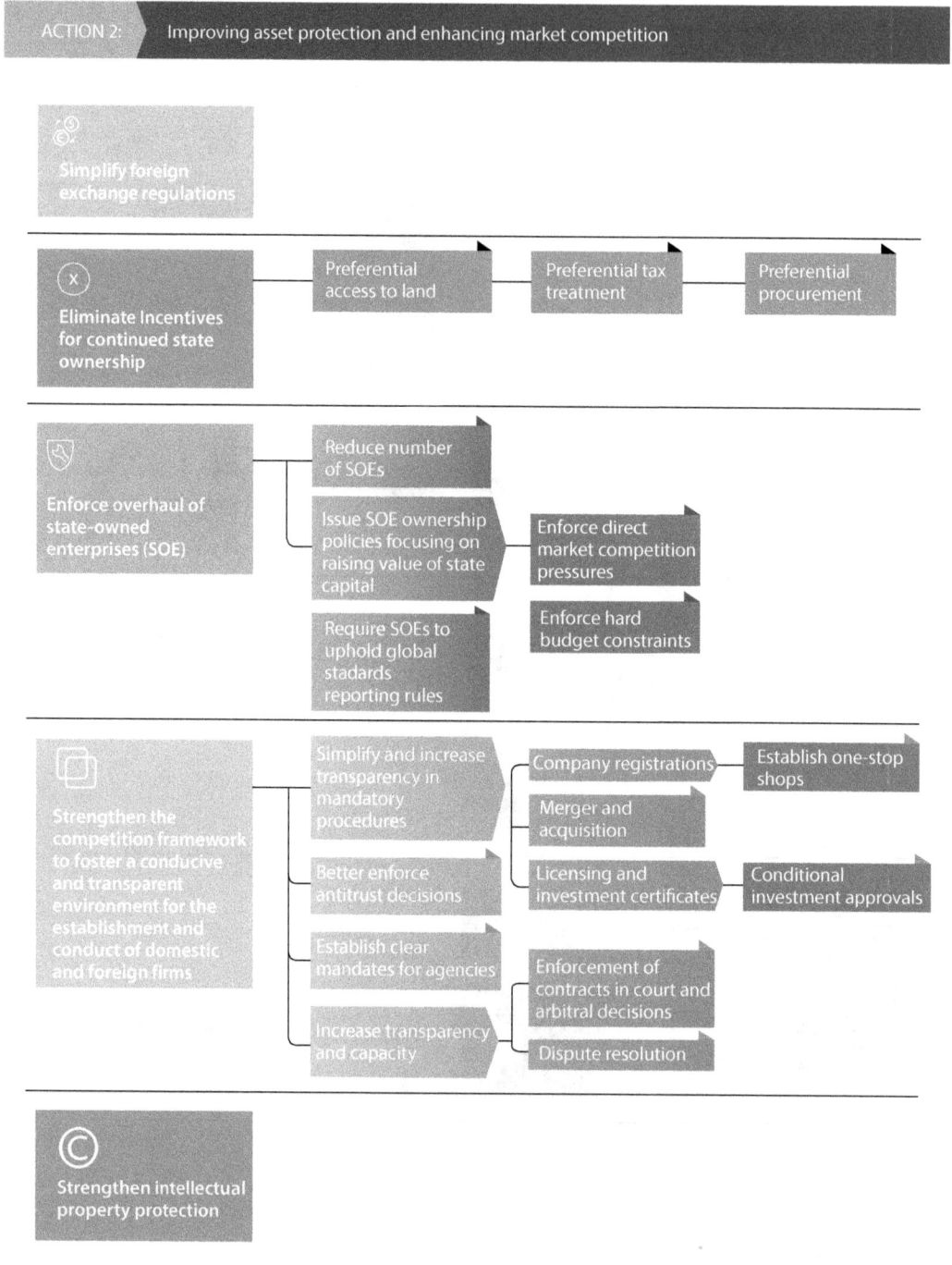

ACTION 2: Improving asset protection and enhancing market competition

Simplify foreign exchange regulations

Eliminate Incentives for continued state ownership
- Preferential access to land
- Preferential tax treatment
- Preferential procurement

Enforce overhaul of state-owned enterprises (SOE)
- Reduce number of SOEs
- Issue SOE ownership policies focusing on raising value of state capital
  - Enforce direct market competition pressures
  - Enforce hard budget constraints
- Require SOEs to uphold global stadards reporting rules

Strengthen the competition framework to foster a conducive and transparent environment for the establishment and conduct of domestic and foreign firms
- Simplify and increase transparency in mandatory procedures
  - Company registrations
    - Establish one-stop shops
  - Merger and acquisition
- Better enforce antitrust decisions
  - Licensing and investment certificates
    - Conditional investment approvals
- Establish clear mandates for agencies
  - Enforcement of contracts in court and arbitral decisions
- Increase transparency and capacity
  - Dispute resolution

Strengthen intellectual property protection

figure continues next page

Figure 1.6 Eleven Action Agendas *(continued)*

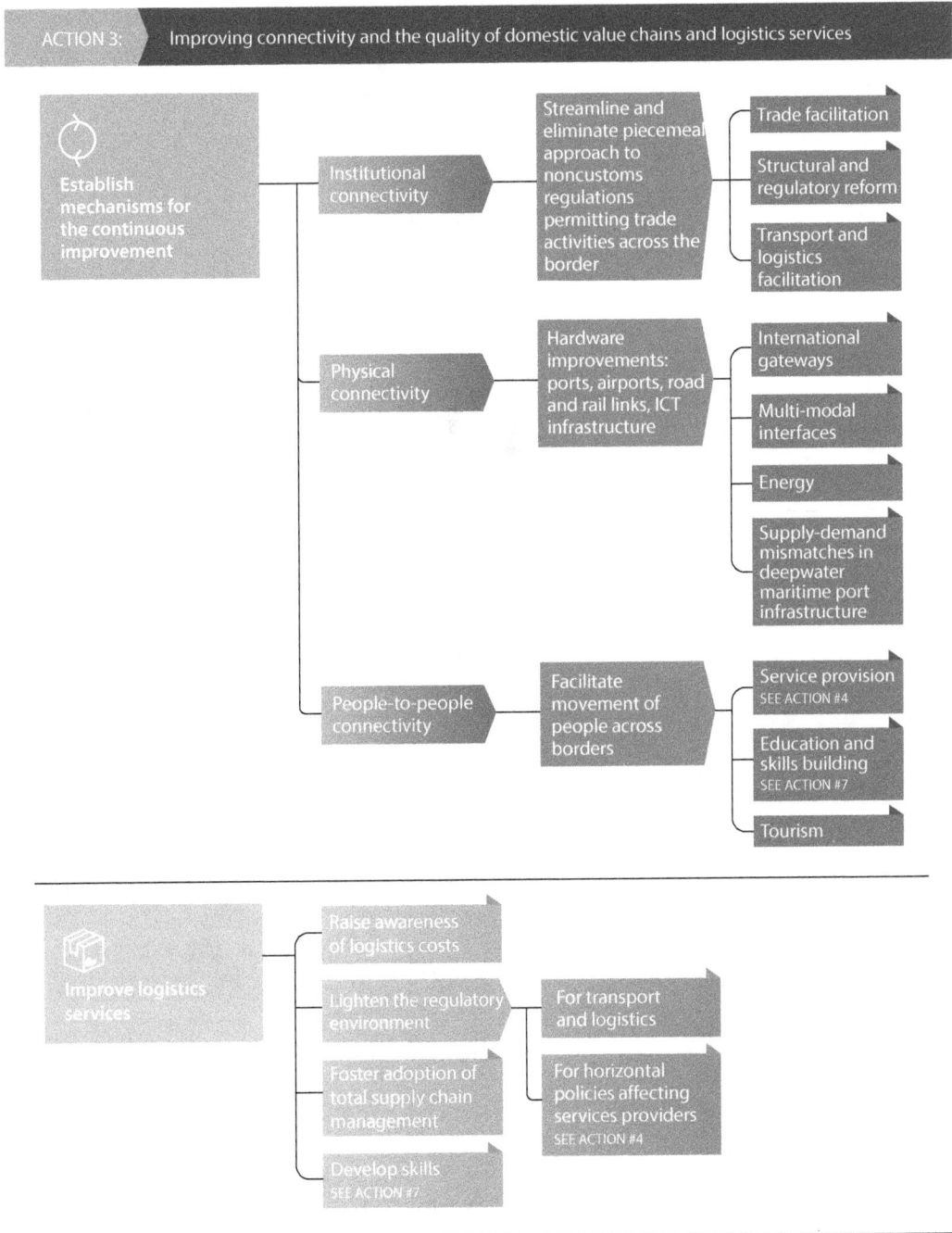

ACTION 3: Improving connectivity and the quality of domestic value chains and logistics services

Establish mechanisms for the continuous improvement

Institutional connectivity → Streamline and eliminate piecemeal approach to noncustoms regulations permitting trade activities across the border → Trade facilitation / Structural and regulatory reform / Transport and logistics facilitation

Physical connectivity → Hardware improvements: ports, airports, road and rail links, ICT infrastructure → International gateways / Multi-modal interfaces / Energy / Supply-demand mismatches in deepwater maritime port infrastructure

People-to-people connectivity → Facilitate movement of people across borders → Service provision SEE ACTION #4 / Education and skills building SEE ACTION #7 / Tourism

Improve logistics services → Raise awareness of logistics costs / Lighten the regulatory environment → For transport and logistics / Foster adoption of total supply chain management → For horizontal policies affecting services providers SEE ACTION #4 / Develop skills SEE ACTION #7

figure continues next page

Figure 1.6 Eleven Action Agendas *(continued)*

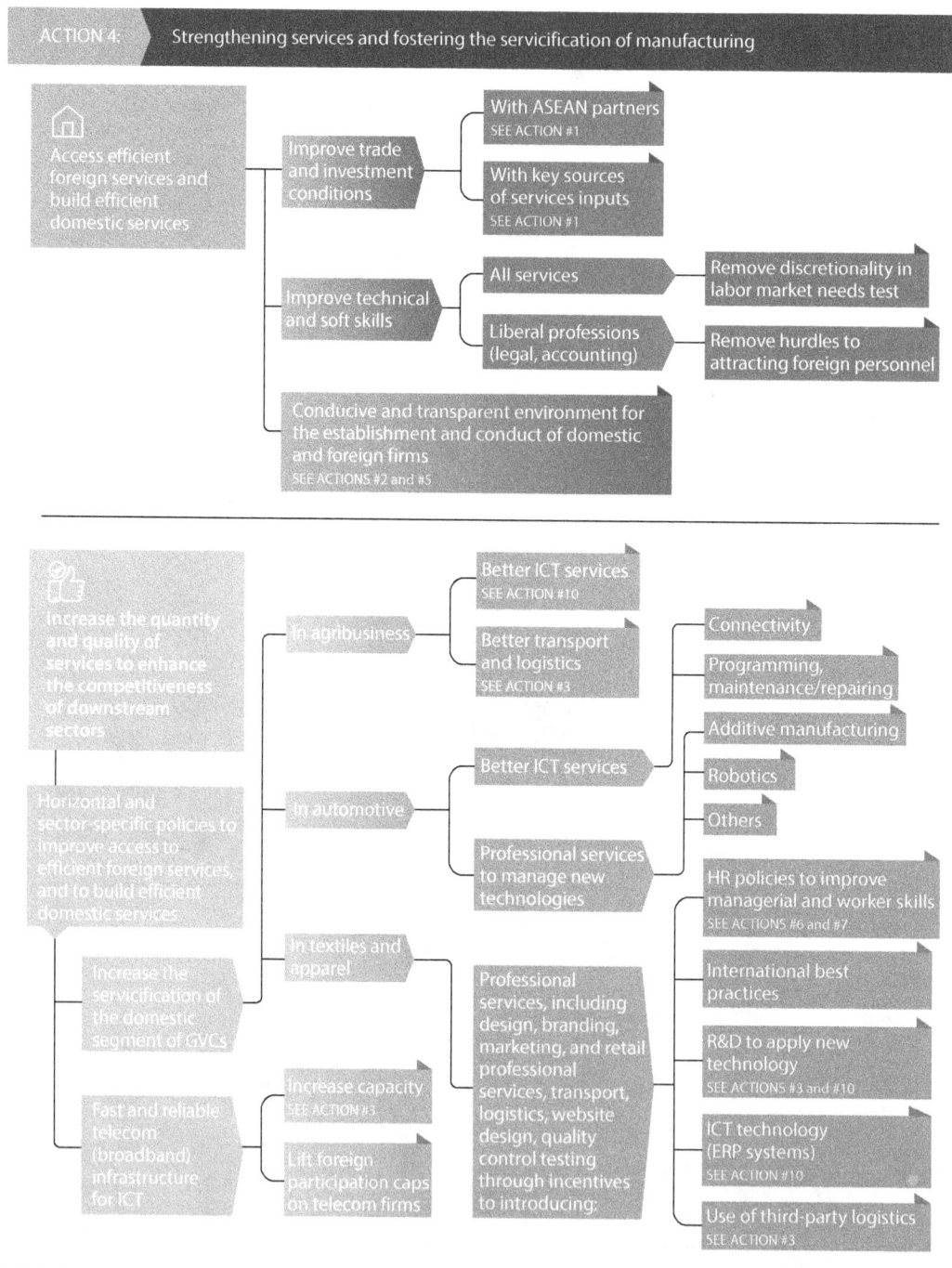

ACTION 4:   Strengthening services and fostering the servicification of manufacturing

Access efficient foreign services and build efficient domestic services

Improve trade and investment conditions
- With ASEAN partners
  SEE ACTION #1
- With key sources of services inputs
  SEE ACTION #1

Improve technical and soft skills
- All services → Remove discretionality in labor market needs test
- Liberal professions (legal, accounting) → Remove hurdles to attracting foreign personnel

Conducive and transparent environment for the establishment and conduct of domestic and foreign firms
SEE ACTIONS #2 and #5

Increase the quantity and quality of services to enhance the competitiveness of downstream sectors

Horizontal and sector-specific policies to improve access to efficient foreign services, and to build efficient domestic services

Increase the servicification of the domestic segment of GVCs

Fast and reliable telecom (broadband) infrastructure for ICT

In agribusiness
- Better ICT services
  SEE ACTION #10
- Better transport and logistics
  SEE ACTION #3

In automotive
- Better ICT services
  - Connectivity
  - Programming, maintenance/repairing
  - Additive manufacturing
  - Robotics
  - Others
- Professional services to manage new technologies

In textiles and apparel
- Increase capacity
  SEE ACTION #3
- Lift foreign participation caps on telecom firms

Professional services, including design, branding, marketing, and retail professional services, transport, logistics; website design, quality control testing through incentives to introducing:
- HR policies to improve managerial and worker skills
  SEE ACTIONS #6 and #7
- International best practices
- R&D to apply new technology
  SEE ACTIONS #3 and #10
- ICT technology (ERP systems)
  SEE ACTION #10
- Use of third-party logistics
  SEE ACTION #3

figure continues next page

Figure 1.6 Eleven Action Agendas *(continued)*

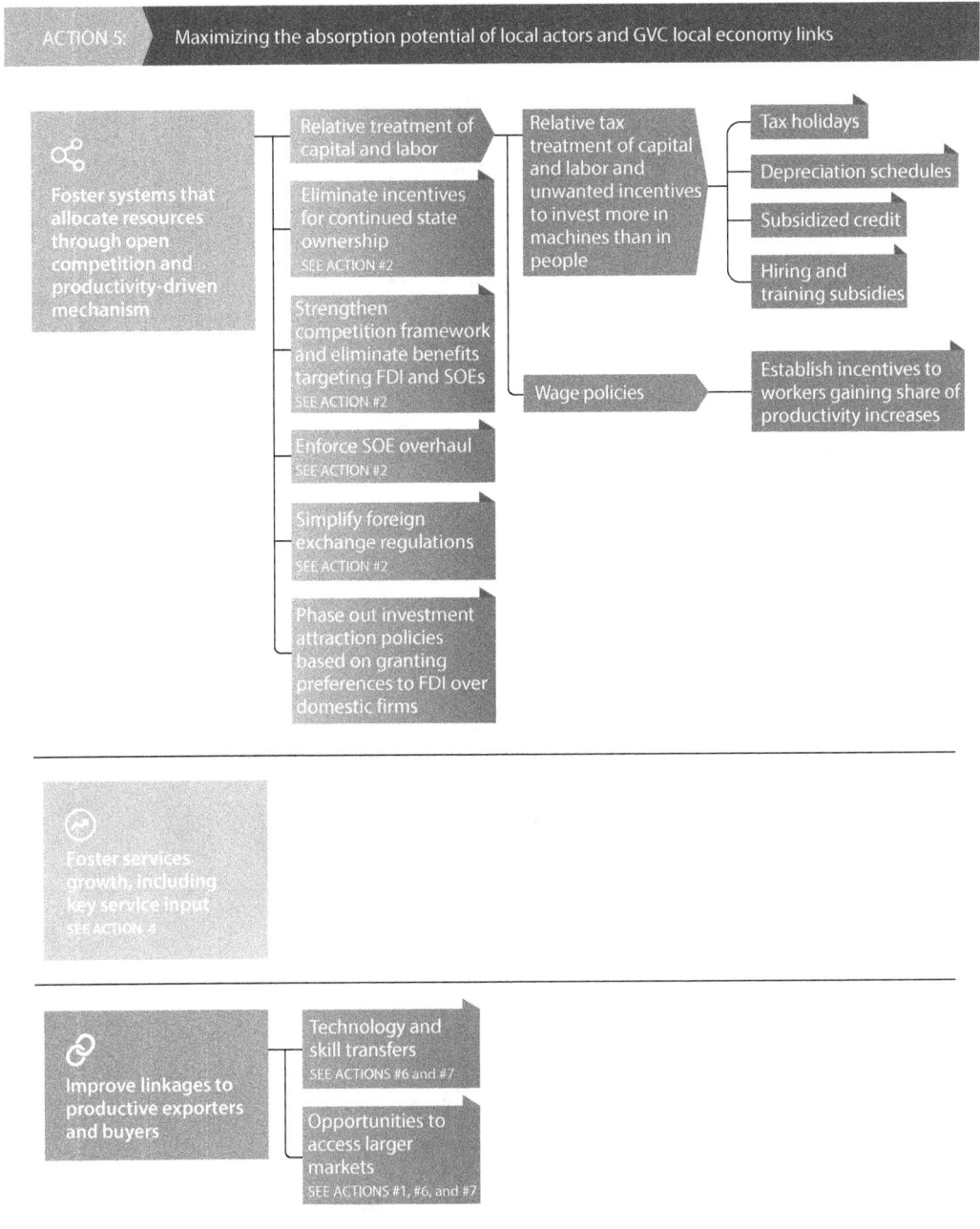

ACTION 5:   Maximizing the absorption potential of local actors and GVC local economy links

Foster systems that allocate resources through open competition and productivity-driven mechanism

- Relative treatment of capital and labor
  - Relative tax treatment of capital and labor and unwanted incentives to invest more in machines than in people
    - Tax holidays
    - Depreciation schedules
    - Subsidized credit
    - Hiring and training subsidies
  - Wage policies
    - Establish incentives to workers gaining share of productivity increases
- Eliminate incentives for continued state ownership
  SEE ACTION #2
- Strengthen competition framework and eliminate benefits targeting FDI and SOEs
  SEE ACTION #2
- Enforce SOE overhaul
  SEE ACTION #2
- Simplify foreign exchange regulations
  SEE ACTION #2
- Phase out investment attraction policies based on granting preferences to FDI over domestic firms

Foster services growth, including key service input
SEE ACTION #4

Improve linkages to productive exporters and buyers

- Technology and skill transfers
  SEE ACTIONS #6 and #7
- Opportunities to access larger markets
  SEE ACTIONS #1, #6, and #7

figure continues next page

Figure 1.6 Eleven Action Agendas *(continued)*

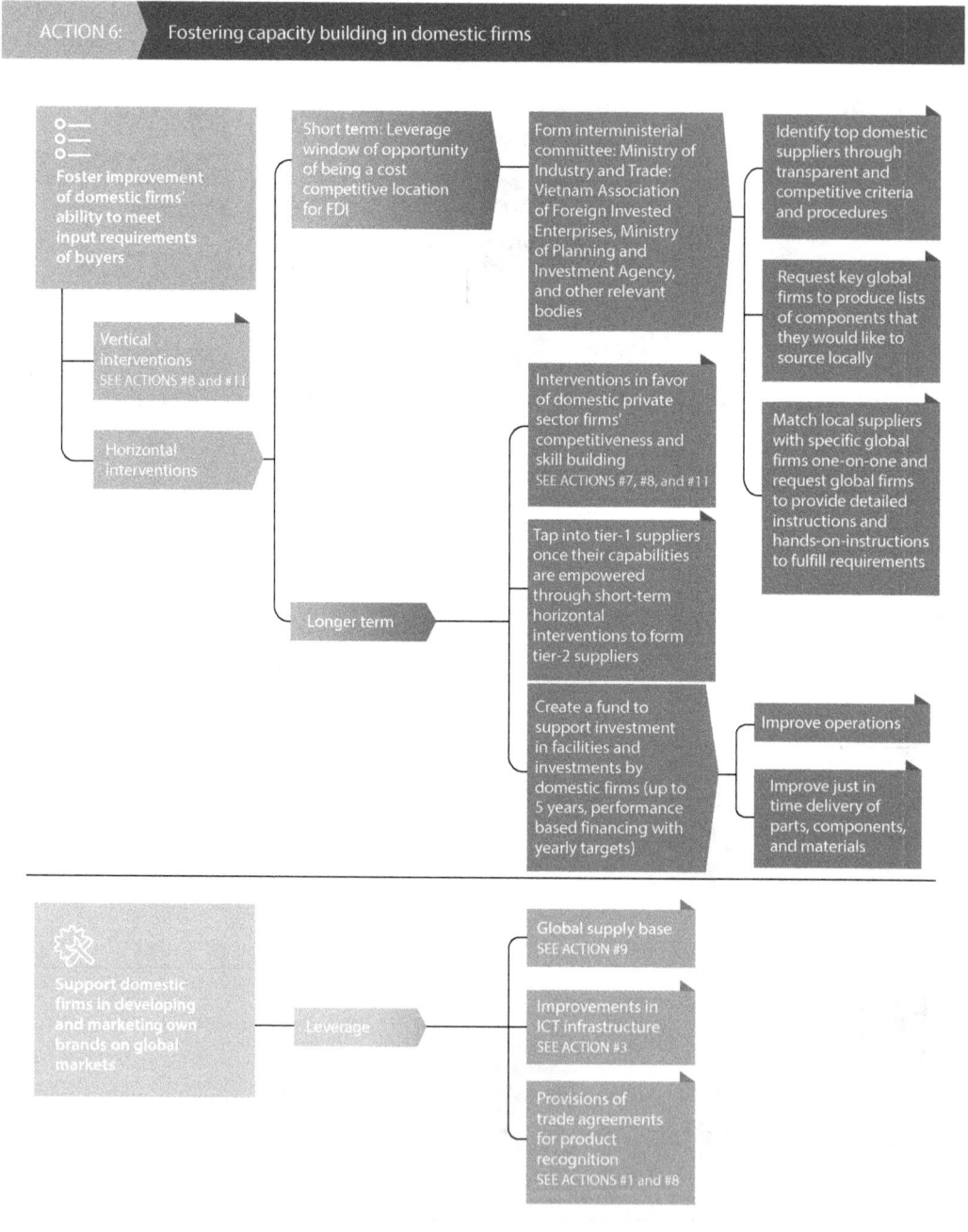

ACTION 6:   Fostering capacity building in domestic firms

Foster improvement of domestic firms' ability to meet input requirements of buyers

- Vertical interventions
  SEE ACTIONS #8 and #11
- Horizontal interventions

Short term: Leverage window of opportunity of being a cost competitive location for FDI

Form interministerial committee: Ministry of Industry and Trade; Vietnam Association of Foreign Invested Enterprises, Ministry of Planning and Investment Agency, and other relevant bodies

- Identify top domestic suppliers through transparent and competitive criteria and procedures
- Request key global firms to produce lists of components that they would like to source locally
- Match local suppliers with specific global firms one-on-one and request global firms to provide detailed instructions and hands-on-instructions to fulfill requirements

Longer term

- Interventions in favor of domestic private sector firms' competitiveness and skill building
  SEE ACTIONS #7, #8, and #11
- Tap into tier-1 suppliers once their capabilities are empowered through short-term horizontal interventions to form tier-2 suppliers
- Create a fund to support investment in facilities and investments by domestic firms (up to 5 years, performance based financing with yearly targets)
  - Improve operations
  - Improve just in time delivery of parts, components, and materials

Support domestic firms in developing and marketing own brands on global markets

Leverage

- Global supply base
  SEE ACTION #9
- Improvements in ICT infrastructure
  SEE ACTION #3
- Provisions of trade agreements for product recognition
  SEE ACTIONS #1 and #8

figure continues next page

Figure 1.6 Eleven Action Agendas *(continued)*

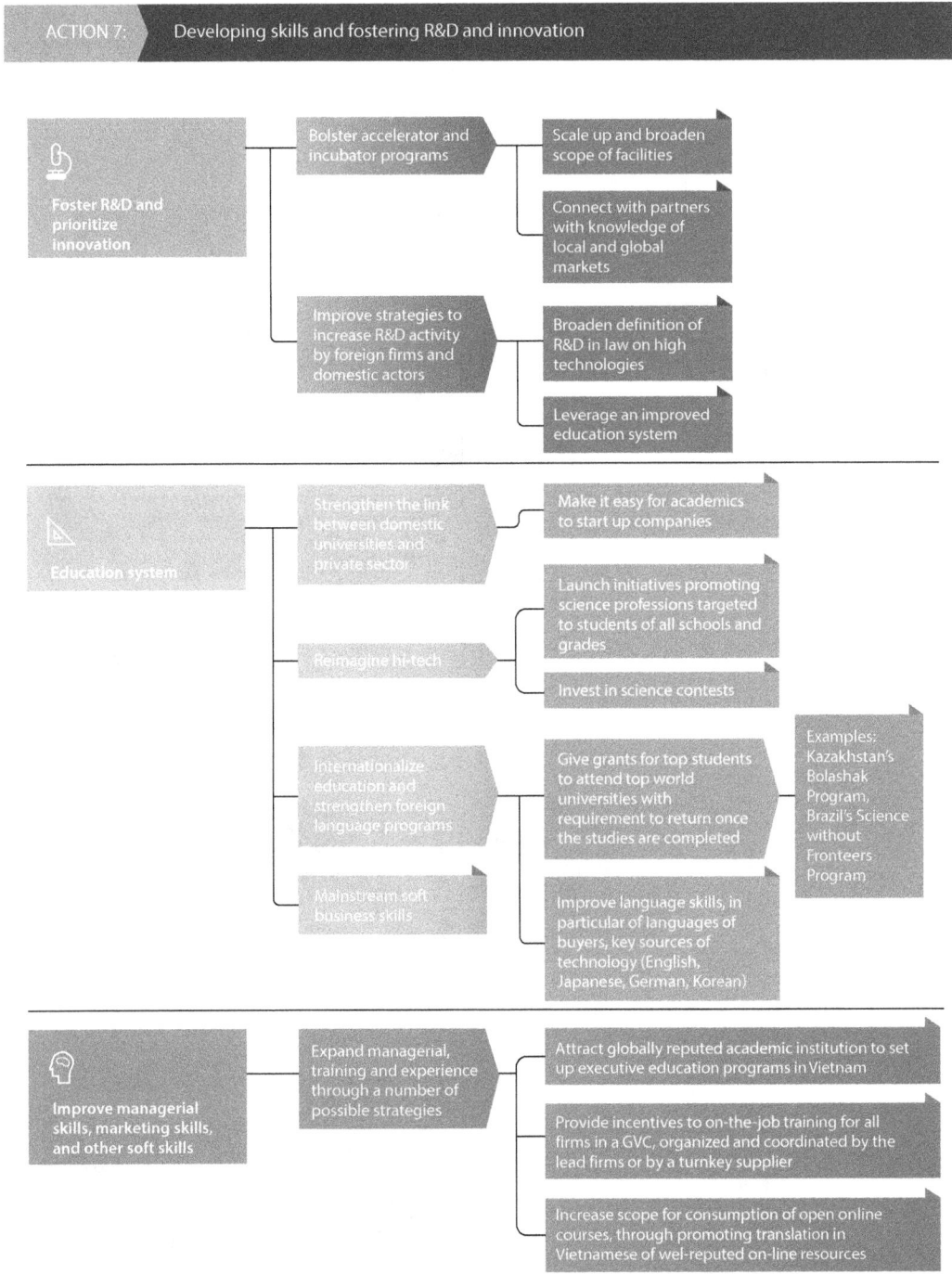

ACTION 7:   Developing skills and fostering R&D and innovation

Foster R&D and prioritize innovation

- Bolster accelerator and incubator programs
  - Scale up and broaden scope of facilities
  - Connect with partners with knowledge of local and global markets
- Improve strategies to increase R&D activity by foreign firms and domestic actors
  - Broaden definition of R&D in law on high technologies
  - Leverage an improved education system

Education system

- Strengthen the link between domestic universities and private sector
  - Make it easy for academics to start up companies
- Reimagine hi-tech
  - Launch initiatives promoting science professions targeted to students of all schools and grades
  - Invest in science contests
- Internationalize education and strengthen foreign language programs
  - Give grants for top students to attend top world universities with requirement to return once the studies are completed
    - Examples: Kazakhstan's Bolashak Program, Brazil's Science without Fronteers Program
- Mainstream soft business skills
  - Improve language skills, in particular of languages of buyers, key sources of technology (English, Japanese, German, Korean)

Improve managerial skills, marketing skills, and other soft skills

- Expand managerial, training and experience through a number of possible strategies
  - Attract globally reputed academic institution to set up executive education programs in Vietnam
  - Provide incentives to on-the-job training for all firms in a GVC, organized and coordinated by the lead firms or by a turnkey supplier
  - Increase scope for consumption of open online courses, through promoting translation in Vietnamese of wel-reputed on-line resources

figure continues next page

Figure 1.6 Eleven Action Agendas *(continued)*

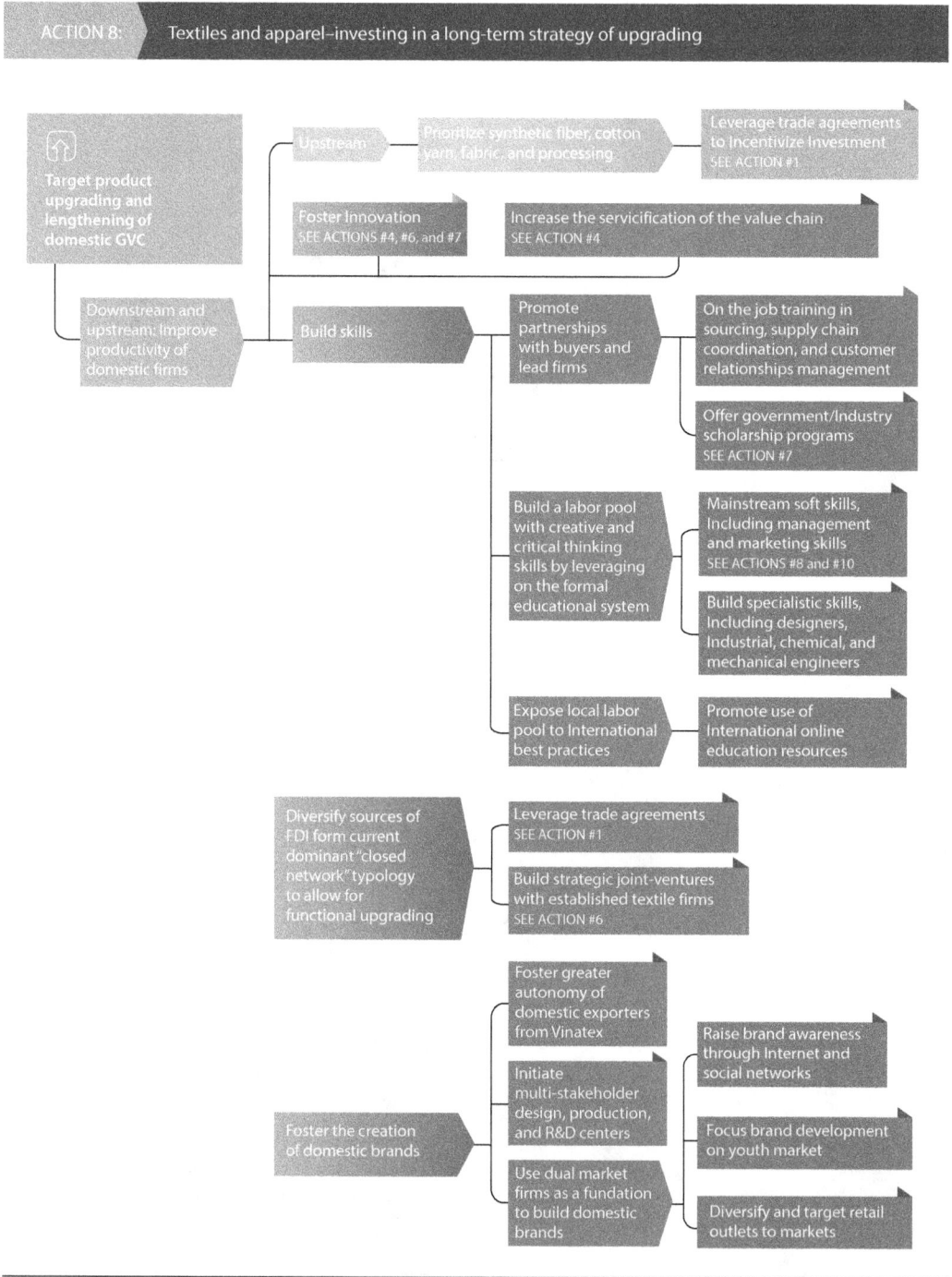

ACTION 8:   Textiles and apparel–investing in a long-term strategy of upgrading

Target product upgrading and lengthening of domestic GVC

Upstream → Prioritize synthetic fiber, cotton yarn, fabric, and processing → Leverage trade agreements to incentivize investment SEE ACTION #1

Foster innovation SEE ACTIONS #4, #6, and #7

Increase the servicification of the value chain SEE ACTION #4

Downstream and upstream: improve productivity of domestic firms

Build skills

Promote partnerships with buyers and lead firms

On the job training in sourcing, supply chain coordination, and customer relationships management

Offer government/industry scholarship programs SEE ACTION #7

Build a labor pool with creative and critical thinking skills by leveraging on the formal educational system

Mainstream soft skills, including management and marketing skills SEE ACTIONS #8 and #10

Build specialistic skills, including designers, industrial, chemical, and mechanical engineers

Expose local labor pool to international best practices

Promote use of international online education resources

Diversify sources of FDI form current dominant "closed network" typology to allow for functional upgrading

Leverage trade agreements SEE ACTION #1

Build strategic joint-ventures with established textile firms SEE ACTION #6

Foster the creation of domestic brands

Foster greater autonomy of domestic exporters from Vinatex

Initiate multi-stakeholder design, production, and R&D centers

Raise brand awareness through Internet and social networks

Focus brand development on youth market

Use dual market firms as a fundation to build domestic brands

Diversify and target retail outlets to markets

figure continues next page

Figure 1.6 Eleven Action Agendas *(continued)*

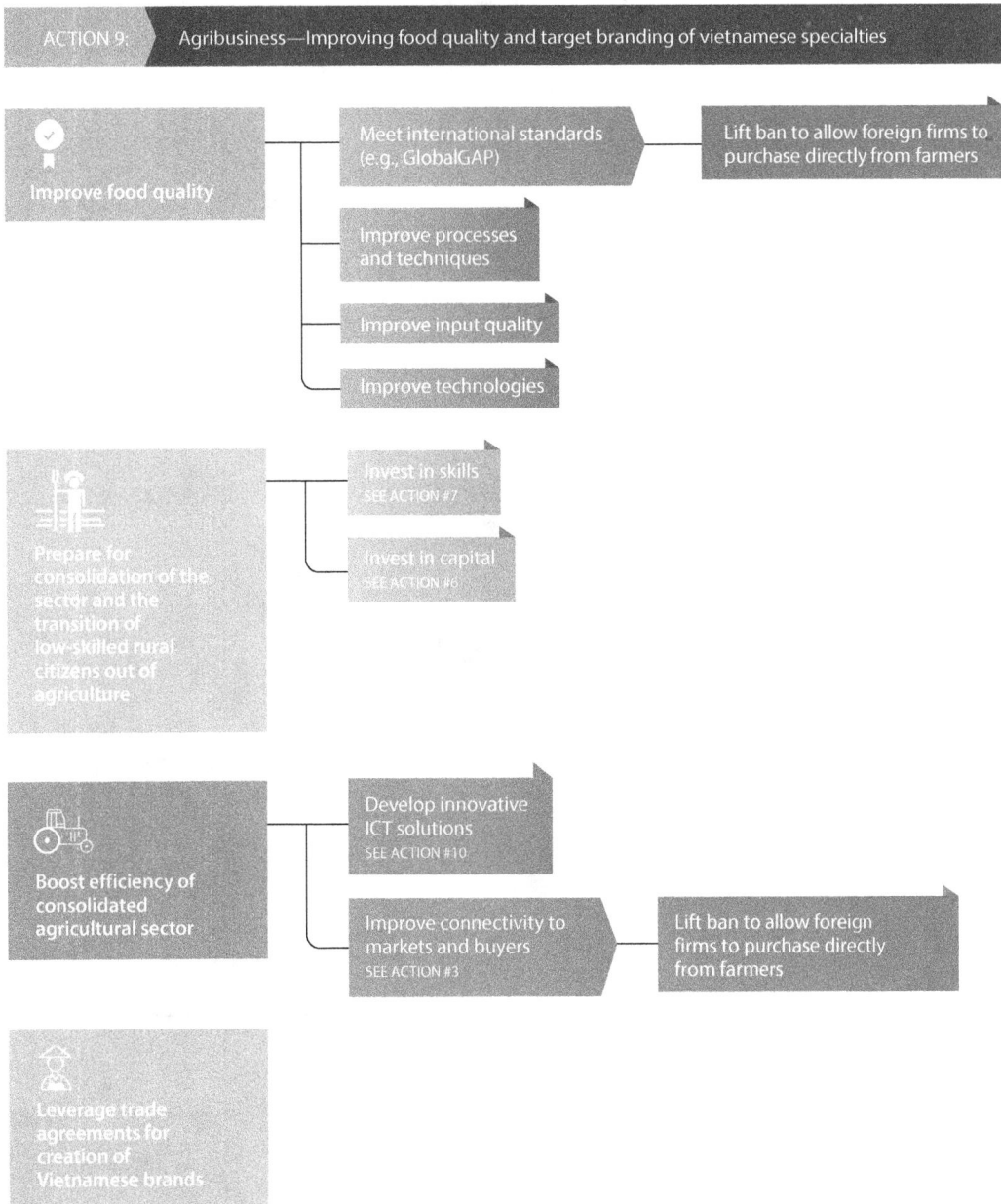

ACTION 9: Agribusiness—Improving food quality and target branding of vietnamese specialties

Improve food quality

- Meet international standards (e.g., GlobalGAP)
  - Lift ban to allow foreign firms to purchase directly from farmers
- Improve processes and techniques
- Improve input quality
- Improve technologies

Prepare for consolidation of the sector and the transition of low-skilled rural citizens out of agriculture

- Invest in skills
  SEE ACTION #7
- Invest in capital
  SEE ACTION #6

Boost efficiency of consolidated agricultural sector

- Develop innovative ICT solutions
  SEE ACTION #10
- Improve connectivity to markets and buyers
  SEE ACTION #3
  - Lift ban to allow foreign firms to purchase directly from farmers

Leverage trade agreements for creation of Vietnamese brands

figure continues next page

Figure 1.6 Eleven Action Agendas *(continued)*

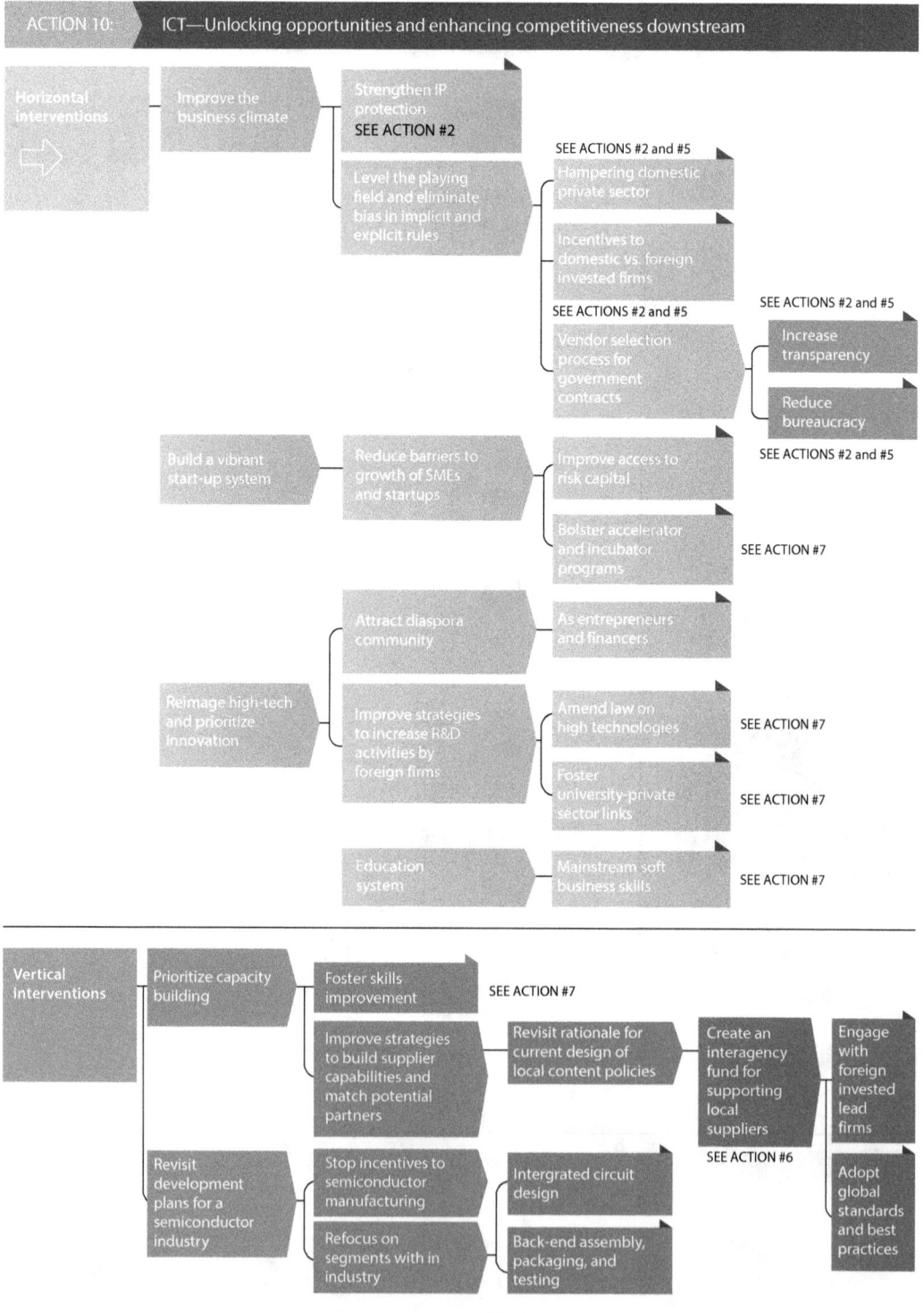

ACTION 10: ICT—Unlocking opportunities and enhancing competitiveness downstream

Horizontal interventions

Improve the business climate
- Strengthen IP protection — SEE ACTION #2
- Level the playing field and eliminate bias in implicit and explicit rules
  - Hampering domestic private sector — SEE ACTIONS #2 and #5
  - Incentives to domestic vs. foreign invested firms — SEE ACTIONS #2 and #5
  - Vendor selection process for government contracts — SEE ACTIONS #2 and #5
    - Increase transparency — SEE ACTIONS #2 and #5
    - Reduce bureaucracy — SEE ACTIONS #2 and #5

Build a vibrant start-up system
- Reduce barriers to growth of SMEs and startups
  - Improve access to risk capital
  - Bolster accelerator and incubator programs — SEE ACTION #7

Reimage high-tech and prioritize innovation
- Attract diaspora community
  - As entrepreneurs and financers
- Improve strategies to increase R&D activities by foreign firms
  - Amend law on high technologies — SEE ACTION #7
  - Foster university-private sector links — SEE ACTION #7
- Education system
  - Mainstream soft business skills — SEE ACTION #7

Vertical Interventions

Prioritize capacity building
- Foster skills improvement — SEE ACTION #7
- Improve strategies to build supplier capabilities and match potential partners
  - Revisit rationale for current design of local content policies
    - Create an interagency fund for supporting local suppliers — SEE ACTION #6
      - Engage with foreign invested lead firms
      - Adopt global standards and best practices

Revisit development plans for a semiconductor industry
- Stop incentives to semiconductor manufacturing
  - Intergrated circuit design
- Refocus on segments with in industry
  - Back-end assembly, packaging, and testing

figure continues next page

Figure 1.6 Eleven Action Agendas *(continued)*

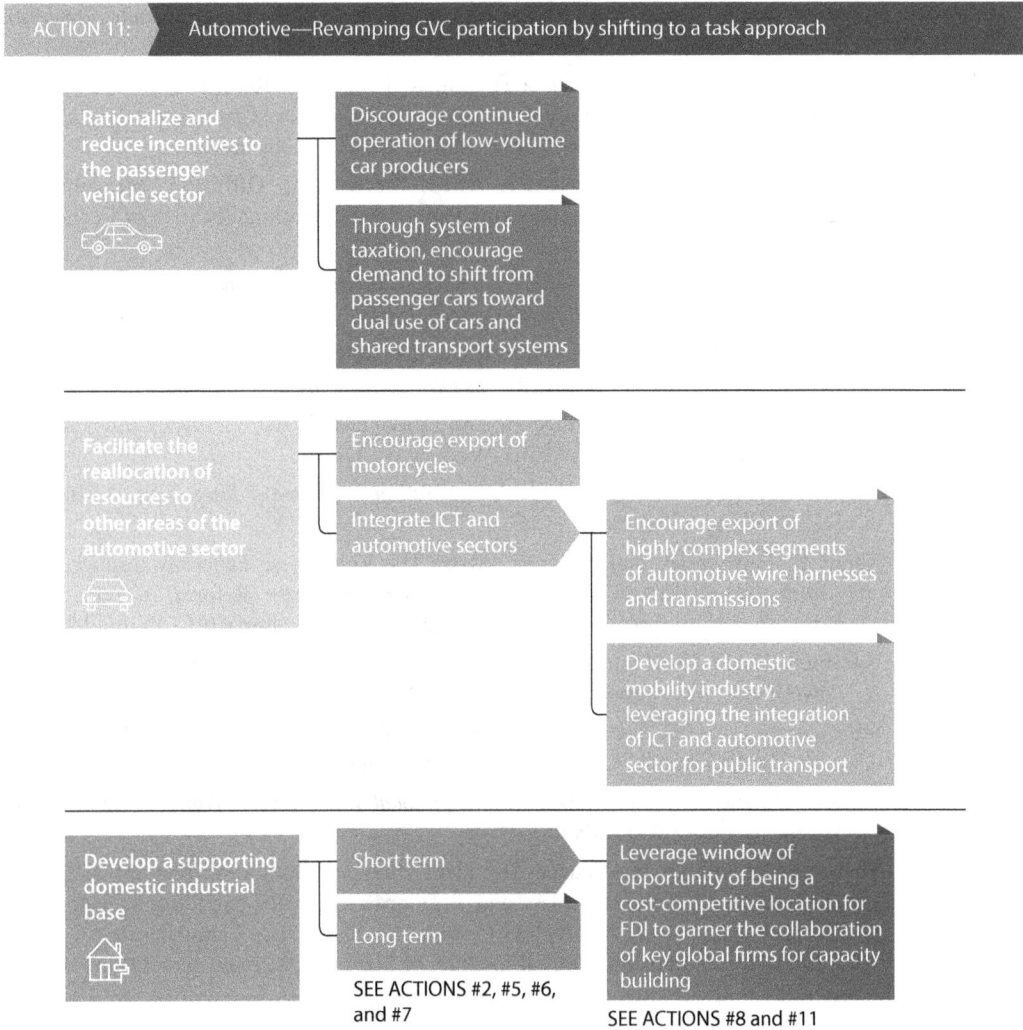

ACTION 11:	Automotive—Revamping GVC participation by shifting to a task approach

Rationalize and reduce incentives to the passenger vehicle sector
- Discourage continued operation of low-volume car producers
- Through system of taxation, encourage demand to shift from passenger cars toward dual use of cars and shared transport systems

Facilitate the reallocation of resources to other areas of the automotive sector
- Encourage export of motorcycles
- Integrate ICT and automotive sectors
  - Encourage export of highly complex segments of automotive wire harnesses and transmissions
  - Develop a domestic mobility industry, leveraging the integration of ICT and automotive sector for public transport

Develop a supporting domestic industrial base
- Short term
  - Leverage window of opportunity of being a cost-competitive location for FDI to garner the collaboration of key global firms for capacity building
- Long term

SEE ACTIONS #2, #5, #6, and #7

SEE ACTIONS #8 and #11

Notes

This chapter draws on the analysis in a background note to the Vietnam 2035 report: "Vietnam's Integration in Global Value Chains" (Kummritz et al. 2016).

1. The New World Bank dataset on content of PTAs is an extension of Horn et al. (2010) and WTO (2011) datasets, and contains 280 PTAs signed by 180 countries between 1980 and 2015, with a total of 51 potential policy areas that are identified in the PTAs.
2. The discussion of GVC products ultimately embodies the idea of complexity of activities and tasks, which are the drivers of and the lens to view sophistication and diversification.

Bibliography

Antràs, P., and R. Staiger. 2012. "Offshoring and the Role of Trade Agreements." *American Economic Review* 102 (7): 3140–83.

Berger, A., D. Bruhn, A. Bender, J. Friesen, K. Kick, K. F. Kullmann, R. Roßner, and S. Weyrauch. 2016. *Deep Preferential Trade Agreements and Upgrading in Global Value Chains: The Case of Vietnam*. Bonn: German Development Institute.

Comin, Diego, and Marti Mestieri. 2013. "Technology Diffusion: Measurement, Causes and Consequences." Working Paper 19052, National Bureau of Economics, Cambridge, MA.

Gershenkron, A. 1962. *Economic Backwardness in a Historical Perspective, a Book of Essays*. Cambridge, MA: Harvard/Belknap.

Horn, H., P. C. Mavroidis, and A. Sapir. 2010. "Beyond the WTO? An Anatomy of EU and US Preferential Trade Agreements." *The World Economy* 33 (11): 1565–88.

Kummritz, K., G. Santoni, D. Taglioni, and D. Winkler. 2016. "Vietnam's Integration in Global Value Chains." World Bank, Washington, DC.

Lawrence, R. Z. 1996. *Regionalism, Multilateralism, and Deeper Integration*. Washington, DC: Brookings Institution.

Minor, P., T. Walmsley, and A. Strutt. 2016. "The Vietnamese Economy through 2035: Alternative Baseline Growth, State-Owned Enterprise Reform, a Trans-Pacific Partnership and a Free Trade Area of Asia and the Pacific." ImpactECON, Boulder, CO.

Nakamura, David. 2016 "Buoyed by U.S. firms, Vietnam Emerges as an Asian Manufacturing Powerhouse." *Washington Post*, 21 May, Washington, DC.

Stinchcombe, A. 1965. "Social Structure and Organizations." In *Handbook of Organizations*, edited by J. G. March. Chicago, IL: Rand McNally.

Taglioni, D., and D. Winkler. 2016. *Making Global Value Chains Work for Development*. Washington, DC: World Bank.

Thanh, Vo Tri, Anh Duong Nguyen, Thu Hang Dinh, and Binh Minh Tran. 2015. "Impact of Current and Proposed FTAs and BITs on Vietnam's Long Term Development Goals: A Case Study of Food Processing and Electronics Manufacturing Sectors." Action Aid Vietnam and Central Institute of Economic Management, Hanoi.

Whittaker, D. H., T. Zhu, T. Sturgeon, M. H. Tsai, and T. Okita. 2010. "Compressed Development." *Studies in Comparative International Development* 45 (4): 439–67.

World Bank. 2016a. *Vietnam 2035: Towards Prosperity, Creativity, Equity, and Democracy, Overview*. Washington, DC: World Bank.

———. 2016b. "World Bank Measuring Export Competitiveness (database)." https://mec.worldbank.org/. Accessed September 2016.

———. 2016c. "World Bank Labor Contents of Export (database)." http://data.worldbank.org/data-catalog/lacex. Accessed September 2016.

PART 1

Cross-Cutting Determinants of GVC Participation

CHAPTER 2

Enterprise Dynamics and Job Flows in Vietnam 2004–12

Implications for Continued Dynamism

Reyes Aterido and Mary Hallward-Driemeier

Key Takeaways

Vietnam has achieved one of the highest sustained rates of growth over the last 30 years, second only to China. Since 1986, real gross domestic product (GDP) growth has averaged 7 percent. Looking forward, there are a number of issues policymakers must address to sustain this momentum. A central issue is how to increase the dynamism of the domestic private sector. Three shifts are needed.

First, the allocation of resources should be driven by open competition and productivity. Preferential access to subsets of firms can help them succeed, but can have larger costs on productivity, innovation, and growth for the economy as a whole. Second, Vietnam must develop a vibrant services sector that can contribute to productivity and growth but also more broadly as supplying important inputs to industry and commercial agriculture. Third, linkages between foreign-owned exporting firms and local suppliers need to be tightened to enable a greater number of domestic firms to move up the productivity ladder.

Using panel data of firms from 2004 to 2012, this chapter looks at the determinants of firm dynamics, jobs flow, and productivity to analyze the nature of job creation and determine if there is scope to improve conditions for further productivity and employment growth to help Vietnam achieve its vision for 2035.

Challenges Confronted

Since the introduction of Đổi Mới, Vietnam has embarked on significant reforms (Hau and Dickie 2006). While Vietnam's growth and poverty reduction have been impressive (Vietnam Academy of Social Sciences 2011; World Bank 2011), the concern is that it is not being driven by gains in productivity. Previous literature does not indicate significant growth in total factor productivity in Vietnam—and recent years have seen a declining rate of productivity growth.

Since the early 2000s, the contributions of capital deepening and structural transformation from agriculture to manufacturing and services have picked up markedly (McCaig and Pavcnik 2014; Tarp, Roland-Holst, and Rand 2003). Conversely, growth in total factor productivity, which accounted for the bulk of productivity growth in the 1990s, has fallen significantly in the post-millennium period (World Bank 2016). Productivity growth will require greater attention, as productivity and innovation eventually will need to become the main drivers of growth.

The playing field is not level for all firms in Vietnam (Hansen, Rand, and Tarp 2009). There are distinct advantages—and disadvantages—for three types of firm ownership. Foreign-owned private firms enjoy preferential access to land and tax treatment. State-owned enterprises (SOEs) also have preferential access to land and to credit, as well as to government procurement, and SOEs continue to have a monopolistic position in certain sectors, including some services sectors that serve as important inputs to other sectors. But domestic private firms do not enjoy these benefits. Looked to as prime drivers of productivity, growth, and hiring going forward, domestic private firms face disadvantages relative to the other ownership groups. These imbalances must be addressed to enable such firms to play a larger role in driving Vietnam's future.

Solutions Proposed

Vietnam has three main options:

- Continue with the current policy framework while monitoring productivity and employment growth. This approach facilitates growth of foreign firms and SOE activity in Vietnam while monitoring spillover effects to the domestic private sector as they contribute to the economy's overall growth rate.
- Support development of Vietnam's services sector as a bridge between domestic and foreign firms. This sector is in its infancy, and the state continues to play a significant ownership role in several important subsectors. It has room to grow, participating in services global value chains (GVCs) more intensely, while also acting as an input to industry and commercial agriculture in particular.
- Take a forward-looking perspective that aims to balance the playing field for all firms. This option involves supporting resource allocation according to productivity and competition (not preferential treatment), bolstering the services sector, and linking export firms to local suppliers.

This chapter proposes that Vietnam take a proactive and forward-looking approach to increasing the dynamism of the domestic private sector. This involves conducting a detailed policy review, including assessing:

- Incentives for continued state ownership and conditions for competition.
- Relative tax treatment of capital and labor.
- Wage policies in support of workers gaining a share of productivity increases.

Lessons to Be Learned

Imbalances in market participation and productivity by firms can be a result of policies that target certain firms in preference to others. SOEs, domestic private firms, and foreign-owned private firms all have a role to play in sustaining Vietnam's productivity and growth. However, concerns exist about an uneven playing field by ownership type. Particularly if SOEs underperform, even with some of their preferential treatment, the case for reform is stronger. This work finds differences in the performance of these three types of firms in their contribution to employment, job creation, and productivity growth over time.

Preferential access to land, tax treatment, credit, and procurement skew market participation opportunities from domestic private firms. This can erode productivity, innovation, and growth for the economy as a whole. The government should take a comprehensive approach to economic growth by implementing regulatory and incentive systems that foster greater balance in participation and productivity among the three types of firms (Athukorala 2006).

Common Lessons and Potential for Replication in Other Countries

This comprehensive approach can be adapted by countries facing the same imbalances in firm market participation and productivity. Common lessons include:

- By understanding firm micro-data, as opposed to aggregate whole-of-country or household data, more detailed investigation of the determinants of productivity growth is possible. We learn what types of firms are creating jobs and how patterns may be evolving across the ownership, size, and age classes that can inform the policy debates. Of particular interest is knowing whether higher-producing firms employ more people, and the extent to which resources, including human resources, are allocated to firms that are becoming more productive. This information will help us ascertain whether productivity growth is likely, or if steps are needed to free the movement of resources across sectors and firms.
- Productivity and growth require the participation of SOEs, domestic private, and foreign-owned private firms to be harmonized. To sustain growth, the collective functioning and contributions of each firm type should serve to complement one another, supporting and not undermining the productivity of each.

Current Conditions and Challenges

Doubling of Formal (Mainly Private) Wage Jobs in the Productive Sector

Vietnam created 5.6 million net new formal wage jobs from 2004 to 2012. Some 4.4 million (almost 80 percent) were in firms with at least 20 employees, indicating that it is not just a result of the expansion of micro firms. Job growth occurred through firm entry and firm growth, though SOEs created fewer jobs and their share of employment has declined. The role of entry has been particularly strong.

Employment Still Tilted toward Larger Firms

Of formal wage workers, 40 percent work in large firms (with 500 or more employees). While there are relatively few such firms, they still account for a significant share of total employment. Policies that shape their behavior or incentives to hire will disproportionately affect employment patterns.

The total number of workers in these very large firms is expanding. There were 1,000 additional such firms by 2012 relative to 2004. The average size in this category increased from 1,479 to 1,693 employees. The share of employment in these large firms declined, however, as the rate of entry and expansion among small and medium firms was even higher.

While the composition of firms is shifting toward smaller firms, the share of employment of the largest 5 percent of firms remained around 65 percent (figure 2.1).

- A relative cutoff (largest 5 percent of firms) rather than an absolute employment size cutoff (500+ workers) reinforces the important role that larger firms play in overall employment.
- In manufacturing firms with 20 or more employees, the employment share of the largest 5 percent of firms is just over 50 percent, and rising.

The high rates of entry are a sign of dynamism, but the concentration of employment among larger firms underscores the need to look at broader dynamics, mainly whether scale efficiencies are being realized among smaller firms and whether there is evidence that these smaller and younger firms can gain productivity and market share and grow.

Figure 2.1 Share of Largest Firms in Total Employment

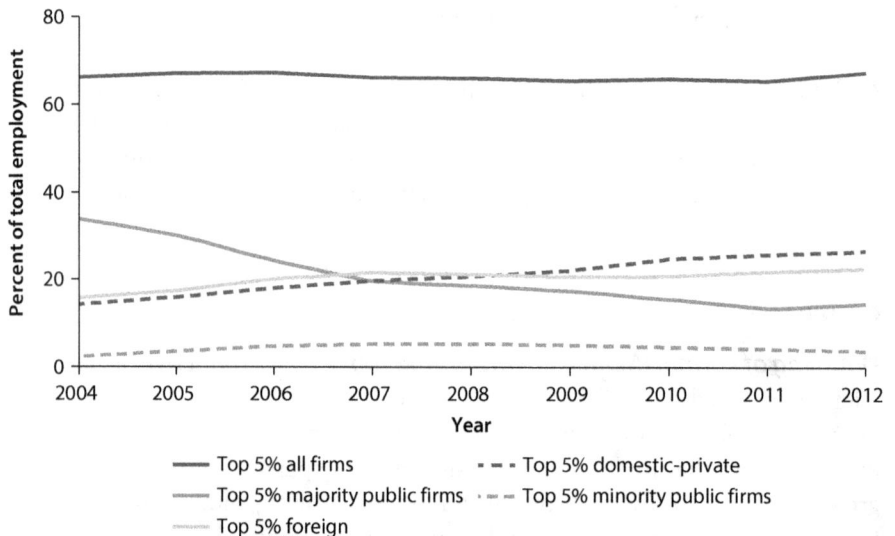

Source: Calculations using Vietnam's Enterprise Data, 2004–12.

Distinct Patterns of Employment and Job Creation by Ownership Types

SOEs' contribution to job creation comes in the form of entry of new, large establishments, which then typically do not grow. These establishments, with access to credit, are able to achieve scale from the beginning. Foreign entrants tend to be relatively large (though there is a range of sizes), but continue to expand even after entry; there is more dynamism in this type of firms. In contrast, domestic private firms tend to be small at entry, and do not grow much over time; achieving large status is very rare.

Foreign direct investment (FDI) has expanded dramatically (from 2.8 percent of GDP in the early 1990s to 7 percent by 2010), but somewhat at the expense of the domestic private sector. Rather than serving as a broader catalyst for growth with spillovers to the domestic private sector—in the form of increased demand for inputs, access to new technology and managerial techniques, demonstration effects, and agglomeration benefits—FDI has not enabled the domestic private sector to expand its share of GDP to the same extent.

By ownership composition of employment across the firm size distribution, among the smaller firms (fewer than 50 employees), employment is overwhelmingly in domestic private firms (figure 2.2). The private sector has expanded its share of overall formal employment somewhat from 2004 to 2012, largely due to expanded entry of small firms and small-scale growth among micro and small firms.

What is striking is the shift at the top end of the size distribution, where the share of workers in SOEs has dropped from 2004 to 2012, while the share in foreign-owned firms has risen sharply. While there are fewer large domestic firms—and they employ only a relatively small share of workers in these largest firms—the share has shown some increase. However, the expanded role of the private sector also is notable at the top: of the largest 5 percent of employers, the share of employment in domestic private firms has doubled since 2012, accounting

Figure 2.2 Ownership Composition of Employment

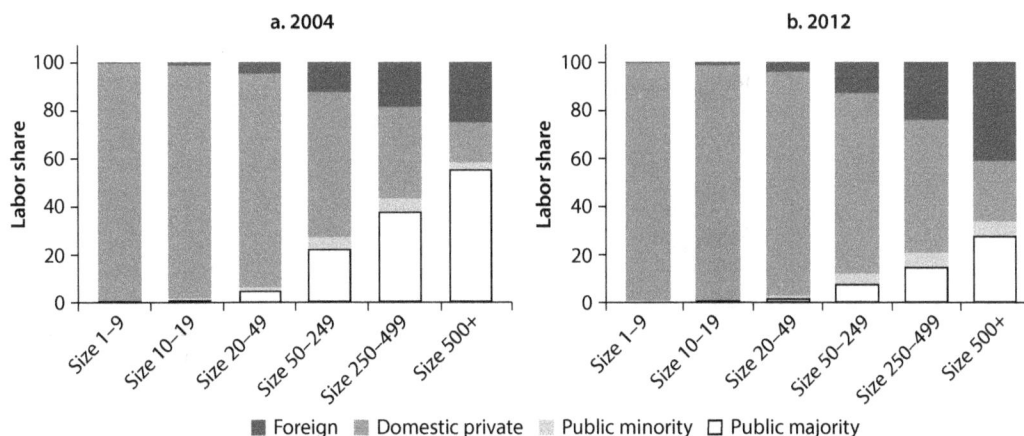

Source: Calculations using Vietnam's Enterprise Data, 2004–12.

for more employment than the SOEs. (Some of this is due to the change in composition of the top 5 percent as the population of firms has disproportionately grown at the bottom of the size distribution.)

Dynamism in Manufacturing, but Less so in Traditionally Higher Value-Added Services

During the 2000s, more than 3 million additional workers were absorbed by manufacturing, primarily in subsectors that already were large employers. Employment in services also has grown, but mainly in retail. Growth in business-support–related services has been more muted. This has implications for the ability of the private sector more broadly to increase its productivity and dynamism.

Fall in Market Concentration across Almost All Sectors

This decline is consistent with greater competition, though some sectors remain dominated by a few players, including some that remain under state control despite lacking a clear rationale for excluding the private sector.

Comparing Herfindahl indices over time (or measures of market share of the top four players), the degree of market concentration has fallen across a majority of sectors (figure 2.3).

Yet in the most concentrated sectors, competition remains limited. This is true for some publicly owned services sectors that have important inputs into other sectors (such as telecommunications and financial services) or sectors where the economic case for a government monopoly is not clear (dairy, pharmaceuticals).

Figure 2.3 Vietnam's Market Concentration Has Fallen across a Majority of Sectors

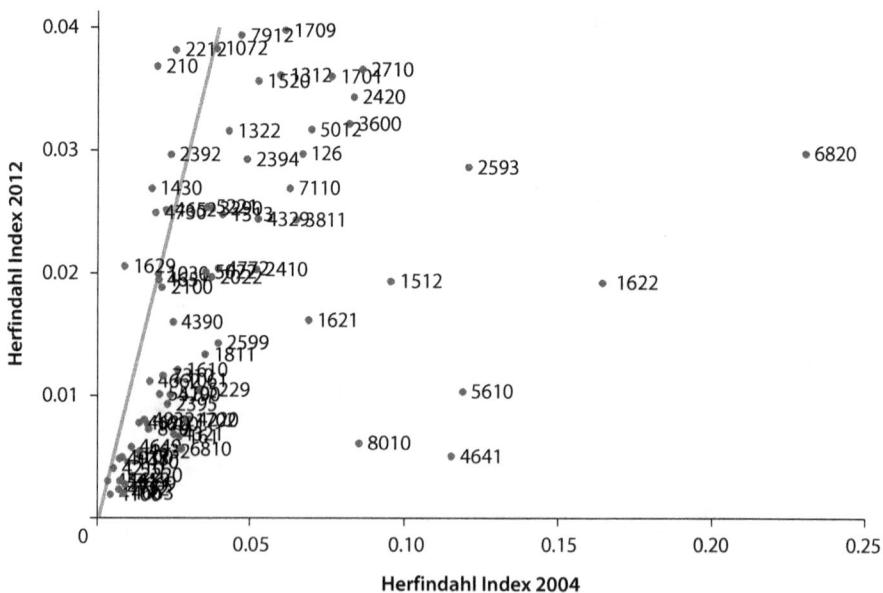

Source: Calculations using Vietnam's Enterprise Data, 2004–12.
Note: Sectors with an employment share ≥0.001 and a 2012 Herfindahl index calculated using labor shares <0.04.

The pattern of market concentration differs dramatically by ownership type, with SOEs dominating mining and utilities, foreign-owned firms dominant in some manufacturing sectors, and the domestic private sector dominant in most other services.

Apparent Reallocation of Resources to More Efficient Uses, but Somewhat at Labor's Expense

Static efficiency measures (that is, the distribution of resources at a point in time) suggest that firms with a higher level of productivity tend to employ a relatively larger share of workers.

Dynamic efficiency measures (how resources are moving over time) suggest that those with a higher level of productivity are not necessarily growing or hiring more workers. Those firms with improving productivity (showing a positive change in productivity rather than a high level of productivity) are growing market share but are not expanding their share of employment.

Thus, some efficiency gains are being realized by labor-saving technological changes or by shifting production to become more capital intensive. This could have important implications for the ability to create jobs for an expanding population, for developing domestic markets, and for ensuring sustainable, balanced growth.

Employment Growth Unlikely to Keep Up with Output Growth As Capital Intensity Rises

There is evidence of shifting patterns of capital intensity, particularly among domestic private firms and some SOEs. Domestic private firms have always been less capital intensive than SOEs or FDI firms, but the gap has been narrowing sharply as these domestic private firms expand their investments (figure 2.4).

While SOEs' share of employment has fallen, their share of output remains significant, consistent with shifts in production technology and a deepening of capital intensity in these firms.

Monitoring the relative productivity and incentives affecting the choices between labor and capital is important not only to maintain growth, but to ensure that employment also expands and enables Vietnam's workers to share in these gains.

Wage Gains Not Always Commensurate with Productivity Improvements

Foreign firms and most SOEs pay significantly higher wages than domestic private firms, even controlling for firm size, sector, and age. The smallest firms pay lower wages, but for those with at least 10 employees, there is little effect of firm size on average wages. As firms expand their employment, wages tend to fall, particularly in SOEs. Wage gains are often lower in firms with the highest labor productivity. However, firms that raise productivity tend to raise wages too, although domestic private firms less so.

Figure 2.4 The Capital-Intensity Gap Is Narrowing

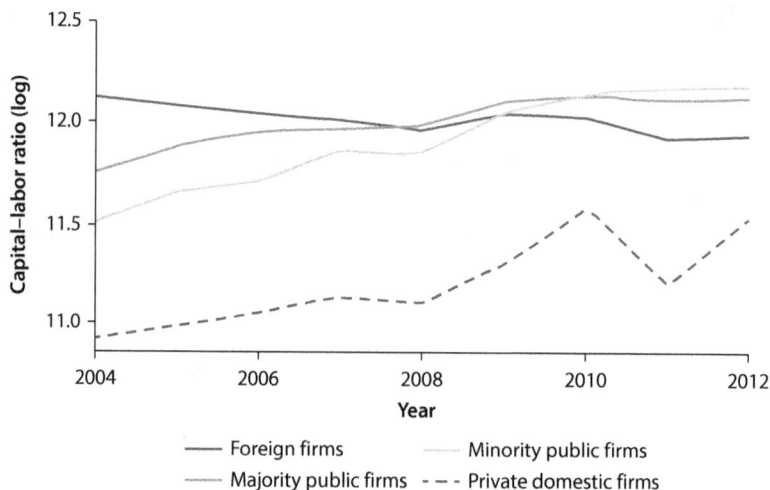

Source: Calculations using Vietnam's Enterprise Data, 2004–12.

Concrete Actions

Changes at the policy level should be targeted and should include:

- Addressing inequalities in the regulatory environment, such as access to finance, infrastructure, and markets by ownership, and where possible, removing the disadvantages domestic private firms face to enable them to drive productivity and employment growth.
- Reviewing the continued presence of SOEs in certain sectors, particularly those that provide important input services.
- Encouraging stronger links between domestic private firms and foreign private firms to encourage technology transfers and opportunities to access larger markets.
- Given rising capital intensity, reviewing the policies encouraging firms to invest more in machines than in people, including tax holidays (particularly for FDI), depreciation schedules, access to subsidized credit, and hiring and training subsidies.
- Reviewing wage policies to support workers in gaining a share of productivity increases, although the smallest firms may face challenges in maintaining the pace of mandated increases.

Key Outcomes

Above all, productivity growth, which has been on a long-term decline, will require greater attention as productivity and innovation eventually must become the main drivers of growth. What explains this productivity stagnation?

Public investment in infrastructure, skills development, and support for market institutions has not always been efficient and well coordinated, in part reflecting a fragmented state structure. The large presence of the SOE sector has also been raised as contributing to this pattern, though in fact most SOEs are relatively efficient producers, even if they are generally not innovating or improving their efficiency as are FDI firms. Rather, the steady erosion of productivity growth in the domestic private sector is most worrisome. There are opportunities to raise productivity, by improving competitive markets, improving the linkages with more productive FDI firms, expanding and diversifying exports. The question for policymakers is whether they are willing to embark on the next round of reforms to help realize these opportunities.

Drivers and Enablers

A better balanced playing field for firms operating in Vietnam can improve productivity growth and employment. Among other elements, the reform agenda to unleash strong and sustainable economic growth must create an enabling environment for domestic enterprises. Restructuring and equitizing SOEs will remain important, but ensuring more competitive and productive domestic enterprises demands even greater policy attention. This will involve strengthening the institutional foundations of the market economy (by protecting property rights and enforcing competition policies); creating and maintaining a stable, well-regulated, and inclusive financial sector; promoting transparent and functioning land markets; facilitating a stronger services sector; and furthering a more extensive transport and network connectivity across the country and with trading partners.

Barriers, Threats, and Challenges

The reform agenda will be demanding. Even if a balanced playing field is created, it is not enough. Creating an enabling environment for a vibrant private sector to grow and become lead firms in the global economy will require more policy action—deepening the skills of workers and managers, improving markets for credit and other financial and business services, addressing issues of access to land, providing reliable access to infrastructure, maintaining a solid macroeconomic foundation, and supporting an innovation system that will enable greater productivity growth in the future. While new technology offers opportunities, it also risks significant disruptions. Global economic trends, including the slowdown and rebalancing of growth in China, the growth of FDI and exports in other Southeast and South Asian economies requires more nimble policy responses. International agreements such as the Trans-Pacific Partnership offer Vietnam an opportunity to deepen its involvement in international markets, while reinforcing the need to reform at home. Vietnam has much to build on, but sustaining its growth performance will take renewed efforts.

Bibliography

Athukorala, Prema-Chandra. 2006. "Trade Policy Reforms and the Structure of Protection in Vietnam." *The World Economy* 29 (2): 161–87.

Hansen, Henrik, John Rand, and Finn Tarp. 2009. "Enterprise Growth and Survival in Vietnam: Does Government Support Matter?" *Journal of Development Studies* 45 (7): 1048–69.

Hau, Chu Thi Trung, and Paul M. Dickie. 2006. "Economic Transition in Viet Nam: Doi Moi to WTO." PPTP Study Series 1/2006, Asian Development Bank, Manila.

McCaig, Brian, and Nina Pavcnik. 2014. "Export Markets and Labor Allocation in a Low-Income Country." Working Paper 20455, National Bureau of Economic Research, Cambridge, MA.

Tarp, Finn, David Roland-Holst, and John Rand. 2003. "Economic Structure and Development in an Emergent Asian Economy: Evidence from a Social Accounting Matrix for Vietnam." *Journal of Asian Economics* 13: 847–71.

Vietnam Academy of Social Sciences. 2011. *Poverty Reduction in Vietnam: Achievements and Challenges*. Hanoi: Vietnamese Academy of Social Sciences.

World Bank. 2011. *Vietnam Development Report 2012: Market Economy for a Middle-Income Vietnam*. Washington, DC: World Bank.

———. 2016. *Vietnam 2035: Towards Prosperity, Creativity, Equity, and Democracy*. Washington, DC: World Bank.

CHAPTER 3

Servicifying the Vietnamese Economy

Claire H. Hollweg

Key Takeaways

A changing trade landscape offers Vietnam an opportunity to reposition itself higher in global value chains (GVCs), transitioning from assembly functions to more sophisticated products or tasks. To leverage these opportunities, Vietnam will need to create an enabling environment that supports a nascent set of dynamic, innovative, and autonomous domestic firms to grow, diversify, and move up the value chains in which it participates. This includes the agribusiness and ICT GVCs the government considers strategic, as well as the automotive and textiles and apparel GVCs in which global competition is fierce and the country is locked at the low end of the value chain. Enhancing the competitiveness of the domestic services sector to enable servicification—the role of services, not only as inputs into the economy, but as a means to change the way value is created—is an essential component of this dynamic transition.

Because the high-value added segments of GVCs are often rich in services content, servicification would simultaneously enable upgrading to more sophisticated products or tasks in GVCs and allow for the capture of more value added domestically. In the 21st century, efficient services are a major determinant of export competitiveness as inputs into manufacturing, agriculture, and other services, and it is in services that the majority of value is added within the chain. And once the domestic services sector is competitive enough by international standards, direct services exports themselves provide an opportunity to diversify exports and can be used as an engine of growth.

Yet the forward linkages to export sectors from the backbone services sectors necessary for competitive industry are weak. Enhancing the performance of the services sector involves ensuring an open and liberal regulatory environment for service providers; targeting supply-side factors including workforce skills and infrastructure; and leveraging trade agreements to allow greater access to low-cost services from abroad, while enabling the economy to become a regional supplier of modern services such as ICT.

Challenges Confronted

The services sector in Vietnam is in its infancy. Services' contribution to GDP is low, given the country's level of development, and has declined since 1995. Services have increased Vietnam's integration in the global economy, acting as a source of export diversification. But gross services exports are lower than expected by international standards. As Vietnam emerged as an assembly platform, services contributed significantly to expanding domestic value added in gross exports, including those in the automotive, electronics, agribusiness, and textiles and apparel sectors. But this strong growth was from a low base. Services are less important for creating domestic value added embodied in exports than in comparator countries, and Vietnam's exports became less reliant on services since 1995.

Domestic services contribute to Vietnam's exports primarily as direct exports rather than as inputs into other sectors' exports. In relative terms, Vietnam's exports in GVC-intensive sectors use less domestic services inputs for their exports than those in comparator countries and less than the economy at large. These sectors rely little on productive, modern services as inputs, such as financial and business services, and instead rely heavily on wholesale and retail trade, construction, and real estate services. This may be for economic reasons, where Vietnam's position in these sectors' GVCs does not demand high value-added services. But evidence from firm-level interviews also suggests that Vietnam has yet to establish a vibrant domestic modern services sector to act as inputs into downstream production.

Not having access to well-functioning and efficient services—domestically or through foreign provision—may be a constraining factor for manufacturing and commercial agriculture to leverage global integration through higher value-added participation in GVCs. There is room for the sector to grow, but binding constraints to servicifying the domestic economy and exports include regulatory issues as well as horizontal constraints specific to the services sector.

Solutions Proposed

A priority will be to ensure that the domestic economy has access to modern, productivity-enhancing services as inputs to manufacturing and commercial agriculture. In textiles and apparel, services such as design, marketing, transportation, retail, and utility provision arguably would help facilitate sectoral growth into higher value-added activities. For agribusiness, improvements to information and communications technology (ICT) and transport services would help the sector adapt to globalized supply chains. ICT service improvements can facilitate a networked, multimodal system of mobility and build connectivity throughout the country. This will require a strong service component to design, operate, and monitor the system. Exports of ICT services themselves would directly translate export growth into value-added growth.

To facilitate services sector change to support exports, a focus on forward linkages is necessary. Actions that can develop the domestic services sector and enable servicification involve:

- Targeting supply-side limitations including workforce skills such as human capital, technical skills, and managerial capacity, all of which matter for the provision of modern services.
- Ensuring an open and enabling domestic regulatory environment governing services providers.
- Investing in and upgrading other enabling factors that support the development of the domestic services sector, including the business environment, infrastructure, and institutions.
- Leveraging regional trade agreements for Vietnam to have greater access to low-cost services from abroad, such as transport and logistics; to attract foreign investments and professionals to modernize the domestic services sector; and to become a regional supplier of modern services, such as ICT.

Common Lessons and Potential for Replication in Other Countries

Servicification has become increasingly important as production internationalizes. The GVC revolution has been accompanied by key changes in the services sector, underscoring the importance of the goods–services nexus. For example, managing the complexity of the value chain and preserving production throughout the chain require strong coordination that relies on efficient services such as auditors, lawyers, and managers (Taglioni and Winkler 2016). It is in services such as design, marketing, and retailing that the majority of value added is captured within the chain, while others such as transport and distribution exhibit higher labor intensity. Governments and policy practitioners should not undervalue the role that services play for export competitiveness, value-added capture through GVC participation, and making exports more inclusive by supporting jobs and wages.

Current Conditions and Challenges

Different measures are used to assess the export performance of Vietnam's services sector. Gross trade statistics capture both the direct value added embodied in the production of the export as well as all domestic and imported intermediate inputs, measured at the transaction value. Gross trade statistics tend to undervalue the services sector's real contribution to exports. This is because services indirectly support other sectors' exports, when they act as inputs to production. Value added trade statistics capture the total domestic value added embodied in the production of the export, which takes into account the forward linkages of services with other sectors' exports.[1]

Services in the Domestic Economy

An initial indication of Vietnam's underdeveloped domestic services sector is the share of services value added in GDP. At 43.1 percent in 2013, this is low by international standards given the country's level of development and has declined since 1995. Employment in services also is low given the size of the services sector, absorbing 32 percent of the workforce. Although the share of industry value added in GDP—at 36.9 percent in 2013—is above that predicted for Vietnam's level of economic development, industry constitutes 86.1 percent of exports (79.7 percent for manufacturing) against only 21.2 percent of employment. Agriculture instead absorbs 46.8 percent of employment. This suggests unexploited opportunities for the domestic economy to move toward more sophisticated and high-quality export products, and to further diversify into services.

Continued structural transformation away from agriculture toward manufacturing and services could support the development of a productive, modern services sector. This, in turn, could support a competitive private sector in Vietnam and enhance the economy's global integration. This is because services play a dual role in building export competitiveness. Services are a source of competitiveness as inputs into manufacturing and agriculture, and direct exports of services provide an opportunity to diversify exports and can be used as an engine of growth.

Gross Services Exports

Services exports have increased Vietnam's integration in the global economy. Gross services export values more than doubled since 1995, faster than most comparator economies (China; the Republic of Korea; Malaysia; Singapore; Taiwan, China; and Thailand). But gross services exports are lower than expected internationally, given Vietnam's level of development, accounting for only 7.5 percent of Vietnam's total exports in 2013. Services exports have not yet acted as a source of export diversification, which have declined over the past decade as a ratio to GDP and remain dominated (95 percent) by travel and transport services, rather than other commercial services.

Total Services in Gross Exports

The following analysis uses the Organisation for Economic Co-operation and Development–World Trade Organization (OECD–WTO) Trade in Value Added (TiVA) database to measure the contribution of services to the domestic value added in Vietnam's gross exports, how services contribute to gross exports (directly or indirectly as inputs to other sectors' exports), and which services sectors contribute.

Between 1995 and 2011, the services sector made a major contribution to expanding domestic value added in Vietnam's gross exports, including automotive, electronics, agribusiness, and textiles and apparel. Domestic services value added embodied in gross exports saw a compound annual growth rate (CAGR) of 15.1 percent in the period, outperforming all regional comparators except China. The growth of domestic services value added in gross exports of each of Vietnam's GVC-intensive sectors ranked the fastest among its comparators, apart from electronics, automotive and agribusiness exports in China.

But this strong growth was from a low base, and domestic services contribute a lower share of gross exports in Vietnam—only $25.0 in 2011 for each $100 of gross exports—than comparator countries except Malaysia and countries at a similar level of economic development. The GVC-intensive sectors in Vietnam also rely less on domestic services for their exports than comparator countries, and less than the economy at large (figure 3.1).

The value added growth of services was less than the growth of total value added embodied in gross exports. As a result, Vietnam's exports became less reliant on services, either directly or indirectly, since 1995—$37.3 of domestic value added in 1995 was services for each $100 of gross exports. The textiles and apparel sector was the only sector where gross exports became more reliant on domestic services value added between 1995 and 2011.

The main channel through which domestic services contribute to Vietnam's gross exports is direct domestic value added. In 2011, 57 percent of services value added embodied in gross exports was generated directly within services sectors. The value added generated as inputs to other sectors' exports through forward linkages equaled 43 percent.

This indirect contribution remains underdeveloped by international yardsticks. Vietnam's forward linkages of services with other export sectors of the economy also are among the lowest in the TiVA database, indicating that Vietnam's services sector may be providing inadequate support to export activities.

Indirect Services in Value-Added Exports

These linkages are explored in more detail by focusing on where services inputs are supplied, and where manufacturing inputs are sourced (figure 3.2).

Figure 3.1 Share of Domestic Services Value Added Embodied in Gross Exports, 2011

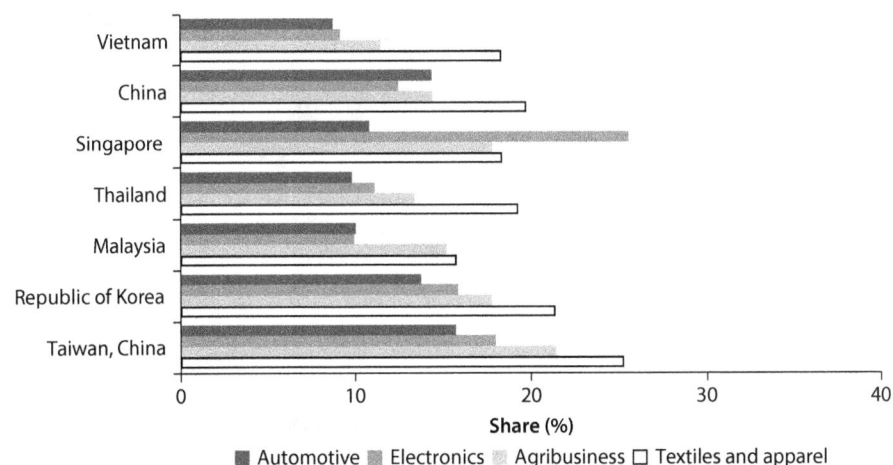

Source: Calculations using data from OECD–WTO TiVA database.

The structure of forward and backward linkages with export activities in Vietnam differs from that in comparator countries. Services contribute 39 percent of total exported value added in Vietnam—the lowest share relative to its comparators. One third of the value added is exported indirectly through manufacturing and primary production activities. In contrast, the forward linkages to manufacturing export sectors from backbone services sectors necessary for a competitive industrial base is much higher in China; Korea; and Taiwan, China. Services also generate very few linkages with each other in Vietnam.

There are several theories about these weak forward linkages. One is that the services linkages in Vietnam are in low value-added activities, such as wholesale and retail trade. Another is that Vietnam's export sectors are in low-value added activities, or are not services intensive, or that Vietnam's position in these sectors' GVCs does not demand high value-added services. Or alternatively, Vietnam's firms may rely on imported services.

Despite accounting for 80 percent of gross export values, the manufacturing sector adds relatively little value added. Manufacturing contributes 47 percent of total exported value added in Vietnam—again the lowest share relative to its comparators except Singapore. The low value-added content of manufacturing exports also is associated with low services content, as are exports of Vietnam's GVC-intensive sectors. Although high-income countries generally use services more intensively in manufacturing, Vietnam's manufacturing exports rely on fewer services as inputs than those of comparators, in a pattern that extends to the agribusiness, automotive, and electronics sectors (servicification of textiles and apparel exports is relatively advanced).

Figure 3.2 Inputs from Services into Manufacturing Exports, 2011

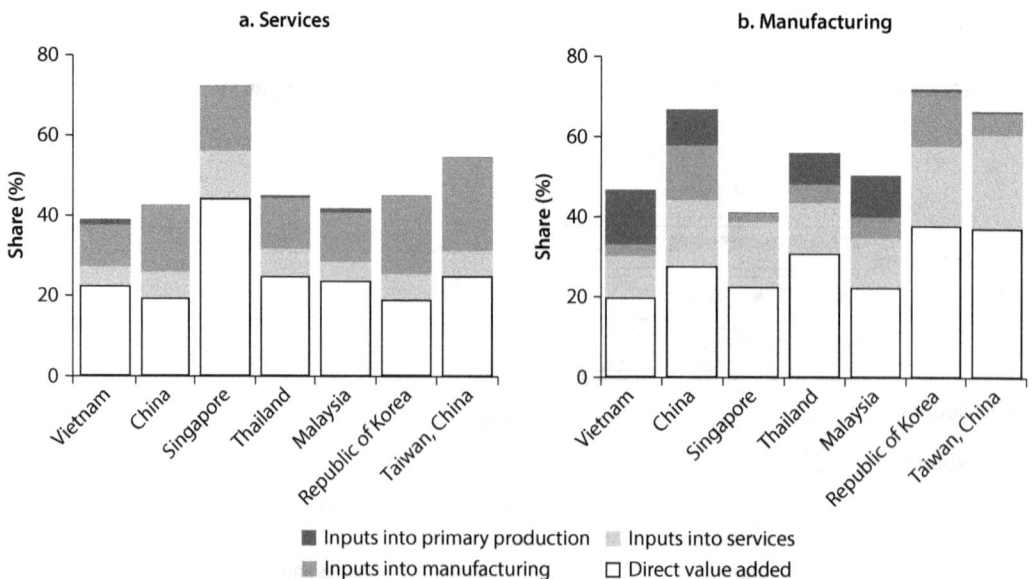

Source: Calculations using data from OECD–WTO TiVA database.

Vietnam's manufacturing sector creates few forward linkages, and other economies rely more on manufacturing as inputs for exports. That sector also creates few backward linkages, such that manufacturing growth in its current activities will have limited pull on the domestic economy unless these domestic linkages are strengthened. Upgrading in GVCs through servicification may thus be one avenue for Vietnam to strengthen its domestic manufacturing sector's forward and backward linkages, and help drive the structural transformation of the economy from agriculture.

Vietnam's exports, including manufacturing exports of GVC-intensive sectors, rely little on financial services, post and telecommunications, research and development, other business services, and computer services, instead depending heavily on construction, wholesale and retail trade, and real estate. The support that financial intermediation provides to export activities is extremely underdeveloped by international yardsticks. The use of electricity, gas, and water supply also is lower in Vietnam than the average economy at a similar level of economic development. Among the four GVC-intensive sectors (figure 3.3), the share of

Figure 3.3 Composition of Domestic Services Inputs into Manufacturing Exports, 2011

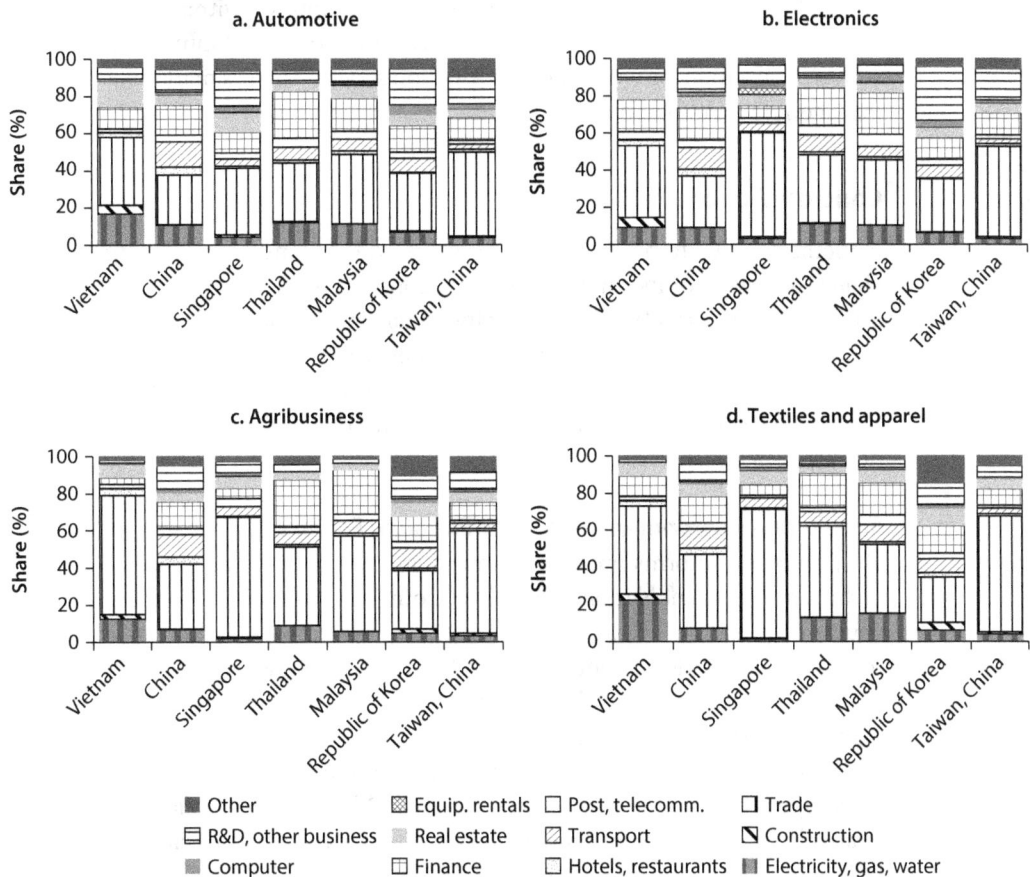

financial and nonfinancial modern services embedded in exports is significantly lower in Vietnam than in comparator economies.

Challenges

The above review suggests that Vietnam has yet to establish a vibrant domestic modern services sector to act as inputs into downstream production. This finding stems in part from Vietnam's industrial structure and positioning within these GVCs, where Vietnam is focused primarily on assembly activities, with limited processing or value addition in the domestic industrial sector. (The services dominating the linkages with manufacturing are primarily construction, wholesale and retail trade and real estate, as seen.) Few assembly activities demand modern services as inputs, domestic or imported, particularly when the supply chains are controlled and coordinated by foreign lead firms. For example, the parts and components are imported into Vietnam, which are transported to the assembly plant, assembled, and then transported to the port and exported.

Inadequate services supply may inhibit upgrading into more sophisticated products or tasks in GVCs. Modern services (especially professional and backbone services) can also be an important value-added creating segment of these value chains. In many GVCs, the greatest value added is captured within pre-production services such as the initial idea based on research and development, design, and commercialization, or within post-production services such as marketing, advertising, and retail and brand management.

Concrete Actions

If Vietnam wants to move into higher value-added manufacturing in these value chains—as many of its comparators have done—it must ensure that its firms can access efficient, modern, productivity-enhancing services. These services can be provided either domestically or by foreign services providers, and regional trade agreements and FDI in the services sector will be important. But for Vietnamese private firms to become lead firms, many of these services capabilities will be needed domestically.

Regulatory Environment and Other Enabling Factors

Despite major reforms introduced in the last two decades by many Association of Southeast Asian Nations (ASEAN) countries, including Vietnam, ASEAN countries have, on average, more restrictive services policies than any other region in the world except the Gulf States (Gootiiz and Mattoo 2015). The Services Trade Restrictions Index of the World Bank for the region is 60 percent higher than the global average. Among ASEAN members, however, the restrictiveness of applied policies varies widely. Cambodia and Singapore have the most open policies in the sectors covered. Myanmar and Vietnam are also relatively open, with some restrictions, while the rest (Indonesia, Malaysia, the Philippines, and Thailand) have significant restrictions. Vietnam's index falls below the ASEAN average in all services sectors, reflecting the effect of market-opening reforms (figure 3.4). Nevertheless, major services trade restrictions exist in Vietnam's financial, telecommunications, transportation and professional services sectors.

Vietnam should further leverage ASEAN integration to promote services exports and expand services provision domestically by local and foreign providers. The ASEAN Economic Community is a potential market of more than 600 million people with $2.3 trillion in GDP, and can foster competition and productivity while expanding the supply of intermediate services for manufacturing and other services. To that end, Vietnam should strive to advance the removal of the remaining formal restrictions to trade and investment in services between ASEAN partners, such as foreign equity limits. In addition, enhancing regulatory cooperation in services is necessary to ensure a true single market in services, which will reduce regulatory compliance costs for ASEAN services providers and improve conditions for expanding and upgrading Vietnam's services sector.

Aside from the regulatory environment, a range of other enabling factors are necessary for servicifying the domestic economy. Enabling factors include foreign investment in services; the promotion of private small and medium enterprises; human capital, including skills and entrepreneurial ability; infrastructure, such as a telecommunications network that facilitates the delivery of services; and institutions, such as the quality of a country's rule of law or regulatory environment (Sáez et al. 2014). Countries can be confined to the bottom of the value chain not only because of regulatory barriers in services, but also because of gaps in these other areas.

Firm-level interviews in three GVC sectors in Vietnam inform how better use of services can support upgrading in each.

Figure 3.4 Services Trade Restrictiveness Index, ASEAN Countries, 2012

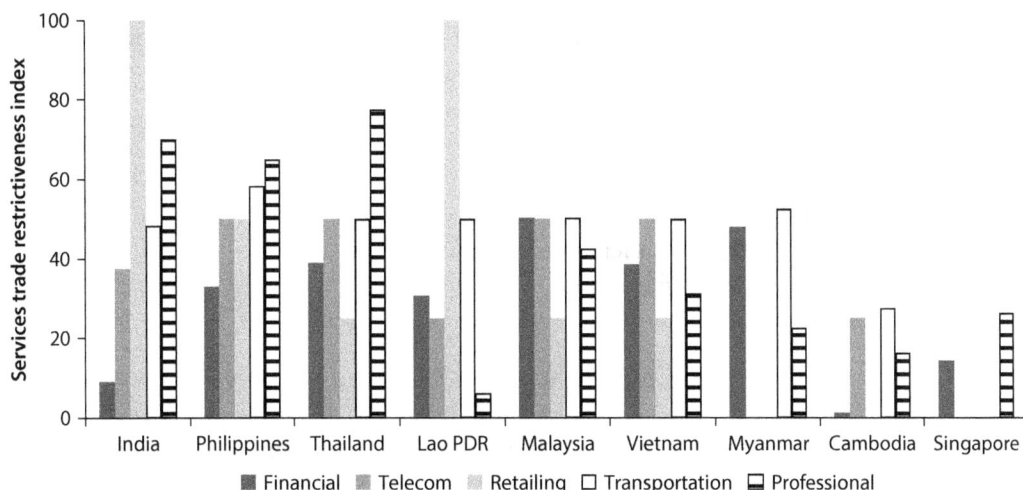

Source: Gootiiz and Mattoo 2015.

Textiles and Apparel

Services will be critical for Vietnam to move up the value chain in apparel, to develop a strong supporting industry, and ultimately to take advantage of market-access opportunities granted under preferential trade agreements (PTAs). Over the next 20 years, Vietnam will get the chance to expand and diversify into higher value-added activities in apparel. This opportunity is largely due to PTAs (see chapter 6), including the ASEAN–Japan Free Trade Agreement (FTA) and trade agreements with yarn-forward conditions for preference. Yet Vietnam has a weak textiles industry, which will limit its ability to exploit the opportunity. Although substantial spinning takes place, less investment has been made in textiles or dyeing due to high costs (chemicals and treatment systems) and other bottlenecks.

The capacity to develop along the textiles and apparel GVC will rely heavily on services, in particular design and marketing, but also professional skills, transport, and utilities. Moving along the apparel GVC involves moving from contract cut-make-trim (CMT) to free on board (FOB)—where a foreign retailer will place an order with a Vietnamese factory, which then produces the garment and ships to the retailer—to original design manufacturing (ODM), and eventually moving beyond unbranded contract activities to domestic brands. In more detail:

- Vietnamese firms will need to enhance capacity in branding, marketing, and retail services in the domestic and overseas markets. Few Vietnamese firms sell their own brands domestically, and even fewer abroad. Within these firms, branding and marketing generally are performed in house, using few resources, often as merchandising teams responsible for organizing orders from clients rather than sales and marketing teams to drum up business. Website design also will be important, relying on the ICT sector. Many firms create their own websites and do other information technology (IT) services themselves in their back office.

- Investing in a technically skilled workforce with professional qualifications will enable development of supporting industries in textiles and footwear. Skills mismatches exist, particularly in a textiles industry that relies heavily on qualified technicians and engineers to dye and finish. The footwear and leather-goods industry—a complementary but higher value-added GVC—is skill intensive, as workers are needed to produce leather pieces or work with chemicals to dye the leather. Workers without adequate skills working as chemical engineers, for example, can create large losses very quickly for firms from small mistakes in the production process.

- As the textiles industry expands, additional support services will be needed, creating more specialized but high value-added services jobs. For example, a domestic textiles research institute provides a variety of support services to private textiles enterprises. Two important services it offers for textiles companies include research and development to introduce applications of technology in the textiles industry, and quality control tests of products for textiles inspection and certification.

- Improving managerial skills and other soft skills of workers will become increasingly important to improve competitiveness. Management can be a bottleneck for labor productivity in domestic apparel firms, with marked differences in management techniques between foreign and domestic companies. Successful upgrading from CMT—where everything is arranged by the foreign contractor—to FOB and ODM—where firms source their own inputs—requires a more sophisticated management system.

- There are applications for ICT to improve management within firms operating in the textile and apparel industry, such as enterprise resource planning systems. These systems integrate internal and external management information across an entire organization, automating this activity with an integrated software application. Likely only a few domestic firms in the industry use them.

- Access to finance is important for supporting industries to develop, but also for apparel firms to move into higher value-added activities. For firms to move from CMT to FOB or ODM involves sourcing materials and other inputs themselves, requiring the firm to be in a much stronger financial position, with access to its own liquidity or external loans.

- Rapid growth of the industry will demand sound physical infrastructure and transport. Many textiles and apparel companies perform their own transport in house. While this may be for economic reasons, Vietnam should ensure there are no constraints to the availability of third-party transport companies, which can lower costs for smaller firms. Most textiles and apparel firms are in Hanoi and Ho Chi Minh City, but growth of the industry will add pressures to move outside these metropolitan areas, requiring enhanced connectivity and facilities such as roads, ports, and customs.

- Access to reliable utilities is important, in particular to be able to compete on quality. Water and electricity are basic inputs for yarn and textiles producers. Synthetic fiber producers also need reliable power, without which low- or inconsistent-quality output results.

Agribusiness

Vietnam's vision is to transform its agriculture sector from low value-added commodities to high value-added and high-quality processed goods by integrating into regional and global agribusiness supply chains. Many of Vietnam's agricultural products are exported as commodities in raw, unprocessed form with minimal value added. These products are then processed and sold outside Vietnam as packaged and branded goods in international markets at much higher prices.

This transformation can only be achieved if Vietnam improves the efficiency and competitiveness of agriculture, through higher productivity, quality, and value added. It will be driven by less resource-intensive and more technology-intensive agricultural growth. ICT and transport services are critical for agribusiness to make these shifts:

- Technology adoption in agribusiness will be important for productivity growth, and application of ICT will play a big role. ICT services can become an important productivity-enhancing input for farmers, providing the information and tools necessary for modernization, technology transfer, and risk management.

- ICT can improve the quality of agricultural products—important because quality standards are integral to participating in GVCs. A severe constraint is in improper or inadequate methods of using agricultural inputs (a majority of Vietnamese farmers do not, for example, use the seeds, fertilizers, and crop-production products best suited to their outputs). Farmers can use ICT for advisory services on integrated pest management, satellite imagery on crop/aquaculture expansion, automated sensor-based irrigation systems, or satellite-based precision applications of fertilizer and pesticides. Current and accurate information on weather conditions allows farmers to plan planting and adjust inputs accordingly.

- ICT services can help farmers coordinate among themselves, or better link domestic sellers to overseas buyers. ICT adoption, including cell phones, would help, allowing for greater consistency in crops among smallholders. It also would improve supply-chain coordination and efficiency, helping reposition domestic products in the global market.

- Transport services will remain important for enabling high value-added agribusiness production and moving products toward the middle and upper segments of the global market. GVCs require goods of exacting standards and consistent quality, delivered on time, in good condition, and ready for further processing for final consumption. Inadequate transportation of products to markets often results in a significant amount of goods being damaged or spoiled before reaching their destination. For lead firms and large global buyers, these issues present serious obstacles to sourcing agricultural products from Vietnam. Improved connectivity of agricultural centers to processing centers or from processing centers to ports will be fundamental, including cold-chain transport. Even for the domestic market, modern chilled warehousing, transport, and packing operations are surprisingly underdeveloped.

Automotive

Two-wheelers are the most common means of transport in Vietnam and dominate the domestic automotive sector, and passenger cars have relatively low market share. As per capita incomes rise, demand is expected to shift from the former to the latter. The adoption of the automobile as a primary means of transport will, however, result in traffic congestion and impaired mobility in large cities. One challenge will be to encourage a shift in transport modes and to develop a new model of mobility, centered on mass public transport systems in dense urban areas. No city has a well-functioning urban transport system, and even regular bus services are not very developed.

A better mobility model would have positive spillovers into other GVC-intensive sectors, for example, it would have linkages with agribusiness. The services sector will need to be ready, in particular ICT software and telecommunications. In further detail:

- The ICT sector can facilitate a networked, multimodal urban mobility system. The new model of mobility will entail a larger network of metropolitan urban infrastructure, including soft infrastructure. Examples include traffic management systems, traffic lights, and speed cameras. Investments in public transport, such as bus rapid transit or light rail systems, will require local digital content and services in public transportation. Examples include GPS tracking of buses or trains where users can connect with up-to-date schedules on cell phones. Vietnam will need to invest in knowledge, capacity, and management of these systems.

- Vietnam should leverage its ICT industry to develop connectivity services and content for the automotive industry, and the software that enables it. The hardware and software sides of the ICT sector stand to make important connectivity services inputs to the automotive GVC. Demand for such services will flourish as automobiles become more digitally enabled.

- Over the next 20 years, it is increasingly likely that robots will replace tasks such as welding, cutting, grinding, polishing, and painting. Vietnam is developing and applying additive manufacturing capabilities in the two-wheeler sector, but robotics and additive manufacturing skills once developed can easily be redeployed to other manufacturing industries. Investing in developing these skills could benefit many of the manufacturing industries in the country.

- Robotics and additive manufacturing are also changing the composition of the industrial workforce, and will demand high-skilled workers. New technologies will generate job opportunities for engineers to work with advanced robots and robotic operating systems as well as programming and maintenance and repair. This should be viewed as an opportunity to create better paying services jobs, and will require an agenda targeted at skills upgrading.

The conclusion to be drawn, therefore, is that more efficient services are needed to grow, diversify, and move up these value chains into more sophisticated products or tasks.

Key Outcomes

Servicification of the domestic economy will release opportunities at three levels: it can accelerate productivity-led growth and competitiveness in the economy at large as an input to downstream activities; it can be a skill generator of domestic capabilities and high value-added jobs in core segments and in connected upstream and downstream activities; and it would have the potential to enable Vietnam to become a leading global or regional player in services exports. This is particularly true for the ICT sector, as discussed in chapter 9 of this volume, but opportunities exist in other services sectors.

Drivers and Enablers

Policy can play an important role in driving and enabling servicification of the domestic economy. Today, binding constraints include regulatory and other horizontal issues such as workforce skills. Promoting trade and investment in services through active policies include reducing regulatory restrictions and improving global trade networks through regional trade agreements.

Ensuring a liberal trade and investment regime for services is part and parcel to developing a domestic services sector. Regulations matter for services provision, domestically and internationally. The deregulation in air and road transport, the abolition of antitrust exemptions for maritime liner transport, the privatization of ports and port services, and the divestiture and breakup of telecoms monopolies are the main examples of regulatory measures reducing the cost of service delivery across borders (Hoekman 2014). Such industry liberalization has helped many countries grow. Generally, there has been a positive link between services trade liberalization and manufacturing productivity (Triplett and Bosworth 2004; Inklaar, Timmer, and van Ark 2008). Complementing openness with a transparent and predictable regulatory environment will help materialize the gains.

Vietnam also must invest in complementary factors that enable services development. The gains from good regulatory practice can be increased by ensuring the right institutional and economic environments are in place for firms (Sáez et al. 2014). A good business environment characterized by competitive markets can attract FDI; trade-related infrastructure, including transportation and telecommunications, can reduce costs for delivery of modern services; and sound institutions, including rule of law, property rights, and the legal system, can foster relationships between private parties. Supporting the development of a domestic services sector also could act as a bridge linking foreign export firms with local suppliers.

Greater upgrading and investment in other enabling factors, including workforce skills, are also needed. Modern, sophisticated services such as professional, ICT, and business services require a skilled workforce that can enhance adoption and use of new technologies. Further efforts are needed to target human capital, technical skills, and soft skills, including managerial and entrepreneurial capacities. Additionally, ensuring that professionals from abroad can enter the country to provide these services can also support the development of a domestic services sector. Vietnam should, for example, look to the ASEAN Economic Community to attract investments and skilled services workers, which could also provide greater opportunities for Vietnam to export ICT services directly.

Note

1. When exports are measured by the value added they create in an economy, it is possible to split the contribution of a sector into its direct and indirect contributions. The direct contribution is the value added a sector generates to produce its own exports directly. If measuring backward linkages, the indirect contribution is the value added a sector pulls from intermediate-input sectors to produce its own exports. If measuring forward linkages, the indirect contribution is the value added a sector generates by supplying intermediate inputs to the production of other sectors' exports.

Bibliography

Gootiiz, B., and A. Mattoo. 2015. "Regionalism in Services: A Study in ASEAN." Policy Research Working Paper 7498, World Bank, Washington, DC.

Hoekman, B. 2014. "The Bali Trade Facilitation Agreement and Rulemaking in the WTO: Milestone, Mistake or Mirage?" CEPR Discussion Papers 10212, Center for Economic Policy and Research, Washington, DC.

Inklaar, R., M. P. Timmer, and B. van Ark. 2008. "Market Services Productivity across Europe and the US." *Economic Policy* 23: 141–94.

OECD (Organisation for Economic Co-operation and Development) and WTO (World Trade Organization). 2015. TiVA (Trade in Value Added) database. https://stats.oecd.org/index.aspx?queryid=66237.

Sáez, S., D. Taglioni, E. van der Marel, C. H. Hollweg, and V. Zavacka. 2014. *Valuing Services in Trade: A Toolkit for Competitiveness Diagnostics*. Washington, DC: World Bank.

Taglioni, D., and D. Winkler. 2016. *Making Global Value Chains Work for Development*. Washington, DC: World Bank.

Triplett, J. E., and B. P. Bosworth. 2004. *Productivity in the US Services Sector: New Sources of Economic Growth*. Washington, DC: Brookings Institution Press.

CHAPTER 4

Connectivity for Growth
Vietnam's Performance and Prospects

Ben Shepherd

Key Takeaways

If Vietnam is to grow rapidly over the next 20 years, it will need to be well connected to world markets for goods, services, capital, and people. Relative to its income level, Vietnam typically performs quite well on connectivity metrics. However, Asia-Pacific is an increasingly competitive environment, and Vietnam will need to upgrade its performance quickly and comprehensively as it transitions to higher per capita income levels.

Challenges Confronted

A country's ability to connect to global markets for goods, services, capital, and people is a key driver of its international competitiveness. Connectivity—a broad concept that encompasses this ability—is an important factor in national attempts to increase participation in global markets, in particular through global and regional value chains. Vietnam has improved its trade costs in recent years but has untapped potential in leveraging connectivity to other countries through international goods exchange. Connections to international trade networks are good but less strong than in neighboring countries, limiting regional competition. While shipping connectivity faces overcapacity, the growth of air transport networks has slowed in recent years. Logistics and trade facilitation is limited by poor efficiency of customs clearance, weak infrastructure quality, and the quality and competence of service providers. Moreover, Vietnam has room to develop in regional value chain trade, including greater network centrality, participation relative to per capita income, and strengthened forward and backward linkages.

Solutions Proposed

Four recommendations are proposed for connectivity upgrading:

- Closing the infrastructure gap through greater mobilization of private financing and a more integrated approach to developing transport corridors.
- Developing competitive services markets in backbone sectors, including through a more liberal stance on foreign direct investment (FDI) and a general reduction in the costs of doing business.

- Streamlining border procedures to make them more transparent and predictable.
- Leveraging current initiatives with China, Japan, and the Republic of Korea to ensure that connections with these regional sources of demand—as well as technology-related investment—are strong.

Lessons to Be Learned

This chapter suggests the following role for private firms and for the public sector:

- For private firms, as Vietnam seeks to close the infrastructure gap and improve its connectivity relative to its neighbors, it will need to mobilize private sources of funding. Public–private partnerships are an important way in which private resources and expertise can be leveraged. Private firms also should work with the public sector to build appropriate domestic regulations that foster competitiveness, particularly in backbone services sectors.
- The public sector must retain an active role in planning infrastructure developments and in prioritizing projects. Ideally, it can provide seed finance that encourages the private sector to crowd in, which would help ensure that every public dollar spent has maximum possible return for country outcomes. On regulation, the public sector should liberalize FDI while reducing the costs of doing business. Logistics and crossborder processing can be standardized to increase trade transparency, predictability, and reliability. In the longer term, the public sector should work to establish strategic economic relationships to strengthen international demand and investment.

Common Lessons and Potential for Replication in Other Countries

- Countries worldwide are becoming more aware that connectivity matters for developing value chains. Lead firms must be able to move component parts quickly, reliably, and at low cost between different points in the production network and assembly facilities. Closing the infrastructure gap, as recommended for Vietnam, is a task that the country has in common with many developing countries. Similarly, the need to leverage the private sector—including for project finance—is common.
- As a result of these commonalities, there is much in the Vietnamese experience that may be of interest to developing countries, including those in other regions. Direct replication is not recommended, but drawing insights from Vietnam's experience could be useful. In particular, the need to carefully plan infrastructure projects to avoid under- and over-capacity is notable. Of course, Vietnam's relatively centralized system makes infrastructure development somewhat more straightforward than in countries with a higher level of civil society involvement in governance. Other countries will need to manage connectivity development in all its dimensions, including its political economy.

Current Conditions and Challenges

Trade Costs

Trade costs refer to all factors that drive a wedge between producer prices in the exporting country and consumer prices in the importing countries. They can be understood as the transaction costs associated with international trade. Countries with lower trade costs are better able to participate in mutually beneficial international exchange, with benefits for consumers (including consumers of imported intermediates) and export-oriented producers.

Among Vietnam, China, Singapore, and the other Association of Southeast Asian Nation (ASEAN) member states, Vietnam has improved its performance on trade costs and is positioned to connect to other countries through international goods exchange, including through global value chains (GVCs).

Trade costs for all comparison countries are much higher in agriculture than manufacturing, which is consistent with the general results reported in Arvis et al. (2016a). At the beginning of the sample period in 2000, Vietnam's trade costs were notably high in comparative terms: 125 percent ad valorem in manufacturing and 205 percent in agriculture. However, there were sharp reductions in those numbers through 2010. Although the final observation for manufacturing seems on the low side, the general tendency is clear: from 2000 to 2010, Vietnam rapidly reduced its trade costs from a relatively high baseline, particularly in manufacturing. On the comparators used here, Vietnam's trade costs appear highly competitive, and are consistent with the rising importance of international trade in its economy.

For manufacturing, Vietnam and China lowered their trade costs at about the same rate until 2008, when Vietnam continued to lower trade costs and China's trade costs appeared to stabilize (figure 4.1). Again, the 2010 observation for Vietnam, which is very low, should perhaps be interpreted with caution. Nonetheless, Vietnam's achievement is significant: it has reduced its trade costs at the fastest rate of any of the comparator countries, by perhaps as much as one-third over 10 years.

In the agriculture sector, Vietnam again reduced trade costs faster than its peers, including China (figure 4.2). It is important to recall, however, that the absolute level of trade costs in agriculture remains far higher than in manufacturing, although this feature is common around the world. Over the decade to 2010, Vietnam reduced its trade costs in agriculture by 25 percent.

Connections to International Transportation Networks

A network analysis[1] of international trade in transport services reveals that Vietnam's connectivity has improved markedly in recent years, but from a low baseline. It caught up with its ASEAN neighbors, but in 2009 it still was not as well connected as Singapore or China (figure 4.3). Vietnam's centrality (network trade share) increased by 14 percent during the 14-year sample period. China's rate of improvement is the next fastest, at 8 percent. However, most of Vietnam's improvement took place in the early part of the sample, between 1995 and 2000.

Figure 4.1 Manufacturing Trade Costs for Vietnam and Selected Comparators, 2000–10

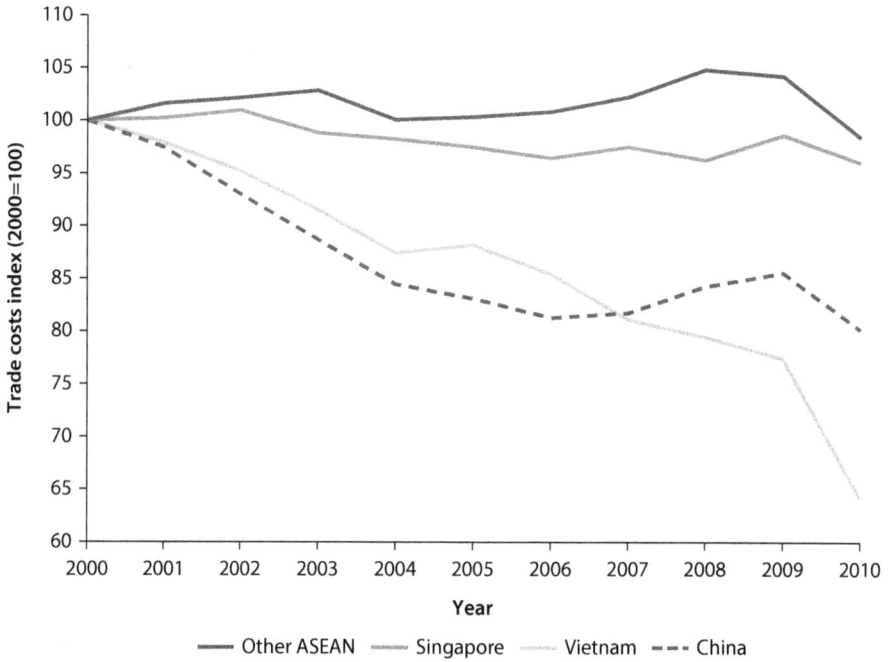

Source: UNESCAP–World Bank International Trade Costs database.

Figure 4.2 Agriculture Trade Costs for Vietnam and Selected Comparators, 2000–10

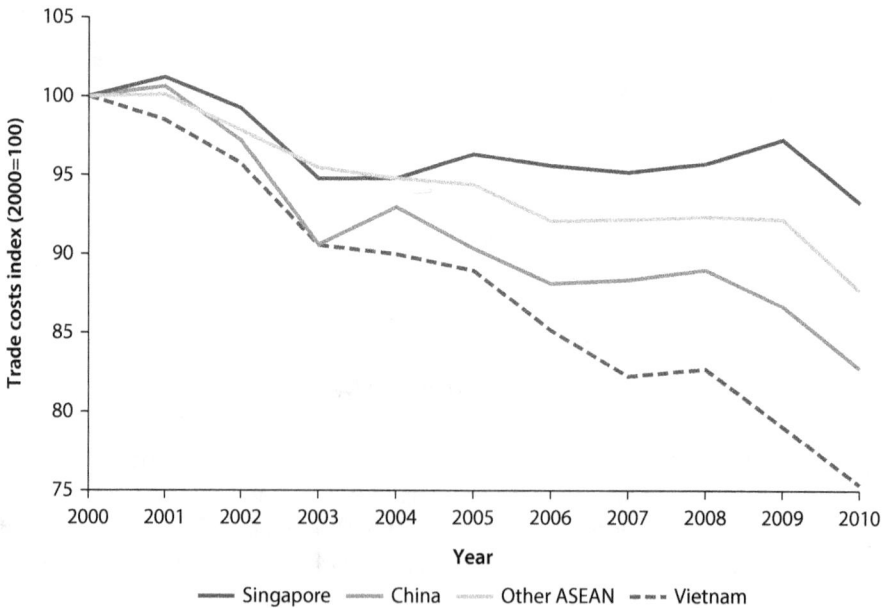

Source: UNESCAP–World Bank International Trade Costs database.

Figure 4.3 Transport Centrality for Vietnam and Selected Comparator Countries, 1995–2009

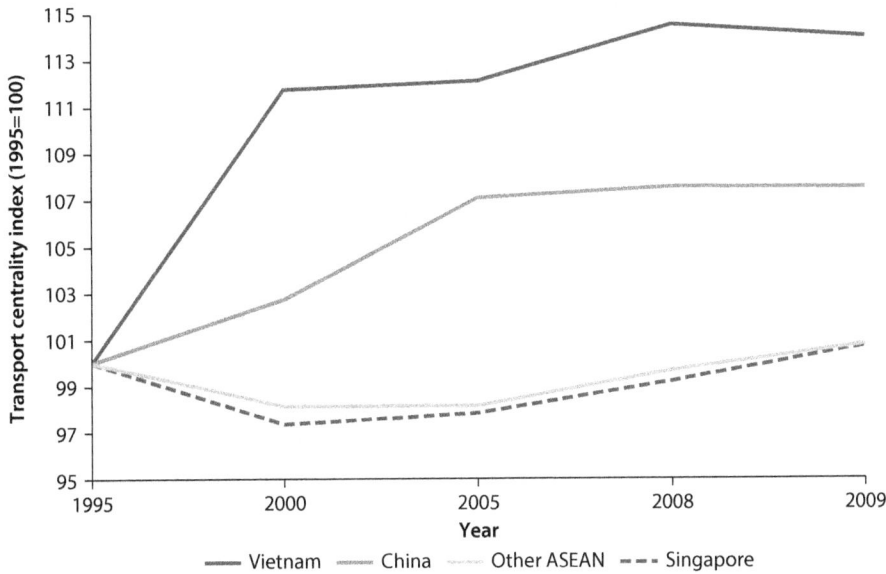

Source: Santoni and Taglioni 2015.

Despite substantial growth in Vietnam's liner shipping connectivity, there is overcapacity in southern ports. UNCTAD's Liner Shipping Connectivity Index, which measures liner shipping connectivity, reveals that by 2014, Vietnam had overtaken its peers in the ASEAN Group (all members but China and Singapore) in scores on this index. Vietnam has moved closer to China and Singapore, though those countries still have much higher index scores. This pattern of change is suggestive of significant improvements in maritime transport connectivity in Vietnam over 10 years; however, the utilization rate at Cai Mep–Thi Vai terminal was only 18 percent in 2012, yet additional large capacity terminals were due to open in following years.

Vietnam's air transport connectivity showed strong performance between 2008 and 2012 but fell sharply in 2012. The World Bank's Air Connectivity Index (Arvis and Shepherd 2016) uses network analysis methods to provide an indication of the extent that different countries are connected to the global network of air transport services. Vietnam's score is the lowest of any of the groups, although it is not far below the ASEAN average.

Logistics and Trade Facilitation

Logistics and trade facilitation is an area in which Vietnam needs to redouble its efforts to ensure that it moves ahead faster than other potential host countries. Using the World Bank's Logistics Performance Index (LPI; Arvis et al. 2016b) to measure Vietnam's performance in facilitating the flow of imports and exports, Vietnam's score gain is impressive—nearly 10 percent in seven years—but that mirrors, more or less, gains among all of ASEAN except China (6 percent). There is evidence that Vietnam is gaining on stronger performers in the region, but only marginally. This is important because the regional environment for participating in GVCs, and attracting GVC-related investment, is competitive. Indeed, Vietnam will need to improve substantially as the country moves to higher income levels; constant, broad-based reforms are necessary to ensure absolute and relative progress.

Looking at the component measures of the LPI (figure 4.4) and their contribution to Vietnam's overall score, some problem areas emerge. Between 2012 and 2014, infrastructure quality improved relatively fast, but customs procedures consistently underperformed. And, although infrastructure investment is a vital part of improving the logistics and trade facilitation environment, it cannot have maximum impact without fast, transparent, and reliable customs clearance procedures. The overall performance of a port, for example, depends on both systems working seamlessly. Other forms of infrastructure cannot be accessed before customs are cleared, which means that border agencies have an important gateway role. Four of the components are packed relatively tightly around Vietnam's overall score, which means that performance is quite consistent in those areas.

Figure 4.4 Components of Logistics Performance for Vietnam and Selected Comparator Countries, 2007–14

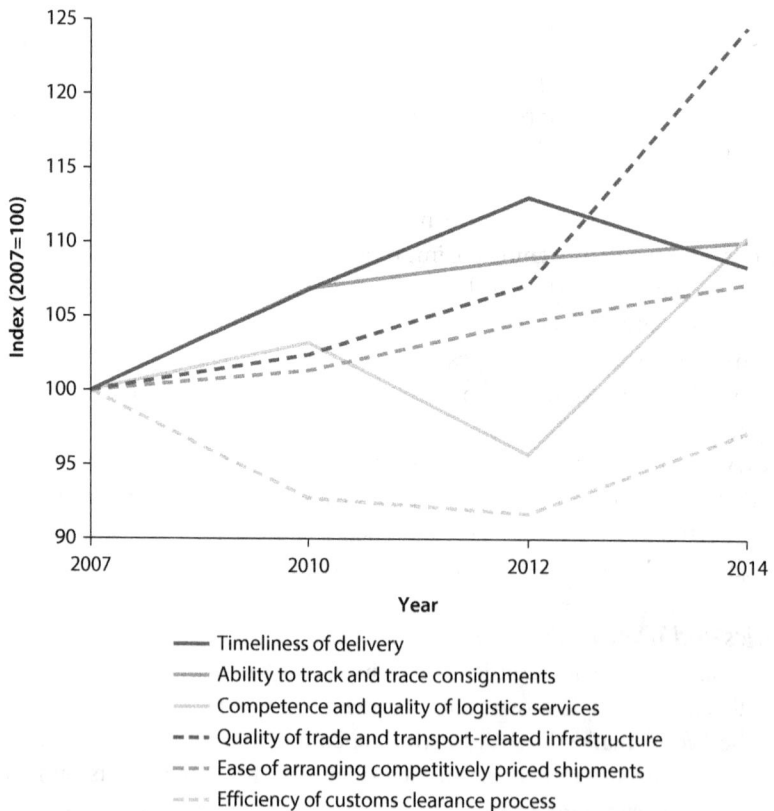

Source: World Bank Logistics Performance Index.

The most serious problems of border clearance may lie in the area of health and sanitary and phytosanitary (SPS) inspections. In this case, not only is there a performance gap between Vietnam and the leader, Singapore, but also between Vietnam and its regional ASEAN peers and neighboring China. In allocating resources, these results suggest that the most urgent priority is to improve performance in health and SPS inspections.

The efficiency of customs clearance, the quality of infrastructure, and the quality and competence of service providers stand out as root causes of the distance between Vietnam's performance and that of Singapore, or even the best developing country score of China (figure 4.5). The reasons for improving customs clearance efficiency have just been given. For infrastructure quality, though Vietnam has made considerable strides in areas such as maritime connectivity, it has much to do to improve its connections with the rest of the world. Vietnam's score on quality and competence of service providers is 22 percent lower than Singapore's, and 11 percent lower than China's. The LPI component results suggest that Vietnam needs to pay additional attention to developing competitive services markets in trade and transport-related areas.

Figure 4.5 Components of Logistics Performance for Vietnam and Selected Comparator Countries, 2014

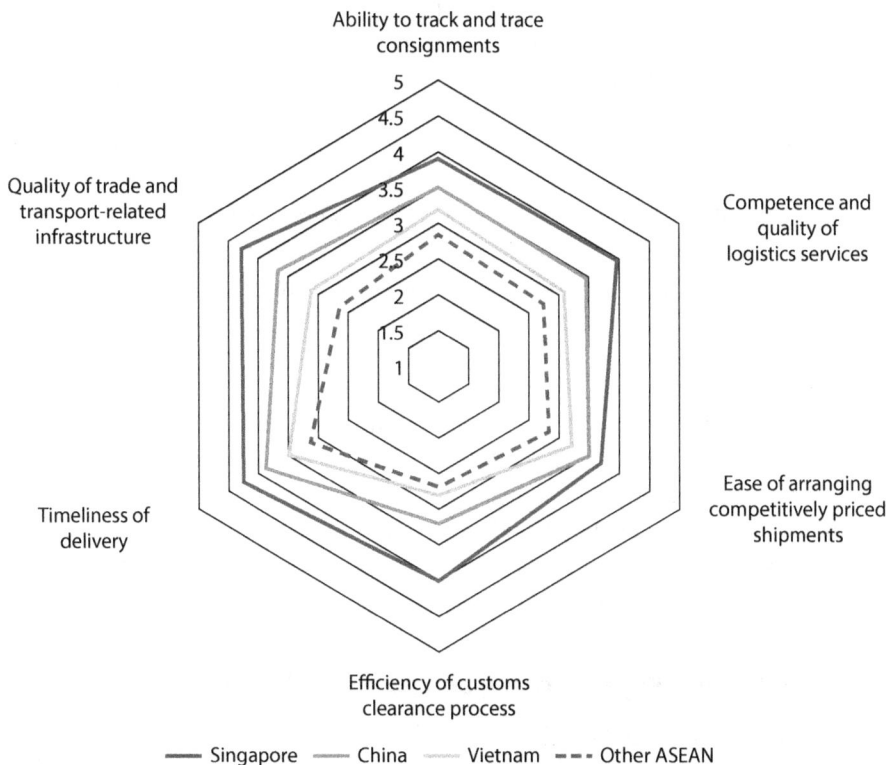

Source: World Bank Logistics Performance Index.

Vietnam at a Crossroads • http://dx.doi.org/10.1596/978-1-4648-0996-5

Value Chain Trade

Vietnam has wide scope to improve in value chain trade in a competitive Asia-Pacific. Where the preceding measures of connectivity focus on input measures, value chain trade focuses on three output measures of connectivity: value chain centrality, participation relative to per capita income, and forward and backward linkages.

Vietnam's value chain centrality varies somewhat by sector. For textiles and apparel, it has increased gradually from a low baseline in 1995, achieving 15 percent of manufacturing value added by 2010. By the end of the sample period, it had surpassed the ASEAN Group average, although wide gaps remain with Singapore and, especially, China. The pattern in other sectors—electrical equipment, machinery, and agriculture—is similar, except the growth rate of the centrality index tapers off at the end of the sample period, a pattern that is consistent with the difficulties experienced in many value chains after the global financial crisis. There still is considerable scope to further improve its integration into GVCs in crucial sectors, as Vietnam remains much less central to them than its large neighbor, China.

On value chain participation relative to per capita income—interpreted as the degree of internationalization of its production processes—Vietnam stands out as performing above expectations, that is, relatively strong for a lower-middle–income country. However, it still lags relative to all other ASEAN countries. In part this is because Vietnam joined regional production structures later than its ASEAN partners, some of which have been involved in Japanese-led value chains for some time.

Forward linkages refer to the contribution of domestically produced intermediates to exports in other countries. Backward linkages, by contrast, represent foreign value added embodied in a country's gross exports, in other words the relative importance of imported intermediates in the export sector. We focus here on an overall participation index that combines the two measures to show Vietnam's degree of integration into value chain trade, using these two types of linkages as proxies. Vietnam's initial participation index is between those of China and the ASEAN Group. Given China's importance in value chain trade, it is perhaps surprising that China's score is not higher. The reason is that its initial backwards participation index is much lower than Vietnam's, perhaps due to the legacy of efforts to develop complete supply chains nationally, rather than to rely on international production structures. In any case, Vietnam has an intermediate level of value chain participation that has increased markedly over time.

Concrete Actions, Key Outcomes, and Potential Constraints

Four important and interlinked issues need to be resolved to enhance the role of policy in boosting connectivity performance and thus competitiveness.

Closing the Infrastructure Gap

This gap will be closed through greater mobilization of private financing and a more integrated approach to developing transport corridors. If Vietnam is to sustain a rapid rate of growth over the next 20 years, it needs to improve that performance even further, and extend it to areas that have received less attention. The LPI revealed that Vietnam's infrastructure is a source of strength in overall logistics performance, but that a major gap exists between Vietnam and China, as well as the best practice example of Singapore. Considerable work remains to be done to develop high-quality infrastructure in areas that affect the ability of firms to do business, especially internationally. Attention to corridor-style development, where intermodal linkages are created, is essential.

Operators need a reliable transport environment, and for that, the quality of infrastructure is crucial. Even though infrastructure is a bright spot in logistics performance, the government will need to shift the emphasis toward quality in the future, while still ensuring that infrastructure is available to the economy in adequate quantity. Attention to balanced investment (from North to South) is necessary to avoid further over- or under-capacity problems.

Better coordination is necessary for effective intermodal linkages. For example, land connections to Vietnamese ports are typically congested, and offer poor service (World Bank 2013). If the benefits of investments in international gateways are to be realized, those facilities need to be effectively linked to the rest of the country. Road links are crucial in the context of an underdeveloped rail sector, and are in need of renewed attention.

There is a need to develop infrastructure within a corridor framework. Developing independent pieces of infrastructure can often lead to poorly coordinated intermodal linkages: a port may be upgraded and receive greater traffic, for example, some years before its connector roads are given a similar upgrade. Viewing infrastructure development through the lens of a small number of key transport corridors can promote an integrated approach to infrastructure upgrading. Transport corridors can improve domestic connectivity, and can promote the free movement of goods and services within the Vietnamese economic space. In addition, by connecting corridors to international gateways, transport corridors become a vital part of the link between producers and consumers on the one hand, and regional and world markets on the other.

Vietnam's infrastructure upgrading has been associated with strong public sector leadership. It is of course appropriate that the public sector should play a major role in planning and coordinating the rollout or upgrading of major infrastructure. However, as Vietnam seeks to close the infrastructure gap and improve its connectivity relative to its neighbors, it will need to mobilize private funding. This area is one in which the country is still gaining experience. With ports, for example, most projects have been undertaken by state-owned Vinalines, with consequent stress placed on its finances (World Bank 2013). There is more that Vietnam can do to bring the private sector into its infrastructure development program, with the aim of achieving superior outcomes and the advantage of less strain on the public purse.

Developing Competitive Services Markets

Carried out in in backbone sectors, resolving this issue entails a more liberal stance on FDI and a general reduction in the costs of doing business. Outward orientation is an important part of a country's overall regulatory stance in services sectors, and opening backbone sectors to international competition can act as a vector for technology upgrading and increased competitiveness. As in goods markets, international openness can bring with it lower prices, increased quality, and greater access to variety for consumers. Importantly, consumers in this case are not only final consumers, but also other businesses that use backbone services, including exporters.

Improving the competitiveness of backbone sectors can have important spillover effects to other parts of the economy, leading to a general increase in domestic and international competitiveness. Services are vital in facilitating exports of manufactured goods—this is embodied services trade. Data from the Organisation for Economic Co-operation and Development–World Trade Organization (OECD–WTO) Trade in Value Added (TiVA) database suggest that services play a significant role in Vietnamese merchandise exports. In textiles and apparel, for example, services value added accounted for 32 percent of the value of gross exports in 2009.

The World Bank's Services Trade Restrictiveness Index (STRI) provides a snapshot of measures affecting trade in services in a range of countries, including Vietnam. Vietnam is more restrictive than its ASEAN neighbors in sectors like telecommunications, retail, and international air passenger transport. In addition, Vietnam and the other ASEAN countries for which data are available are more restrictive than China in the rail and road freight sectors. But the contrast in retail is striking, where Vietnam is the most restrictive of the countries under consideration.

WTO also recognizes sales by foreign affiliates as a type of services trade (Mode 3). Indeed, in backbone sectors, Mode 3 typically is the way that foreign firms enter the domestic marketplace. Most of the trade restrictions summarized in the STRI therefore relate to measures restricting inward FDI in services sectors. Regulatory reform aimed at relaxing at least some of these restrictions will be a key way that Vietnam can leverage trade to promote a vibrant and competitive services sector, which in turn will boost transport connectivity and the performance of goods trade sectors.

Inward FDI restrictions in Vietnam typically take the form of foreign ownership limits—often 49 percent, less for state-owned enterprises—and joint-venture requirements. Foreign investors sometimes also are required to employ a minimum percentage of local workers, although it is not clear if that constraint is actually binding in the sectors under consideration. Ownership limits and requirements as to legal form can be highly trade distorting, because such limits and requirements prevent foreign firms from entering the local market in the most efficient way possible, such that the procompetitive effects of services trade are not completely felt. Vietnam has scope to boost its connectivity by progressively relaxing restrictions on FDI in services sectors.

The contrast with China's regulatory stance is stark in the case of road and rail transport. For these sectors, China imposes no limitations on foreign ownership, which enables foreign competitors to enter the sector in the most efficient manner based on their existing business organization and competitive advantage. This is the difference between the two countries' scores, as Vietnam imposes foreign ownership restrictions. In light of the extensive resources being poured into road and rail infrastructure development in the context of the greater Mekong subregion and the ASEAN Highway Network, it is vital for Vietnam to develop efficient road and rail transport sectors. Land transport is an important way to move goods to and from neighbors, as well as within the country itself. Boosting the competitiveness of the road and rail transport sectors should therefore be a priority in the overall approach to international and domestic connectivity.

In maritime transport, which is not specifically dealt with in the STRI, there is room for Vietnam to adopt a more liberal stance. Cabotage restrictions—the requirement that cargo traveling between Vietnamese ports be carried by a Vietnamese-flagged vessel—could be relaxed, arguably without significantly affecting the market share of existing carriers for domestic cargo (World Bank 2013). There is a need for transshipment of international cargo, especially relating to the underserved (in this sense) Cai Mep–Thi Vai terminals. Relaxing cabotage restrictions would allow international vessels to undertake this activity, resulting in economic gains for Vietnamese producers and consumers.

Although trade policy is important in promoting a competitive services sector, it is not the only aspect of regulatory reform that needs to be considered. The fragmented Vietnamese trucking sector, for example, tends to reduce efficiency and higher costs are passed down through the rest of the logistics system. Working with the private sector to develop domestic regulations that foster competitiveness in backbone services sectors should be a priority. Indeed, the economic gains from nondiscriminatory regulatory reforms—targeting those measures that increase the costs of doing business for all operators, domestic and foreign—are likely larger than those that can be had simply by focusing on ensuring a relatively nondiscriminatory stance in services trade policy.

Streamlining Border Procedures and Making Them More Transparent and Predictable

Border procedures are a particular issue for Vietnam in improving its connectivity. Health and SPS services, in addition to customs proper, appear to be the source of long delays—and thus costs—for traders. Reforming these procedures should be a priority in the short to medium term, all the more so as the country implements WTO's Trade Facilitation Agreement.

For example, the World Bank's Doing Business database reports that it takes 21 days to export or import goods from or into Vietnam—a relatively long time, even though the direct costs involved are not too high globally. Nonetheless,

Vietnam is ranked 75th in this component of the database—superior to China (90th) but far lower than ASEAN partners Thailand (36th) and Indonesia (62nd). Of the 21 days, the bulk is spent on document preparation (12 days) and customs clearance and inspections (four days). There is considerable scope to compress these figures and improve connectivity. Moreover, the region has a stock of experience, proving that countries can make headway in border procedures and related formalities in the short term.

According to the World Bank (2013), a major problem for Vietnam's border clearance regime is that laws and regulations are inconsistently applied and enforced, which creates uncertainty and unreliability for operators and adds to their indirect costs. Unofficial facilitation payments also are used sometimes to try and keep these costs down. The result of these problems at border crossings is that the entire logistics system underperforms relative to regional neighbors.

Vietnam should take advantage of the opportunities offered by the customs components of the Trade Facilitation Agreement, as well as the ASEAN Single Window to upgrade its border-processing procedures. Some steps have been taken, particularly on automating procedures. Much remains to be done, however. In moving toward a paperless single window solution, it will be crucial to ensure interoperability with other regional partners, including, importantly, not just other ASEAN member states but also the vital external markets of China, Korea, and Japan. Asia-Pacific Economic Cooperation's (APEC) Connectivity Blueprint points in this direction and encourages member economies to develop their own single windows by 2020, with an emphasis on interoperability. According to a UNESCAP (United Nations Economic and Social Commission for Asia and the Pacific) survey in 2013, Vietnam was only a partial adopter of paperless trade solutions—an area in which it will need to exert further effort in the short term in line with initiatives underway in some other countries in the region.

Leveraging Existing Initiatives with Major Trade and Investment Partners

To obtain maximum benefit from a policy of outward orientation, Vietnam needs a set of key regional partners. The set is not necessarily large, but two factors need to be taken into account when conceptualizing such a group of regional partners. The first is the need to include partners with relatively large, open markets that can be a source of demand for Vietnam's production. The second is Vietnam's need for foreign investment and technology, which requires partner countries that can act as sources.

This analysis suggests three regional partners of particular importance. The first, of course, is China. It is an important source of demand for Vietnamese exports, particularly in the context of GVCs. In 2013, China was Vietnam's third-largest export market, accounting for just over 11 percent of Vietnam's total exports. Although China's growth probably will slow somewhat over the medium term, it likely will remain a dynamic source of demand for Vietnamese production, and the trade relationship will become increasingly important.

Two richer economies stand out for their demand-side potential for Vietnam: Japan and Korea, respectively the second and fourth most important export partners for Vietnam in 2013. Due to the high level of per capita income, both economies are large regionally and globally. Japan has experienced sluggish economic growth over recent decades, but Korea's economy has been more vibrant. These two markets likely will retain their importance as sources of external demand for Vietnam.

From an investment point of view, the picture changes somewhat. Again, China is a large economy and is potentially a large source of inward FDI for Vietnam. However, China is itself a developing economy, and so the technology that it could export to Vietnam is some distance from the global frontier. But if China's rapid development continues over the next couple of decades, it will grow closer to the global technology frontier; however, it likely will remain some distance from it.

In contrast, Japan and Korea both are important sources of FDI and crucial vectors for technology upgrading throughout Asia-Pacific. They operate at or close to the global technology frontier, and can be important sources for technology upgrading in Vietnam over the medium term. This fact is reflected in UNCTAD's (United Nations Conference on Trade and Development) bilateral FDI data. By 2012 inflows, Japan was Vietnam's most important investment partner, supplying over 15 times as much FDI as China. Korea supplied nearly 3.5 times as much as China. There is considerable scope for leveraging these relationships further, in particular by relaxing FDI restrictions, at least in selected sectors, as discussed above.

On connectivity, the main implication for Vietnam is that while it should focus the bulk of its energies and resources on nondiscriminatory improvements (such as infrastructure upgrading and generalized regulatory reform), where discrimination is necessary, it should choose its partners carefully. Within the scope of the ASEAN+ initiatives, there is some likelihood that trade and investment links with the three key markets will improve over the medium term, though much work still needs to be done in this area. Another body, APEC, includes all important partners, and is committed to free trade and investment in the region. However, the prospect of a Free Trade Area of Asia-Pacific remains at the analytical stage after the 2014 APEC Leaders' Declaration. The Trans-Pacific Partnership involves Japan and Korea, but not China, as well as Vietnam itself.

Vietnam must prioritize improving links with major economies in the region, having due regard to the likely role that each of the three major partners can play: China, as a source of demand and limited inward FDI; and Japan and Korea as sources of both demand and technology-related FDI.

Note

1. Network analysis shows intercountry relationships in value-added trade of aggregate micro-level import and export of goods.

Bibliography

Arvis, J. F., Y. Duval, B. Shepherd, C. Utoktham, and A. Raj. 2016a. "Trade Costs in the Developing World: 1996–2010." *World Trade Review* 15 (3): 451–74.

Arvis, J. F., D. Saslavsky, L. Ojala, B. Shepherd, C. Busch, A. Raj, and T. Naula. 2016b. *Connecting to Compete 2016: Trade Logistics in the Global Economy.* Washington, DC: World Bank.

Arvis, J. F., and B. Shepherd. 2016. "The Air Connectivity Index: Measuring Integration in the Global Air Transport Network." *The World Economy* 39 (3): 369–85.

OECD (Organisation for Economic Co-operation and Development) and WTO (World Trade Organization). 2015. "TiVA (Trade in Value Added) database." https://stats.oecd.org/index.aspx?queryid=66237.

Satoni, Gianluca, and Daria Taglioni. 2015. "Networks and Structural Integration in Global Value Chains." In *The Age of Global Value Chains*, edited by João Amador and Filippo di Mauro. Washington, DC: Center for Economic and Policy Research.

UNESCAP and World Bank. 2016. "UNESCAP—World Bank International Trade Costs (database)." http://databank.worldbank.org/data/reports.aspx?source=ESCAP-World-Bank:-International-Trade-Costs.

World Bank. 2013. *Efficient Logistics: A Key to Vietnam's Competitiveness.* Washington, DC: World Bank.

———. 2016. "Logistics Performance Index (database)." http://lpi.worldbank.org/.

CHAPTER 5

Vietnam in 2030

A Logistics and Infrastructure Perspective

Ruth Banomyong

Key Takeaways

Vietnam needs to improve its logistics to sustain economic growth. It should rationalize the institutional environment for logistics rules and regulations. Local logistics service providers are at a disadvantage in offering modern logistics value-added services, and domestic manufacturers suffer from low logistics performance and high costs. Logistics infrastructure and facilitation projects will concentrate growth in the south of the country, thus increasing the burden on current and future infrastructure. Vietnam has started to liberalize its logistics services sector and many foreign providers are making their presence felt in the country, but this competition will be unhealthy to small and medium local service providers if they cannot serve niche customers' segments.

Challenges Confronted

Logistics is a relatively new concept in Vietnam and no official authority has overall responsibility for it. Thus the government has yet to formulate a comprehensive strategy or orientation for developing it. In infrastructure and services, each individual mode of transport suffers from limited capacity and capability. There is a lack of understanding of the role of logistics and how it can help improve firms' competitiveness.

Solutions Proposed

Two solutions are proposed here. The first relates to logistics infrastructure and services upgrading through traditional global value chain (GVC) strategies. Domestic infrastructure upgrading is critical if Vietnam is to benefit from enhanced GVC integration. The improved domestic infrastructure will not only facilitate connectivity to and from Vietnam but will also enable firms to be located deeper inland and still be integrated in value chains. Domestic logistics services upgrading will support higher reliability, thus assuring connectivity within GVCs.

The second concerns the logistics regulatory environment, which needs to be streamlined to enable service providers to offer the full spectrum of services that will enable firms to connect efficiently and effectively in GVCs.

Lessons to Be Learned

Logistics and connectivity infrastructure are essential for strong economic growth across sectors. For forward and backward market linkages to connect efficiently, connectivity infrastructure needs to be in place and accessible to market participants of all sizes according to their needs. An appropriate regulatory environment should facilitate the design, management, and operation of logistics and connectivity within and among countries.

Logistics services and infrastructure form a lucrative economic sector in its own right. The contribution of the logistics industry to GDP can be as high as 10–15 percent in developed economies and has the potential to boost Vietnam's economic development—but improved infrastructure is a necessary condition for this to occur.

Healthy market competition among logistics service providers is necessary to ensure domestic firm participation and modern linkages with regional and international market providers, yet investment regulation, spatial concentration of logistics hubs, and concentration of market power currently inhibit such competition. A better balance of domestic and foreign market participation is required to maximize spillover effects while ensuring more equitable service provision.

Multimodal connectivity is essential and should be a priority in national connectivity designs. Coordination of transport experts is required to ensure appropriate infrastructural, regulatory, and servicing linkages.

This chapter suggests the following role for private firms and the public sector:

Private firms should finance, either independently or through public–private partnership arrangements, logistics infrastructure upgrades and development. They should emphasize research and development, human resources, and efforts to lower trade costs.

The public sector should continue efforts to streamline regulation and design macro-based logistics infrastructure. It should focus on enhancing multimodal domestic and regional linkages, and should create incentives for private sector development, according to macro-based logistics plans, to ensure appropriate implementation of the design strategies. The public sector also should emphasize spillovers when attracting foreign investment so as to support domestic firm development and healthy competition.

Common Lessons and Potential for Replication in Other Countries

For logistics to improve connectivity and integration into GVCs, infrastructure, the legal framework, logistics service providers, and firms' needs should be connected. This will enable a holistic approach to developing logistics.

Current Conditions and Challenges

Despite a railway across the country from north to south, cargo volumes transported by rail are small and have fallen largely due to poor service. In 2009, a number of Vietnamese shipping companies reacted to the global crisis by transferring tonnage to the domestic coastal market (north–south transportation), but it made little difference to the declining trend as illustrated in Table 5.1. The reduction in the share of river and coastal carriage is largely due to improved road infrastructure.

The government has approved a general transport development plan for 2020 and a vision for 2030, with individual 2020 modal master plans for inland waterways, roads, marine transport, and air transport. What is lacking, however, is the integration of the modal plans for infrastructure and service development. Investment, regulatory policies, and sector promotion are not viewed in a coherent manner and are thus not conducive to integrated logistics infrastructure.

Seaports

Many logistics operators and users feel that the country's ports are not suited to cater to modern maritime transport for physical reasons, underlining the urgency to further support deep-sea port development and improve port capability. Sea transport is the most important mode for Vietnam's imports and exports.

The national seaport system comprises three main groups, of which the Southern group (Saigon, Vung Tau) is the most developed, handling around 70 percent of Vietnam's foreign trade. Saigon New Port is considered one of the best operated port facilities in the country with the fastest vessel turnaround time.

Built before 1939, the majority of Vietnamese seaports are now outdated with insufficient water depth for large modern seagoing vessels and few terminals adapted to container handling. Many physical structures are deteriorated and have little or no maintenance. However, some deepwater seaports with modern facilities, especially for container handling, have started operations. In early 2010, a new container port opened at Cai Mep, about two hours south of Ho Chi Minh City, and some ocean carriers have added the port to their international rotations.

Table 5.1 Freight Modal Share in Vietnam

Percent

Mode of transport	2006	2007	2008	2009	2010	2011	2012
Road	65.92	68.6	72	70.6	74.65	73.86	75.28
Train	2.63	2.4	1.4	1.15	1.11	0.82	0.73
Inland waterway	21.19	18.93	18.14	19.4	16.63	18.08	17.56
Sea (coastal)	10.23	10.04	8.44	9.9	7.58	7.22	6.41
Air	0.03	0.03	0.02	0.02	0.03	0.02	0.02

Source: General Statistics Office of Vietnam 2014.

Other seaports such as Hai Phong, Cailan, Saigon New Port, Vietnam International Container Terminal (VICT) in Ho Chi Minh City, and Da Nang are relatively well equipped and can handle modern vessels and containers, but not large vessels. Modern equipment and operating systems such as full-truck scanners, automated gate entry, and commercial information and communication technology systems are not yet widely available in Vietnamese seaports. The terminals at Saigon New Port and VICT are leading in that area.

Ports are grouped based on geographic regions—north, central, and south. Each region has its designated major ports, small subordinate ports, and independent industrial private ports. In the north, Hai Phong port is the main gateway port, but because it is at the mouth of a river and often affected by sedimentation, vessels of more than 10,000 deadweight tonnage (DWT) cannot call there. Cai Lan Port, 40 km to the northeast of Hai Phong, is a deepwater seaport that can accommodate vessels up to 40,000 DWT.

In the center, Da Nang port functions as a gateway for that region and for transit to and from the Lao People's Democratic Republic (Banomyong and Beresford 2001). Tien Sa port in Da Nang can accommodate vessels of up 30,000 DWT, with a throughput capacity of 4.5 million tons. The three other major ports serving the central coastline—Cua Lo, Quy Nhon, and Nha Trang—can receive vessels only up to 10,000 DWT. Another problem with ports in the central region is that scheduled liner services are scarce due to a limited hinterland that cannot generate enough cargo to attract the main line operators.

In the south, the Saigon River is the busiest navigational route. It has numerous ports that can accommodate various kinds of vessels with a maximum capacity of 20,000 DWT. The Vung Tau–Thi Vai port area is becoming a focal point for new deepwater seaports in the south, notably Cai Mep.

The total design capacity of the seaport system in 2010 was 170 million tons, but by the end of 2007 the total throughput reached 190 million tons (VINAMARINE 2014). The government has an aggressive infrastructure investment program for seaports (as well as highways and railroads). Construction started in October 2009 on the Van Phong container port complex north of Ho Chi Minh City, which is designed to be a mammoth transshipment port. The project was scheduled to be constructed in four phases, with completion planned for 2015. The latest news is that construction has stopped due to a lack of funds (Tuoi Tre News 2012).

Ports play an increasingly important role in the supply of integrated transport and logistics services. There are more than 200 foreign shipping lines operating liner and container services to Vietnam directly and indirectly through feeder networks with container vessels linking Vietnam to nearby hub-ports such as Hong Kong SAR, China; Kaohsiung; and Singapore, and where containers are transshipped worldwide by mother vessels. The development of ocean and river ports, inland clearance depots (ICDs), and logistics parks is indispensable for Vietnam to promote domestic and international logistics services (Japan International Cooperation Agency 2010). While port

development generally entails major infrastructure work, it is equally important that a framework be created for the relevant high-quality services to be
provided.

Given its central location in Association of Southeast Asian Nations (ASEAN)
and its heavy reliance on trade with China (and less so Thailand), Vietnam has
the potential to develop gradually into a maritime hub for intra-ASEAN and
wider regional trade. Maritime connectivity, including upgraded maritime service quality, will become increasingly important for future integration among
ASEAN countries, a process which so far has been dominated by land transport
(Thai 2008).

Inland Waterways

With 40,998 km of rivers and channels, mainly in the Red River in the north and
the Mekong Delta in the south, inland water transport plays a key role in cargo
movement. In recent years, inland waterway transport has grown by an average
1 percent per year. There are 109 inland waterway ports with 3,111 landing
points throughout the country. Many of the terminals are capable of handling
containers, though none is operated under concession agreements with private
operators. Due to road restrictions in some areas, such as the Mekong Delta
provinces, containers and foreign trade cargo often are moved via inland waterways before (or after) the main sea transport leg. Trade with Phnom Penh,
Cambodia, is largely carried by barges.

The major routes linking seaports with the hinterland include Hai Phong–
Hanoi and Nam Dinh–Viet Tri in the north, and Saigon–Rach Gia-Ha Tien, and
Saigon–Can Tho–Ca Mau in the south. Some inland waterways ports also have
rail connections, but these are underused. Some major ICDs around Hai Phong
and Hongai have distribution facilities or a free trade zone within or next to their
inland waterway terminals. These facilities include customs-bonded storage.
Similar to maritime transport, inland waterways' carrying capacity is high and the
cost is low against other transport modes.

Although inland waterway transport of goods has increased over the last few
years, the river system, especially in the northern area, has not been exploited to
its potential, though the Mekong river system is comparatively well developed.
One reason is that only about 40 percent of the river system in Vietnam is regularly dredged and thus navigable all year. The difference in water level and draft
between the rainy and dry seasons also is very high, especially in the south, which
adversely effects cargo carriage.

Roads

Road quality must be improved to ensure unimpeded vehicle movement. Road
traffic accounts for more than 70 percent of domestic cargo volume. Traffic
density in major urban areas has led to general bans on trucks operating within
city limits, while limited capacity of bridges and bad roads affect cargo
transport, especially container haulage. Road access to big seaports such as
Hai Phong, Da Nang, and Saigon needs to be rehabilitated and some must be

built to help local logistics services providers expand their activities to neighboring countries for transit and border trade with China, Cambodia, and the Lao PDR.

Trucks and articulated vehicles ply the roads, though a significant share of the commercial trucking fleet (six wheels and above) is at least 10 years old. Despite capacity limitations and infrastructure shortcomings, road transport is highly flexible and remains by far the first choice among domestic consignors.

Rail

According to Banomyong, Thai, and Yuen (2015), most of the existing rail lines are below international standard: 44 percent are below technical standards with at least 25 percent of the lines needing replacement sleepers. Many structurally weak bridges keep freight trains' operating speeds down to an average of 15–20 km/hour. There are an estimated 430 locomotives, with an average age of 20 years. Locomotive traction power is limited to around 2,000 horse power.

Trains' carrying capacity is also limited, both single-wagon capacity and train length and traction power. The rail network is used mainly for passengers and for domestic cargo. Vietnam lacks tracking systems for freight and a central train control system (for monitoring train movements with train identification and automatic route setting or other types of advanced train control systems). Some areas have 24-hour freight terminal operations. Bad weather causes frequent service interruptions, especially in the central region.

Container transport by rail is minimal, as Vietnamese shippers prefer road transport given rail inefficiencies and long and unpredictable transit times. The Vietnam railway system has only 500 flat-bed wagons for containers among a total of 5,000, and only a few stations have container loading and unloading equipment. Container carriage by rail transport takes place mainly along two routes: Hai Phong–Yen Vien–Viet Tri–Lao Cai and the North–South railway. Statistics for container freight are unavailable, but the total movement was estimated at some 8.4 million tons in 2008.

Regional railway connectivity, particularly between China and Vietnam, is threatened by the gauge used: trains from China run on the standard gauge (1.435 meter) while the Vietnamese system is based on the 1 meter gauge. Vietnam's railway system has been connected to China through the Lao Cai border gate since 1996, after a service disruption in 1975. Since 1996, cargo volume transported between the two countries has slowly increased and trade with south China will require further rail support. There is a possibility to run trains between Hai Phong seaport and Kunming, China, a connection that would eventually become part of the Singapore to Kunming railway line. However, since December 2010, Chinese authorities stopped using the 1 meter gauge and focused solely on the standard gauge for rail transport between Hekou and Kunming, severely affecting railway connectivity between Lao Cai and Hekou. Lao Cai needs an interchange before rail freight with China can move seamlessly.

Air

Airfreight services are concentrated at the two main airports of Noi Bai in Hanoi and Tan Son Nhat in Ho Chi Minh City. Regular air flight services operate at all 20 civil airports run by the Civil Aviation Administration of Vietnam. The country has six international airports. Airfreight services are also concentrated at the two main airports. Import/export cargo for Da Nang and Hue must be transshipped via Noi Bai or Tan Son Nhat. Activities at these smaller international airports are mainly for passengers, and only a small proportion is for cargo.

In 2012, the volume of total air freight through airports in Vietnam was around 649,000 tons, reflecting growth of 6.3 percent from 2011. Vietnamese airlines accounted for about 201,000 tons of this (Civil Aviation Authority of Vietnam 2012). The two main airports have cold storage facilities for perishables and storage facilities for dangerous goods, but capacity is limited. Separate areas provide warehousing and office space for freight operations.

The Vietnamese air fleet is composed primarily of chartered passenger planes. A license to provide domestic air cargo services was granted in 2008 to Trai Thein Air Cargo, but was later revoked because of its failure to launch any services within 12 months (Vietnam Breaking News 2011). Air cargo transit remains limited to chartered cargo planes.

Inland Clearance Depots

ICDs are inland locations that can act as a dry port, offering services such as loading and unloading of containers and customs clearance. The development of ICDs in Vietnam is seen as a self-derived development and thus they have not really functioned well as important nodes in the integrated logistics network (Transportation 2013). The majority of ICDs were set up between 2003 and 2008, and two large ICDs were commissioned in 2010 in the north (at Hai Duong and My Dinh). The ICDs established after 2008 were designed to be on a par with international standards.

Most ICDs in the south are linked to road and inland waterway networks, while those in the north are only accessible by road.

Eight northern ICDs were set up to serve 50 large industrial zones along major trunk roads connecting Hanoi and Hai Phong port. There are nine southern ICDs that serve around 70 industrial zones spread out over Ho Chi Minh City, Dong Nai, Binh Duong, and the Ba Ria–Vung Tau area. Most of those in the south are around Saigon port. However, as container traffic concentration will shift dramatically from near the city center to Cai Mep in coming years and down south to Vung Tau subsequently, the best locations for logistics operations or ICDs should be studied carefully to enable capacity expansion.

Regulation and Services

Transport logistics is administratively fragmented, whether provincial and national regulations or, to some extent, implementation of multilateral and regional agreements. Nor does Vietnam have overarching logistics legislation, as each mode is governed by its own legal framework. Conflicting overlaps create difficulties for logistics users and providers in business registration and liability.

International agreements[1] have affected logistics in Vietnam as they have resulted in Vietnam liberalizing its logistics services sector, while at the same time facilitating trade and logistics activities with partner regions and countries.

Customs clearance procedures, which are based on facilitation instruments such as the Single Administrative Document, the World Customs Organization Harmonized System Code, and WTO's Customs Valuation agreement, must be improved. The automation and modernization of the customs clearance process based on a domestically developed automation system is in its final trial phase. Logistics and multimodal transport can benefit from more customs-bonded warehouses inland from the borders and ports (including ICDs and free trade zones) at which goods can be customs cleared based on national transit procedures.

The quality of local logistics services remains low, with no real ability to compete with foreign providers. Domestic operators tend to provide only some elements of the chain, rather than integrated services. Transfer of know-how and capital injections will be required, whether providers act as independent suppliers or as partners to international companies.

The presence of global operators facilitates traders' access to foreign markets; however, these operators face a lack of adequately trained personnel. Competitive pressures based on foreign companies' presence will further increase once market access restrictions have been gradually taken back or relinquished (Anderson and Banomyong 2010). Currently, large foreign service providers are making their presence felt in the domestic market.

Few Vietnamese trading companies are aware of the importance of managing logistics and the supply chain, or of the potential benefits. Thus they often equate logistics with transport, and the outsourcing of nontransport services is the exception rather than the rule. This is still consistent with the findings by Razzaque (1997). According to a survey carried out in Vietnam (SCM Consulting and Research Services 2008), traditional logistics activities including transportation, warehousing, customs clearance and forwarding are still the most out-sourced activities. The most services in-sourced are reverse logistics, cross-docking, supply chain consulting, custom clearance and distribution. The situation will probably gradually change as outsourcing of end-to-end logistics activities emerges. As the management of supply chains becomes more complex, the trend for outsourcing is expected to develop.

On December 31, 2015, the 10 ASEAN member countries established the ASEAN Economic Community, with the objective to create a single market and single production base. As a member of ASEAN, Vietnam is expected to contribute to the single market's success. ASEAN has produced a Master Plan on ASEAN Connectivity (ASEAN Secretariat 2011), which views connectivity in physical, institutional, and people-to-people terms—the most challenging of which is institutional, due to different legal traditions among the ASEAN member countries.

Concrete Actions

Four key recommendations are suggested:

- Develop and increase the awareness related to the role of logistics and logistics costs in firms' operations to Vietnamese manufacturers and traders. It is necessary to encourage manufacturing and export–import enterprises to raise their efficiency of logistics management by reducing non–value-added activities. This can only be done through an initial baseline survey to evaluate the current logistics performance of firms in Vietnam. Such data will highlight areas where logistics can be improved and where the non–value-added activities are in firms. Benchmarking with other countries can then be carried out to develop competitiveness policies.

- Conduct continuous investments in logistics infrastructure from a macro perspective to create an enabling environment for improved logistics. Investments should not only be in transportation infrastructure but also in other dimensions such as the institutional framework and the promotion of logistics service standards that could be offered by local providers.

- Give priority to investing in human resources development by providing necessary skills for all levels of authorities and enterprises. An initial skill need analysis should be conducted to identify current levels against expected levels, from an employer's perspective. The gaps identified will help develop targeted human resource development programs.

- Because logistics is a crucial part of supply chain management, total supply chain management should be developed and implemented by firms, which will benefit entrepreneurs by increasing the efficiency of production, planning, and monitoring and evaluation. To manage the supply chain, it is critical to establish coordination and collaboration mechanisms between trading partners. Joint planning and forecasting can be an initial starting point for total supply chain management, which would benefit the government sector in supporting growth of manufacturers and traders.

Key Outcomes

A list of logistics infrastructure and facilitation related projects was identified, ranked, and validated by Vietnamese experts in July 2014 (table 5.2). There is only one clearly defined trade facilitation project (the national single window project). The others are infrastructure related, with a focus on freight and passenger logistics. The best case scenario reflects the on planned time-completion of these projects while the most likely case, as validated by the Vietnamese experts, the most likely completion dates. These 2 scenarios, are then fed into a simulation model to predict their respective impact on Vietnam.

Table 5.2 Vietnam's Logistics Projects and Scenarios

Logistics related project	Best case	Likely case
High speed train link Lao PDR–Vietnam	2025	2030
Highway expansion	2015	2015
Vietnam's Cam Ranh Airport in Khanh Hoa (passenger)	2025	2030
Provincial road development	2015	2015
Inland and coastal waterway transport improvement	2015	2020
Lachhuyen deep seaport (Hai Phong Expansion)	2030	2035
Highway North–South (Route 1) upgrade	2015	2015
Longthanh Int'l. Airport (Ho Chi Minh City) upgrade	2030	2035
National single window	2020	2025
Hanoi–Ho Chi Minh City Expressway	2025	2030

Under a best case development scenario, where all listed projects and recommendations have been fully implemented, economic growth will be concentrated in a few provinces and thus will put an extra burden on provincial and regional infrastructure. It is important, therefore, that Vietnam considers the kind of infrastructure that is needed in the provinces to help sustain growth.

Note

1. Such agreements include the ASEAN Framework Agreement on the Facilitation of Goods in Transit, ASEAN Framework Agreement on Multimodal Transport, the ASEAN Framework Agreement on the Facilitation of Inter-State Traffic, and the GMS Cross Border Transport Agreement.

Bibliography

Andersson, A., and R. Banomyong. 2010. "The Implications of Deregulation and Liberalization on the Logistics Service Industry in Lao PDR." *International Journal of Production Economics* 128 (1): 68–76.

ASEAN Secretariat. 2011. *Strategic Transport Action Plan 2011–2015*. Jakarta: ASEAN. http://www.asean.org/wp-content/uploads/images/archive/documents/BAP%20 2011-2015.pdf.

Banomyong, R., and A. K. C. Beresford. 2001. "Multimodal Transport: The Case of Laotian Garment Exporters." *International Journal of Physical Distribution and Logistics Management* 31 (9): 663–85.

Banomyong, R., V. V. Thai, and K. F. Yuen. 2015. "Assessing the National Logistics System of Vietnam." *The Asian Journal of Shipping and Logistics* 31 (1): 21–58.

Civil Aviation Authority of Vietnam. 2012. *Annual Report 2012*. http://www.caa.gov.vn /Default.aspx?tabid=0&catid=436.438&articleid=9026.

General Statistics Office of Vietnam. 2014. "Volume of Freight by Types of Transport." http://www.gso.gov.vn/default_en.aspx?tabid=473&idmid=3&ItemID=13925.

Japan International Cooperation Agency. 2010. *The Comprehensive Study on the Sustainable Development of Transport System in Vietnam (VITRANSS2)*. Logistics Technical Report 5, Ministry of Transportation of Vietnam and Japan International Cooperation Agency, Hanoi.

Razzaque, M. A. 1997. "Challenges to Logistics Development: The Case of a Third World Country—Bangladesh." *International Journal of Physical Distribution and Logistics Management* 27 (1): 18–38.

SCM Consulting and Research Services. 2008. *The 2008 Logistics Survey*. Ho Chi Minh City, Vietnam.

Thai, V. V. 2008. "Service Quality in Maritime Transport: Conceptual Model and Empirical Evidence." *Asia Pacific Journal of Marketing and Logistics* 20 (4): 493–518.

Thai, V. V., and D. Grewal. 2005. "An Analysis of the Efficiency and Competitiveness of Vietnamese Port System." *Asia Pacific Journal of Marketing and Logistics* 17 (1): 3–31.

Transportation. 2013. "Investment in ICD: Why Is It Still Inefficient?" http://giaothongvantai .com.vn/giao-thong-phat-trien/quan-ly/201308/dau-tu-cang-can-vi-sao-chua-hieu -qua-334707/.

Tuoi Tre News. 2012. "Ceased Transshipment Port Opens Door for Investors." http:// tuoitrenews.vn/features-news/1266/ceased-transshipment-port-opens-door-for -investors.

Vietnam Breaking News. 2011. "Transport Ministry Revokes Private Cargo Airline License." http://www.vietnambreakingnews.com/2011/12/transport-ministry-revokes -private-cargo-airline-license/.

VINAMARINE (Vietnam Maritime Administration). 2014. "Statistical Data: Port Throughput." http://www.vinamarine.gov.vn/Index.aspx?page=report&tab=hhrvcb.

CHAPTER 6

Vietnam's Preferential Trade Agreements
Implications for GVC Participation and Upgrading

Axel Berger and Dominique Bruhn

Key Takeaways

Vietnam is a lower-middle–income country and, like many of its peers, faces the challenge of upgrading to higher value-added tasks in global value chains (GVCs). Upgrading typically involves moving to different tasks within or between value chains (functional upgrading), improving the efficiency of production processes (process upgrading), or improving the quality and value of outputs (product upgrading) in order to capture more value along the chain.

Participation and upgrading are not an arbitrary policy objective: both may be of decisive importance for Vietnam's future economic development path. While the economy currently is highly competitive in relatively low-skilled, labor-intensive tasks, history has shown that wages eventually will rise and this comparative advantage will erode. In order to avoid the middle-income trap—where a country can compete neither in low value-added stages due to rising labor costs nor in higher value-added stages due to a lack of adequate skills and technologies—the Vietnamese government has embarked on a path toward deeper integration with the world economy. While other middle-income countries hesitate, Vietnam is signing deep preferential trade agreements (PTAs) with economic heavyweights such as the EU, the United States, and Japan. However, committing to the comprehensive rulebooks of today's PTAs is not a guarantee for good GVC performance and requires accompanying policy initiatives at the domestic level.

Challenges Confronted
Since its accession to the World Trade Organization (WTO) and involvement with PTAs, partly in the framework of the ASEAN, Vietnam already is quite active in regional and GVCs. The conclusion of a number of deep PTAs, as well as the potential conclusion of the Regional Comprehensive Economic Partnership (RCEP),

promises Vietnam a further surge in exports and foreign direct investment (FDI) due to preferential access to large markets and their consumers. A number of studies identify Vietnam as the main beneficiary of these agreements (see Vietnam in the PTA Landscape below). However, the complex standards and rules of origin make it difficult for many domestic firms to make use of preferential market access. Moreover, it is unclear whether the agreements lock in the status quo, that is, foster Vietnam's current comparative advantage in production stages associated with low value added, or promote a dynamic transition to more sophisticated and higher value-added tasks.

Besides improving access to global markets, Vietnam's more recent PTAs are so broad in scope and high in standard that they have implications for a number of policy areas beyond international trade. On the one hand, the coverage of rules on investment, intellectual property rights (IPRs), public procurement, and many more behind-the-border issues may be seen as a necessary response to the activity of multinationals and trade within GVCs and as a credible signal for a reliable policy and business environment. On the other hand, these rules go beyond WTO commitments and may have implications for formulating economic policies intended to support Vietnamese firms to move to production stages with higher value added.

The domestic business sector seems not entirely ready to benefit from deeper international integration. Despite a spectacular export performance, labor productivity has been shrinking since the end of the 1990s. Export growth is driven mainly by foreign-invested companies. Vietnam has indeed been successful in attracting FDI and the recently signed PTAs will accelerate this trend further. FDI flows are welcome as they create additional employment opportunities for Vietnam's young and growing population. However, linkages between foreign and domestic companies often are lacking, suggesting that domestic companies are unable to compete in the current business environment and cannot provide inputs at a quality and quantity demanded by multinational companies.

Solutions Proposed

Vietnam owes much of its impressive growth performance of the last decade to international economic integration. This certainly is one reason why the country is embracing the new generation of deep PTAs that promise to improve its access to global markets. However, the challenges just outlined illustrate that economic benefits will not materialize automatically. We make the following recommendations how Vietnam can therefore make best use of the agreements coming into force and use the momentum of deep PTAs to push domestic policy reforms while acknowledging and addressing potential caveats.

Identify Potential and Remaining Policy Instruments

The new generation of PTAs is so comprehensive in scope and strength of commitments that it is almost impossible to identify at first sight the positive and negative implications. Fully understanding the opportunities and challenges, as well as trade-offs, associated with deep PTAs will allow Vietnam to better harvest the benefits of further integration. Moreover, the government needs to identify the policy instruments available to support upgrading in GVCs so that the potential opportunities materialize. Investments in infrastructure and human capital (in particular vocational training) and a more efficient allocation of capital do not breach international rules, such investments increase Vietnam's attractiveness for foreign investors and encourage linkages with domestic firms. At the same time, increased efforts in intergovernmental coordination will be necessary to assure compliance with the commitments made under deep PTAs.

Raise Awareness and Build Capacities

Vietnam needs to ensure that domestic firms are aware of the preferential treatment they are entitled to under the PTAs. Experiences with previous PTAs show that many companies, in particular small and medium firms, either are unaware of the improved market access opportunities or do not have the capacities to take advantage of them. The gains from tariff reductions should not be offset by transaction or compliance costs, hence the need for awareness raising and capacity building among Vietnamese firms.

This is true also for firms to realize upgrading potential. Upgrading to higher value-added tasks requires capacities to assume new stages of production, produce at higher quality, meet international standards, or improve the efficiency of processes. Building up these skills is economically valid—irrespective of any challenges and opportunities implied by PTAs—if Vietnam wants to progress on the path of economic development.

Lessons to Be Learned
Negotiate to Achieve Outcomes That Promote GVC Participation and Upgrading

When negotiating comprehensive PTAs, it is important for countries to strike the right balance between signaling a reliable policy and business environment and safeguarding areas sensible for national economic development strategies. The commitments Vietnam has agreed to undertake are a credible signal for international investors and almost certainly will increase Vietnam's attractiveness as a partner in GVCs. However, to achieve this credibility, Vietnam will need to embark on rather painful policy adjustments.

In any case, it is important for Vietnam to be aware of the implications, positive or negative, of the comprehensive PTA provisions and take them into account when negotiating PTAs. Many aspects have the potential to attract investors and increase GVC participation, yet sometimes it remains unclear the extent to which the domestic economy will benefit from expansion in low value-added production stages while having fewer policy instruments to support upgrading to higher value-added tasks. An important precondition to benefit from PTAs is to have a clearly identified national development strategy before entering the complex negotiations, including the means and instruments needed to achieve these goals, and to assess final PTAs and their implications against this background.

Strengthen Economic Framework Conditions Complementary to Trade Policy Decisions

To realize the potential benefits, policymakers can use the momentum of deep PTAs to reform the national policy environment and strengthen economic framework conditions. Upgrading in GVCs does not necessarily need vertical or discriminatory industrial policies in the sense that specific sectors or major national players enjoy preferential treatment. The use of some traditional instruments such as reverse engineering or local content requirements is no longer available because of the international commitments Vietnam has undertaken in WTO and in recent deep PTAs. Instead, Vietnam could increase investments in horizontal measures that are beneficial for the economy at large, in particular private businesses, by improving infrastructure, human capital, vocational training, and the rule of law, and by establishing a level playing field between foreign and domestic, and private and state-owned enterprises. These measures would complement trade policy, attract foreign investors, and encourage fruitful linkages with the domestic sector.

Common Lessons and Potential for Replication in Other Countries

The above findings are relevant not only for Vietnam but also for a range of other middle-income countries that aim to upgrade in GVCs and may face the decision to sign deep PTAs, which have become the trade instrument of choice of the major trading powers. As Vietnam shows, it is important to be aware of the challenges and opportunities arising from PTAs, to negotiate the agreements against the background of their implications for national development strategies, and to carefully weigh the benefits of market access against potential restrictions of national policy space for supporting industrial development. If gains from market liberalization are high enough, countries should seize these opportunities for GVC participation and upgrading, and identify the policy instruments that are available to support these objectives. Policy instruments that do not discriminate against foreign investors and do not favor specific firms or sectors likely are compliant with PTA commitments. They include investments in infrastructure or human capital that ultimately will benefit foreign and domestic firms. Deep PTAs can serve as instruments to initiate crucial domestic reforms that improve countries' conditions for upgrading.

Vietnam in the PTA Landscape

After multiple multilateral trade rounds in the context of the General Agreement on Tariffs and Trade—where the international community picked the low-hanging fruits of trade liberalization resulting in a remarkable reduction of tariffs and increased economic activity and exchange in the postwar era—trade negotiations in the forum of WTO have become increasingly sluggish since the turn of the century. Progress in the remaining issue areas is too slow to keep pace with the rapidly evolving nature of international trade. While WTO's Doha Round is in virtual deadlock, PTAs have proliferated and are shaping the international trade system.

Unlike many developing countries, Vietnam has seized the opportunity and is negotiating deep PTAs. In 2015 alone, it concluded four PTAs, among them the TPP signed by the United States, Japan, and 10 other countries of the Pacific rim, and EVFTA.[1]

The new generation of PTAs includes rules that go beyond WTO in two ways: first, they demand much larger commitments in areas that are part of WTO's rulebook; second, they cover disciplines outside the current WTO mandate (Horn, Mavroidis, and Sapir 2010). Four core disciplines that feature in a large share of PTAs and go beyond the WTO rulebook (or do not exist in WTO agreements at all) are competition policy, IPRs, investment, and the movement of capital (WTO 2011). Other provisions that are included regularly in recently signed PTAs include rules on public procurement, services, the environment, and labor and human rights. Evidently, such deep PTAs go much further than the trade rules of WTO and shift their focus to regulatory measures, whereas the focus of shallow PTAs rests under the WTO roof and on tariff measures.

PTAs have become much deeper since the 1990s, with the last decade witnessing another major deepening (figure 6.1). One of the main factors in this may be the expansion of GVCs. The rise in GVC trade creates new incentives for signing deep PTAs for two reasons: first, trade costs—tariffs and nontariff barriers—are

Figure 6.1 Deepening Trade Agreements

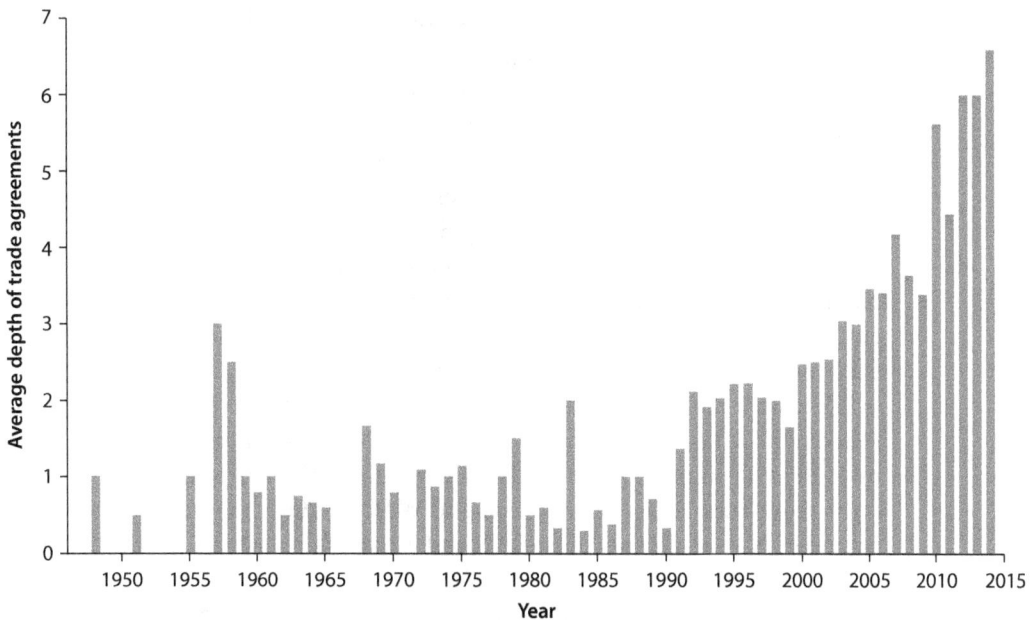

Source: Illustration based on DESTA database.
Note: The data are taken from the DESTA database (version Februrary 2016). Dür, Baccini, and Elsig (2014) have developed an additive indicator that measures the depth of PTAs along seven dimensions (elimination of tariffs, services trade, investments, standards, public procurement, competition, and intellectual property rights), ranging from 0 (the shallowest) to 7 (the deepest). Figure 6.1 shows the average depth of all trade agreements signed in the given year.

magnified within GVCs as products cross borders multiple times; second, GVCs are more affected by behind-the-border policies, such as competition, IPRs and investment, which pose risks for the smooth operation in GVCs and which are not sufficiently addressed at the multilateral level.

From a GVC perspective, the motive for signing deep PTAs is to further reduce or eliminate tariffs and nontariff barriers at the border while addressing behind-the-border issues. Lawrence (2000) was one of the first to point out the importance of harmonizing national policies to ensure that international production networks operate smoothly. Likewise, Antràs and Staiger (2012) argue that multilaterally agreed upon rules—like reciprocity and nondiscrimination—inadequately address the challenges triggered by the increase in offshoring. Instead, trade agreements must cover behind-the-border barriers to fill the governance gap between the countries involved in GVCs.

WTO (2011) finds that countries with higher trade in parts and components relative to total trade are more likely to sign deep agreements. Orefice and Rocha (2013) show that a 10 percent increase in the share of production network trade in total trade increases the depth of an agreement by roughly 6 percentage points. Moreover, the likelihood of signing deeper agreements is higher for countries involved in north–south production sharing and for economies belonging to the Asian region.

PTAs show wide differences in depth depending on the countries engaged. Trade agreements between developed and developing countries are significantly deeper on average than those between countries of similar income level (Bruhn 2014). Agreements among developing countries themselves are the shallowest and focus mainly on eliminating tariffs.

The policy motives for developing countries to adopt deep PTA provisions may vary from one case to another. Deep provisions, such as the protection of IPRs and investment, are important signaling and commitment devices that may help remedy local institutional deficiencies in developing countries and promote FDI. In other instances, developing country governments sign up to deep provisions as a means to overcome domestic reform deadlocks or to tie the hands of future governments by making the reversal of economic reforms more costly. For some developing countries, deep provisions are part of a package deal they must accept to gain access to the markets of major trading powers.

Vietnam is one of the developing countries most actively involved in the evolving PTA network. Thanks to its economic liberalization reforms, it developed from a comparatively closed economy during the 1990s to one of the most open economies today. After acceding to WTO in 2007, the country has signed several PTAs as a member of ASEAN and is one of the first developing countries in the recent wave of ever-deeper PTAs (figure 6.2).

The year 2015 marked a milestone on the path of Vietnam's economic integration. With the signing of the TPP in February 2016, Vietnam has become part of a megaregional trade agreement covering up to 40 percent of global GDP and 25 percent of world trade. In light of the uncertain future of TPP, it is noteworthy that Vietnam signed another three PTAs in 2015. The conclusion of the EVFTA

Figure 6.2 Vietnam's PTA Network

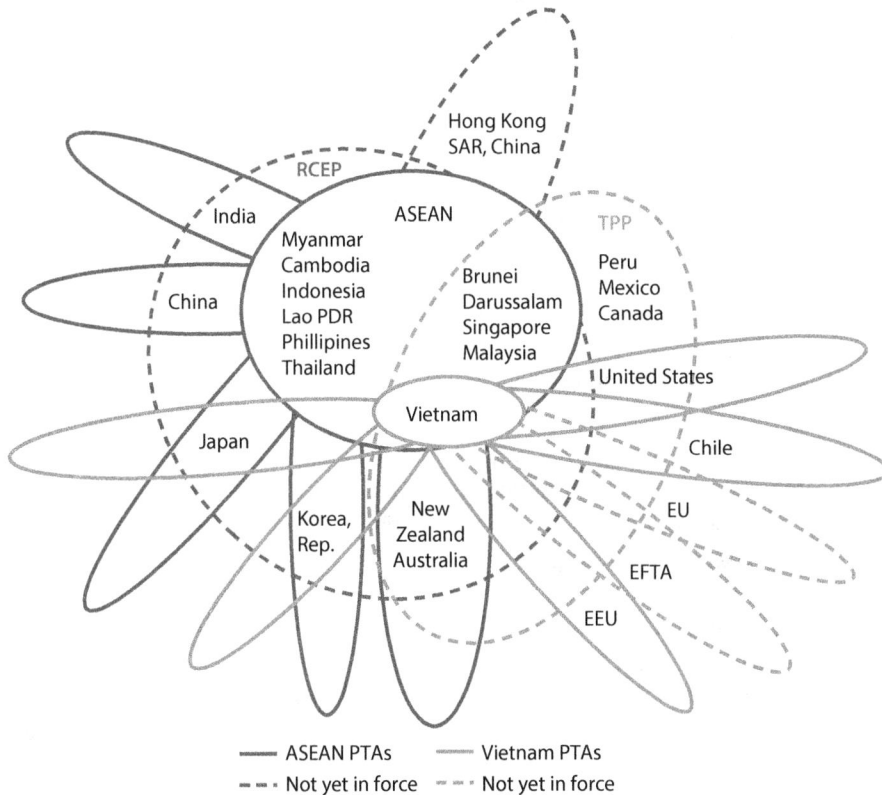

Source: Berger et al. 2016, figure 4: Vietnam's PTA network. Used with permission. Further permission required for reuse.
Note: EFTA = European Free Trade Area; EEU = Eurasian Economic Union; RCEP = Regional Comprehensive Economic Partnership.

negotiations in December 2015 is expected to result in an additional €22.1 billion of products exported annually to the EU, equaling up to 18 percent of Vietnam's total global exports (Sandler and Rosenberg 2015). Vietnam also signed a PTA with Korea and the Eurasian Economic Union (EEU) in 2015. The country also is involved in negotiations for the Regional Comprehensive Economic Partnership (RCEP), another megaregional agreement that—if concluded—would cover up to 30 percent of world trade and account for almost one-third of global GDP. Once (and if) the pending PTAs enter into force, Vietnam will be part of 16 bilateral and regional PTAs, with up to 56 preferential trading partners around the globe.

Vietnam mirrors the global trend of increasing not only the number of PTAs but also their depth. Reviewing Vietnam's commitments in its worldwide network of PTAs using different databases and criteria, Berger et al. (2016) find that Vietnam has moved from PTAs including mainly disciplines covered by the WTO mandate to PTAs with significant commitments in behind-the-border areas. As with PTAs globally, Vietnam's PTAs tend to be deeper when signed with industrialized countries. Two cases in point are the TPP and EVFTA.

As deep PTAs will prospectively be of major importance for Vietnam's future economic development, the publicly available texts of the TPP and the EVFTA, although both agreements have not yet entered into force, are now exemplarily analyzed in detail.

Potential for Vietnam's GVC Participation

We have argued that the proliferation of GVCs is positively related to the depth of PTAs. The rationale of GVCs explaining the formation of deep PTAs also holds the other way around: deep PTAs increase GVC trade for the signing parties by reducing the costs of trade. WTO (2011) shows that PTAs increase trade in parts and components by 35 percent among country members. An additional legally enforceable provision included in the PTA which goes beyond tariff elimination increases trade in parts and components by almost 2 percentage points. Particularly, deep provisions in competition policy and technical barriers to trade have a positive effect on production networks. Noguera (2012) finds growth in value-added trade of 15 percent within the five years following the trade agreement. Dür, Baccini, and Elsig (2014) corroborate that the deeper a PTA, the greater the increase in trade flows between its members. This is driven particularly by nontariff provisions such as service liberalization and IPRs. Investigating differences by industries, Orefice and Rocha (2013) find the trade effect to be larger for industries that require higher levels of regulations, such as automotive parts and information and communications technologies (ICT), and lower for less capital-intensive sectors like textiles.

These general findings are confirmed by estimations of the effects of single PTAs under negotiation. Studies on the potential effects of the Transatlantic Trade and Investment Partnership (TTIP) and the TPP show that their positive impact on trade and GDP are predominantly driven by the reduction of nontrade barriers and converging rules (Egger et al. 2015; World Bank 2016).

Studies suggest that Vietnam will be among the countries that benefit the most from the deep PTAs (Baker, Vanzetti, and Huong 2014; Petry, Plummer, and Zhai 2012; PIIE 2016; World Bank 2016). The TPP and EVFTA could provide Vietnam with preferential market access to the major markets of the United States, EU, and Japan, among others. Vietnam will gain a competitive advantage vis-à-vis its competitors, China in particular, that do not have PTAs in place with these major economies.

Several studies have analyzed the macroeconomic effects of deep PTAs and consistently find that Vietnam will gain from these agreements. With respect to the TPP, we will focus on the two most recent estimations—PIIE (2016) and World Bank (2016)—but both are in the range of projected trade and welfare gains of older studies (such as Petry, Plummer, and Zhai 2012). These studies apply a standard computable general equilibrium (CGE) model to assess the effects of PTAs. Until 2030—the year the agreement could be fully implemented relative to the baseline year 2015—the TPP could yield overall gains of GDP growth of 1.1 percent on average for its members (PIIE 2016; World Bank 2016).

Countries with higher levels of tariff and nontariff barriers, such as Japan, Malaysia, and Vietnam, likely will gain more from the TPP than Canada, Mexico, and the United States, which already have relatively low levels of these barriers due to NAFTA (World Bank 2016). Vietnam, with estimated GDP gains ranging from 8.1 to 10 percent relative to the baseline scenario (PIIE 2016; World Bank 2016), is the country with the biggest potential to benefit from the TPP. Preferential access to the markets of TPP member states will help Vietnam better exploit its comparative advantages in labor-intensive manufacturing. Unskilled labor is projected to gain 14 percent in real wages by 2030. Skilled labor, however, may see its real wages fall, by around 3 percent (World Bank 2016).

EVFTA is expected to yield positive macroeconomic effects in magnitudes similar to those of the TPP. Baker, Vanzetti, and Huong (2014) estimate that EVFTA has the potential to increase Vietnam's GDP in the long run by around 7–8 percent relative to the counterfactual scenario. Vietnam's exports to the EU are estimated to increase by 50 percent and imports by 43 percent. From a sectoral perspective, the textiles and apparel and footwear industries in particular will benefit from EVFTA.

The studies cited above suggest that Vietnam likely will benefit from improved access to the U.S., Japanese, and EU markets because of the TPP and EVFTA. This positive impact stems mainly from the potential to exploit the comparative advantage in low-skilled segments of GVCs, such as textiles and apparel and footwear. The effect will be reinforced because the deeper integration with these three huge markets will lead to trade diversion effects away from Vietnam's competitors. The stringent rules of origin in these agreements, for example, will have the effect that companies are no longer allowed to source yarn and fabrics from China if they want to benefit from the preferential tariff.

While the studies project positive effects of PTAs for Vietnam's GVC participation in general, they also indicate that this will occur mainly in low-skilled labor segments, where Vietnam already has a comparative advantage. The next section sheds some light on the question of whether, and under what conditions, the deep PTAs can also contribute to Vietnam's policy objective of upgrading in GVCs.

Implications for Upgrading

Economic development via industrial upgrading is among Vietnam's priorities. While the preceding section argued that Vietnam's recent PTAs are likely to boost its participation in GVCs mainly due to preferential market access to the EU and United States, their implications for upgrading—moving to higher value-added tasks within or between GVCs—are less clear cut.

Deep PTAs can promote the more stable and reliable trade and investment environment necessary for attracting FDI and increasing exports and value capture. However, the extensive coverage of behind-the-border regulations in deep PTAs can bring about high adjustment costs and restrict the range of national policy instruments available to support upgrading to higher value-added tasks in GVCs (Bruhn 2014). For Vietnam and other lower-middle–income countries, it is important not only to increase value creation

---

Box 6.1 Different Types of Upgrading in GVCs

Process upgrading: Value addition through more efficient production, for example, stemming from enhanced technology and skills or reorganized production systems.

Product upgrading: Value addition through more sophisticated or new products, such as changes in design, branding, and quality.

Functional upgrading: Value addition through an expansion of activities, such as assuming new tasks within the production chain, for example, R&D and design or marketing and sales.

Source: Humphrey and Schmitz 2002.

---

by expanding the scope of activity in the production stages where they already are active and enjoy a comparative advantage, but also to engage in process, product, and functional upgrading, which will help them to take over more sophisticated stages in GVCs (box 6.1) and eventually avoid the middle-income trap.

In the following subsections, we explore whether and how PTAs can spur these processes in Vietnam in three sectors individually—electronics, agriculture, and textiles and apparel—using selected PTA disciplines of the TPP and EVFTA for illustration.

Investment Liberalization and Process Upgrading in Electronics

The TPP and EVFTA both include comprehensive investment chapters, with similar substantive rules on the protection of foreign investments, such as the requirement to guarantee fair and equitable treatment, national treatment and compensation in the case of (indirect) expropriation, and the free transfer of investment-related funds. Both treaties also cover commitments to liberalize market access for foreign investors and prohibitions on the use of performance requirements.

They differ, however, in the design of their dispute settlement mechanisms. While the investment chapter in TPP includes an investor–state dispute settlement mechanism modeled on the U.S. approach, EVFTA includes a novel mechanism—the investment court system. EVFTA is the first treaty to include the new investment court system, promoted by the EU, a departure from the traditional investor–state dispute settlement mechanism. EVFTA's investment court system includes clauses for appointing permanent judges, randomly selecting tribunals, and establishing an appeals mechanism, designed in accordance with WTO's arbitration and public law systems.

While the evidence on the effects of protection provisions in international investment treaties on FDI flows is mixed, studies have found that market access provisions help attract additional investment (Berger et al. 2013). The comprehensive investment rules in TPP and EVFTA therefore potentially lead to increased investment inflows, in particular in previously restricted sectors. In light of recurring complaints by foreign investors about Vietnam's unstable and sometimes discriminatory legal and judicial system,[2] the increased investment protection may provide additional security, potentially further promoting FDI inflows. By increasing FDI, trade agreements such as the TPP and EVFTA in principle may support process upgrading through spillover effects from multinational firms. These effects can lead to a transmission of knowledge and skills from international to domestic firms. While some studies have found positive spillover effects attributed to FDI (Borensztein, de Gregorio, and Lee 1998; De Mello 1997), they also show that the effects are dependent on the supportive host-country framework conditions. Such contextual factors include the technology gap between foreign and domestic firms, the type and motivation of foreign investments, and the linkages to local suppliers.

The promotion of FDI is the main strategy of the Vietnamese government in the electronics sector. Partly due to tax incentives and preferential access to land, in recent years the electronics sector experienced increased FDI inflows of high-tech electronics companies such as Canon, Intel, and Samsung. Foreign-owned firms account for a staggering 90 percent of exports (Thanh et al. 2015). Establishing the important linkages between foreign and domestic firms is regarded as the main challenge in Vietnam's electronics sector. Even though Vietnam has attracted multinational firms investing at large scale, such firms often bring their own supplier network rather than sourcing from local suppliers.

While the TPP and EVFTA may further improve the attractiveness of Vietnam for foreign investors, the positive spillover effects supporting process upgrading are therefore all but guaranteed. In order to build linkages, some countries resort to performance requirements for international investors, such as requiring a certain share of local content in production, the procurement of local goods (or services), and technology transfers. This approach does not seem to be an option for Vietnam for two reasons. First, the investment chapters in TPP and EVFTA prohibit most types of performance requirements, going beyond WTO's rules on trade-related investment measures and Vietnam's former PTAs in their scope and their likelihood of being enforced.[3] Second, the Vietnamese government is no proponent of forcing requirements on FDI, but has chosen the strategy to incentivize foreign investors to locate their production in Vietnam partly by granting them more preferences than domestic firms. Unfortunately, the extent of linkages between domestic and foreign firms in the electronics sector remains below expectations. It seems that many Vietnamese-owned private firms struggle to integrate into GVCs and supply parts and components to MNEs. Box 6.2 gives a brief outline of the challenges Vietnamese firms are facing and suggests conditions that need to be in place to improve firm performance. Only if at least some of these conditions are in place can the comprehensive investment chapters in the TPP and EVFTA that liberalize market access and aim to attract FDI be expected to benefit the local economy and spur process upgrading in the electronics sector.

Box 6.2 Challenges and Policy Options for Improving Private Sector Performance

The private-owned business sector in Vietnam is highly fragmented and consists mainly of small and often informal companies that are unable to make products at a scale and quality required by global lead firms. Distortions within the Vietnamese economy lead to preferential treatment of larger firms—whether state owned or private—effectively shielding them from market pressures and holding back smaller firms.

Without major domestic initiatives addressing these shortcomings, additional FDI inflows threaten to lead to the crowding out of current and future domestic suppliers rather than the creation of linkages between international and national companies. Vietnam needs to create an environment that brings foreign firms to the point where they voluntarily want to establish relationships with local firms. In order to achieve that, support for the domestic private sector is needed in different ways.

First, there should be no reverse discrimination benefiting de facto only large domestic and foreign firms. Second, there should be more support in matching international firms with local suppliers, for example, by promoting business-to-business platforms. Third, assistance is needed to bring Vietnamese firms to a level where they can supply their inputs reliably, in good quality, and in accordance with international standards. One option is to expand vocational training in line with foreign investors' requirements and in cooperation with them.

Intellectual Property Rights and Product Upgrading in Agriculture

IPRs are an important feature of deep PTAs in the context of GVCs. With multinationals' huge crossborder activities, ideas, and inventions such as designs, brands, and technologies need to be protected beyond national territory.

This protection can be achieved through copyrights, patents, designs, trademarks, and geographic indications. Because knowledge-intensive tasks such as research and development (R&D) are undertaken in a developed country headquarters while much of the production is offshored to developing countries, diverging national IPR systems need to be bridged internationally. The new generation of deep PTAs deals with IPRs more comprehensively than the Agreement on Trade-Related Aspects of IPRs, which is part of the WTO rulebook. Notably, the extensive IPR chapter in the TPP further increases the duration of patents and allows enforcement not only via civil but also criminal proceedings.

This increased strength of IPR provisions has generated support and opposition. On the one hand, these rules are crucial to encouraging innovation as well as trade and FDI related to R&D-intensive products and services, which can be beneficial, too, for developing countries participating in the respective value chains. On the other, there is concern that these same rules overstep the mark in favor of powerful companies and prevent developing countries from reaping the benefits from trade and investment linkages. A prohibitively high protection of IPRs may limit developing countries' possibilities that arise from technology spillovers and reverse engineering, which can be essential steps in upgrading to higher value-added tasks.

Discussed less prominently is that developing countries themselves also possess intellectual property and could equally benefit from having their ideas and inventions protected abroad. One prominent aspect where EVFTA's IPRs outstrip the TPP's is EVFTA's extensive coverage of geographic indications.[4] The EU is known to be the biggest promoter of geographic indications, having a wide range of European products of high quality and international reputation such as sparkling wine from Champagne and Parmesan cheese, whose frequent imitations are often regarded as substitutes in foreign markets. Some Vietnamese products have renown, and EVFTA recognizes 39 products of Vietnamese origin on the list of protected geographic indications. One example is Phu Quoc Fish Sauce, which faces fierce competition from Chinese producers, which refer to the Vietnamese island on their product labels. With EVFTA, the Phu Quoc Fish Sauce enjoys exclusive market access to the EU, giving Vietnamese producers a competitive advantage. According to local observers, the prospect of this label being protected in the EU market has spurred investment by Vietnamese fish sauce producers. In this way EVFTA provides incentives to develop a new marketing strategy and place products of Vietnamese origin prominently among foreign consumers.

The coverage of geographic indications opens an opportunity for Vietnam to foster product upgrading, because the value of the products covered can increase with exclusive access to and higher reputation in foreign markets. This upgrading potential through branding, higher quality, and the associated markup in prices obviously reaches beyond fish sauce and applies to many other products in the Vietnamese agricultural and food processing sectors protected under the IPR chapter, such as coffee and fruits.

To reap the potential benefits, however, Vietnam needs to address various shortcomings. First, the Vietnamese brands need to be built and promoted abroad. If foreign consumers have no (or no good) associations when considering such products, the protection of geographic indications will not cater to new markets or benefit Vietnamese producers. This effort will require heavy investment in capacities such as skilled personnel with experience in marketing and distribution. Second, reliable quality control is needed for agricultural products and foodstuffs. Only if Vietnam can export products of a certain quality, complying with EU health and safety standards, can it guarantee market access and make its branding successful. Smaller, local producers especially may need assistance to become aware of these new opportunities, gradually build their capacities, and comply with the standards to achieve product upgrading.

Rules of Origin and Functional Upgrading in Textiles and Apparel

Rules of origin feature in every PTA: they ensure that goods originating only in the PTA member countries enjoy preferential market access and prevent trade deflection. For a product to be assigned a certain origin, rules of origin require either that the product is wholly obtained or has undergone sufficient transformation within the country. In the 21st century, where trade is characterized by GVCs and production is fragmented across borders, sophisticated products increasingly are unlikely to be produced in only one country. As a result, rules of origin have to specify under which conditions the transformation of the product is sufficient to certify its origin within a country. This typically is achieved via one or more of the following criteria: the product has changed classification under the harmonized system due to an activity in the country (harmonized system level to be specified); a certain share of value was added to the product within the country; and one or more product-specific production stages occurred within the country (Draper, Chikura, and Krogman 2016; Elliot 2016). With cumulation, the transformation can take place in any of the PTA partner countries for the product to qualify for preferential treatment.

The design of rules of origin can be criticized on many grounds, however. The complexities stemming from differing rules across products and across (sometimes overlapping) PTAs present many firms in developing countries with serious challenges and can limit the use of tariff preferences. When the cost of compliance is higher than the gains from preferential market access, rules of origin may not even have a trade-creating effect. Their restrictiveness often is higher than needed to prevent trade deflection and results in inefficient sourcing decisions with trade-diverting effects. (Vietnam though, as seen, is destined to be a leading beneficiary of the trade-diverting effects fueled by the rules of origin in EVFTA and the TPP.)

For Vietnam, the rules of origin laid down specifically for the textile and apparel sector are of particular interest, not only because the United States and the EU are Vietnam's biggest export markets with apparel tariffs being relatively high, but also because the structure of the rules of origin in the two PTAs has clear implications for Vietnam's opportunities to upgrade in GVCs. At the moment, Vietnam specializes in the cut-make-trim stages of textile and apparel production. The yarn-forward rule in the TPP and the fabric-forward rule in the EVFTA require that, to be granted preferential market access to the United States, all production stages starting with the yarn (fabric) need to be undertaken within the PTA area (figure 6.3). More precisely, for TPP this means that textiles have to be woven and knitted from yarn produced by TPP countries, the fabric dyed, printed, and finished within TPP countries, and the final fabric cut and sewn in TPP countries (or triple transformation). Only the fiber may be imported from outside the TPP. These rules of origin are more strict than those stipulated in EVFTA, which require a double transformation, that is, fabric forward. However, given the fact that the bottleneck in Vietnam's textiles sector is the making of the fabrics, both rules of origin regimes have similar effects for Vietnam (Berger et al. 2016).

Even though cumulation across member countries is typically provided for in rules of origin regimes, the examples of both the TPP's yarn-forward rule and EVFTA's fabric-forward rule show that Vietnam faces a significant challenge in the short run. Vietnam imports the majority of the inputs needed for textile and apparel production from nonmember countries, namely China and Taiwan,

Figure 6.3 Production Structure in Textiles and Apparel

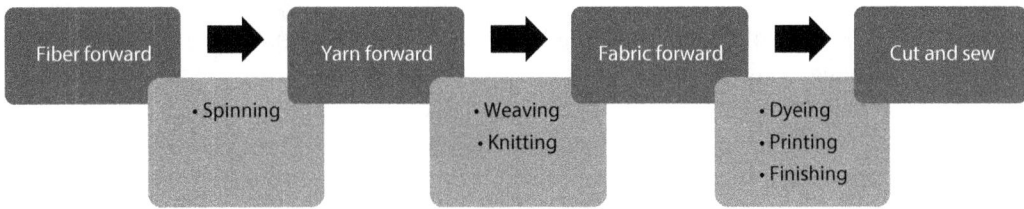

| Fiber forward | ➡ | Yarn forward | ➡ | Fabric forward | ➡ | Cut and sew |
| • Spinning | | • Weaving
• Knitting | | • Dyeing
• Printing
• Finishing | | |

Source: Berger et al. 2016, figure 12: Yarn- and fabric-forward rules of origin. Used with permission. Further permission required for reuse.

China (Elliot 2016). Two broad scenarios could define Vietnam's future in textiles and apparel.

Under the first, Vietnam cannot comply with the strict rule of origins for textiles and apparel. Vietnam sources its inputs from the cheapest suppliers—now, mainly nonmember countries, such as China. Either yarns and fabrics from other countries are not easily available or the costs of information and compliance are so high that they eat up all the potential gains from tariff reductions. Consequently, Vietnamese firms continue exporting their textiles and apparel under the same conditions as without the TPP or the EVFTA, under most-favored-nation rates. The restrictive rules of origin prevent the country from reaping the potential benefits of the agreements.

Under the second scenario, Vietnam succeeds in expanding its own textile and apparel sector to incorporate an additional upstream stage of production. In order for this functional upgrading to be successful, Vietnam needs to produce domestically those inputs—yarn and fabrics—it previously has imported. The rules of origin in the TPP and EVFTA create strong incentives to pursue this second strategy. Once the tariffs are phased out and firms comply with the rules of origin, they can benefit from tremendous tariff cuts. Vietnam already has voiced its intention to expand domestic production facilities. It also seems that FDI in the textile and apparel sector is flowing into the country in search of cheap labor, coupled with preferential market access to the United States and EU, even before the signing and entry into force of the TPP and EVFTA.

To realize these gains, however, Vietnam needs to meet two main conditions. First, it is unclear which actors have enough capacities to build the upstream sector. Either there needs to be a more prominent role for big state-supported companies, which is contested, or there must be more cooperation and better linkages with foreign investors. A particular challenge is fabric making and dyeing, which come with serious environmental consequences. One policy option is to support the clustering of firms in industrial parks. In this way, the government could kill two birds with one stone: encourage linkages between domestic suppliers and foreign firms with financial benefiting from geographic proximity and set up appropriate infrastructure such as wastewater treatment to address environmental concerns. Second, a significant barrier often voiced by Vietnamese policymakers, experts, and firms alike is customs procedures. Lengthy and burdensome administrative processes at the border are a hindrance for firms to make use of tariff preferences.

If it fulfills these two conditions, and raises awareness of tariff preferences among firms, Vietnam stands to benefit from the restrictive design of the rules of origin typically found in recent deep PTAs.

There are two more elements. First, Vietnam needs to achieve competitiveness in these new segments while still under the protective umbrella of the agreements which currently are diverting trade and investment from other countries to the benefit of Vietnam. If other textile and apparel producers join the TPP or sign separate PTAs with the United States and EU, this window of opportunity could close. Second, some tariffs relevant for Vietnam's textile and apparel exports are phased out only slowly, leading to too optimistic projections of export growth in the T&G sector. In fact, Berger et al. (2016) calculate that for 64 percent of Vietnam's garment exports to the United States (in value), the tariffs are completely eliminated only after 10 years. Hence there is a risk that Vietnam becomes just about ready to reap the benefits from its new production stages in textiles and apparel when rising wages make the country a less attractive location for production in general. Thus before making significant investments, the Vietnamese government is well advised to carefully weigh the opportunities and challenges associated with functional upgrading in the textile and apparel sector.

Notes

This chapter stems from a research project conducted as part of the 51st postgraduate training program at the German Development Institute/Deutsches Institut für Entwicklungspolitik (DIE) funded by the German Ministry of Economic Cooperation and Development. The authors warmly thank the research team of Andrea Bender, Julia Friesen, Katharina Kick, Felix Kullmann, Robert Roßner, and Svenja Weyrauch for their outstanding work and continuous commitment throughout the project, and acknowledge their contribution to this chapter. They also express their gratitude to their project and interview partners in Vietnam, in particular the Central Institute for Economic Management, the Vietnamese Chamber of Commerce and Industry, and the Friedrich Ebert Foundation.

1. The main thrust of this chapter was written before the election of Donald Trump as the new president of the United States. Due to the withdrawal of the United States from the TPP in January 2017, the agreement will not enter into force in its current form, as the ratification of the United States is indispensable. We, nevertheless, refrained from substantially rewriting this chapter, because the TPP negotiation process, despite the uncertainty of its actual entry into force, will likely have an impact on Vietnam's economic policymaking and on the upgrading potentials of Vietnamese firms. First of all, the TPP negotiations triggered a number of economic reform initiatives that are likely to be followed up by the Vietnamese government. Second, although the TPP was the lighthouse project for Vietnam, its international integration strategy is based on a much broader footing and includes a number of deep PTAs that have already been signed (for example, the European Union–Vietnam

Free Trade Agreement, EVFTA) or are under negotiation (for example, the Regional Comprehensive Economic Partnership, RECEP). Third, the TPP has been hailed as a pioneering "21st century agreement" and with the full text being freely available, the TPP text will have an impact on future agreements to be negotiated by Vietnam and other middle-income countries.

2. See, for example, the 2016 Whitebook of the European Chamber of Commerce at http://www.eurochamvn.org/node/14697.

3. This is true especially for the TPP. Its investor–state dispute settlement mechanism allows investors to bring claims against states directly in case their rights are being violated, including by the use of performance requirements. The scope of the investment tribunal in the EVFTA, however, is limited to investment protection, most-favored-nation and national treatment with regard to the operation of investments. The WTO is limited to state–state dispute settlement.

4. The TPP does not protect any specific products based on geographic indications. The IPR chapter allows for the establishment of such a system, but at the same time specifies grounds for objecting to certain GIs (see Section E in IPR chapter, TPP text version February 2016 subject to legal review).

Bibliography

Antràs, Pol, and Robert W. Staiger. 2012. "Offshoring and the Role of Trade Agreements." *American Economic Review* 102 (7): 3140–83.

Baker, P., D. Vanzetti, and N. A. T. Huong. 2014. "Sustainable Impact Assessment EU–Vietnam FTA." MUTRAP—European Trade Policy and Investment Support Project, Hanoi.

Berger, A., D. Bruhn, A. Bender, J. Friesen, K. Kick, K. F. Kullmann, R. Roßner, and S. Weyrauch. 2016. *Deep Preferential Trade Agreements and Upgrading in Global Value Chains: The Case of Vietnam.* Bonn: German Development Institute.

Berger, A., M. Busse, P. Nunnenkamp, and M. Roy. 2013. "Do Trade and Investment Agreements Lead to More FDI? Accounting for Key Provisions Inside the Black Box." *International Economics and Economic Policy* 10 (2): 247–75.

Borensztein, E., J. De Gregorio, and J.-W. Lee. 1998. "How Does Foreign Direct Investment Affect Economic Growth?" *Journal of International Economics* 45 (1): 115–35.

Bruhn, D. 2014. "Global Value Chains and Deep Preferential Trade Agreements. Promoting Trade at the Cost of Domestic Policy Autonomy?" Discussion Paper 23/2014, German Development Institute, Bonn.

Draper, P., C. Chikura, and H. Krogman. 2016. "Can Rules of Origin in Sub-Saharan Africa be Harmonized? A Political Economy Exploration." Discussion Paper 1/2016, German Development Institute, Bonn.

De Mello, L. R. 1997. "Foreign Direct Investment in Developing Countries and Growth: A Selective Survey." *The Journal of Development Studies* 34 (1): 1–34.

Dür, A., L. Baccini, and M. Elsig. 2014. "The Design of International Trade Agreements: Introducing a New Dataset." *The Review of International Organizations* 9 (3): 353–75.

Egger, P., J. Francois, M. Manchin, and D. Nelson. 2015. "Non-Tariff Barriers, Integration, and the Transatlantic Economy." *Economic Policy* 30 (83): 541–84.

Elliot, K. A. 2016. "Rules of Origin in Textiles and Apparel, in: Assessing the Trans-Pacific Partnership, Volume 1: Market Access and Sectoral Issues." Briefing 16-1, Peterson Institute for International Economics, Washington, DC.

Horn, H., P. C. Mavroidis, and A. Sapir. 2010. "Beyond the WTO? An Anatomy of EU and US Preferential Trade Agreements." *The World Economy* 33 (11): 1565–88.

Humphrey, J., and H. Schmitz. 2002. "How Does Insertion in Global Value Chains Affect Upgrading in Industrial Clusters." *Regional Studies* 36 (9): 1017–27.

Lawrence, R. Z. 2000. *Regionalism, Multilateralism and Deeper Integration.* Washington, DC: Brookings Institution Press.

Nguyen, D. A., D. Vanzetti, R. Trewin, H. T. Dinh, H. T. Vu, and S. X. Le. 2014. *Assessing the Impacts of the Regional Comprehensive Economic Partnership on Vietnam's Economy.* Hanoi: MUTRAP—European Trade Policy and Investment Support Project.

Noguera, G. 2012. "Trade Costs and Gravity for Gross and Value Added Trade." Job Market Paper, Columbia University, New York.

Orefice, G., and N. Rocha. 2013. "Deep Integration and Production Networks: An Empirical Analysis." *The World Economy* 37 (1): 106–36.

Petry, P., M. Plummer, and F. Zhai. 2012. "The Trans-Pacific Partnership and Asia-Pacific Integration: A Quantitative Assessment." *Policy Analyses in International Economics 98*, Peterson Institute for International Economics, Washington, DC.

PIIE (Peterson Institute for International Economics). 2016. *Assessing the Trans-Pacific Partnership. Volume 1: Market Access and Sectoral Issues.* Washington, DC.

Sandler, T., and P. A. Rosenberg. 2015. *EU and Vietnam Reach Agreement in Principle on FTA.* Sandler, Travis, and Rosenberg Trade Report. http://www.strtrade.com/news -publications-EU-Vietnam-FTA-082115.html.

Thanh, Vo Tri, Anh Duong Nguyen, Thu Hang Dinh, and Binh Minh Tran. 2015. "Impact of Current and Proposed FTAs and BITs on Vietnam's Long Term Development Goals: A Case Study of Food Processing and Electronics Manufacturing Sectors." Action Aid Vietnam and Central Institute of Economic Management, Hanoi.

Vietnam Government Portal. 2016. "Vietnam Strategy on Exports and Imports 2011– 2020." http://www.gov.vn/portal/page/portal/English/strategies/strategiesdetails?cate goryId=30&articleId=10051303.

World Bank. 2016. *Global Economic Prospects. Spillover amid Weak Growth.* Washington, DC: World Bank.

WTO (World Trade Organization). 2011. *World Trade Report 2011: The WTO and Preferential Trade Agreements: From Co-existence to Coherence.* Geneva: WTO.

PART 2

In-Depth Studies of GVC-Intensive Sectors

CHAPTER 7

Vietnam's Textile and Apparel Industry and Trade Networks

Stacey Frederick

Key Takeaways

Vietnam's textile and apparel industry is one of the most important economic sectors in the country. Given the immediate opportunities presented by trade preferences, it makes economic sense to prioritize product and process optimization as a first step before proceeding to functional upgrades. In doing so, Vietnam's advantages in low labor costs, access to backward linkages, and preferential trade agreements (for some) should be leveraged to maximize gains. Simultaneously, workforce gaps in sourcing, technology, design and fashion, management, and textile skills, and the focus on relatively simple, low-value products, should be reduced.[1]

Challenges Confronted

Vietnam has two primary challenges. First, the country depends on imported textiles for apparel exports, and to comply with trade agreements, textiles must be produced within the country.[2] All indicators suggest that backward linkages are expanding rapidly, but the country will need to be sure that textile investments align with the needs of the nation's export-oriented apparel industry.

Second, to remain competitive in the long term, Vietnam will need to move beyond advantages based on manufacturing and selling goods at lowest cost. This shift will require the country to develop a knowledge-intensive workforce and a greater number of export-oriented, domestically owned firms.

Solutions Proposed

With these challenges, Vietnam has two potential paths for upward growth in the textile and apparel value chain. Although it can pursue both simultaneously, the policies and skillsets needed to achieve these two paths are quite different.

The first path focuses on expanding exports, particularly in volume, basic goods (such as knit shirts, trousers, sweatshirts). A subcomponent of this strategy includes expanding domestic backward linkages into textiles. Vietnam's industry currently is aligned with this path and the Trans-Pacific Partnership (TPP) and other trade agreements are driving developments in this area.

The second path is toward functional upgrading into service industries associated with apparel, including sourcing, supply chain management, design, product development, marketing, and branding (that is, functional upgrading).

Three interrelated solutions are proposed and should be pursued in a coordinated manner.

- Vietnam should leverage its trade agreements to incentivize investment in the textile industry. Vietnam has, or is in the process of, establishing unique connections with major import markets—Japan, the United States, and the EU. There is significant opportunity for foreign and domestic investment, aimed at meeting rule-of-origin requirements for key inputs (yarn, fabric, and finishing).
- The country should secure its position in the global textile and apparel sector by participating in high value-added segments of the industry. To this end, it will need to upgrade workforce and educational needs, particularly related to functional upgrading. Vietnam will also need to invest in educational programs that train future industry workers to adapt to global sectoral trends.
- Domestic firms should be promoted with greater autonomy and provided with resources on how the global industry operates. The majority of domestic firms are affiliated with Vinatex, either through partial equity ties or through similar business models. This affiliation (in such volume) tends to restrict innovative perspectives, which when released may help expand the industry. There is also room to develop domestic brands for export, thus diversifying end markets.

Lessons to Be Learned

Vietnam's apparel sector has undergone restructuring and upgrading of its production processes, capabilities, and backward linkages. The main advantages of Vietnam's apparel sector are low labor costs, access to backward linkages, market preferences, and product mix. Key challenges are workforce gaps with regard to sourcing, technological, design/fashion, management and textile skills, and over-concentration on simple, low-value products (Frederick 2016; Frederick and Staritz 2012).

The textile and apparel industry will continue to grow without direct intervention, particularly in the short term. The main challenge will come in the mid to long term in terms of developing sustainable advantages in higher-value activities that are driven not only by trade preferences. The public sector can play a stronger role by incentivizing independent domestic firm growth, and providing resources to domestic firms to understand how GVCs work so as to increase global (not just domestic) participation. To facilitate these efforts, educational programs should seek to develop workforce skills in design, global business, management, branding, and innovation.

Common Lessons Potentially Applicable to Other Countries

First, Vietnam's export-oriented apparel industry is centralized in its sources of foreign direct investment (FDI): Hong Kong SAR, China; the Republic of Korea; and Taiwan, China. FDI represents at least 50 percent of exports and appears to account for the majority of synthetic exports. The challenge here is that these foreign-owned multinational corporations (MNCs) typically operate in closed networks where they import raw materials from global supply networks, and coordinate sales and communicate with buyers (higher value-added activities) from their headquarters located outside Vietnam. Branch plants of MNCs offer benefits for increasing employment and exports with relatively limited ease, but they provide limited spillovers to the domestic economy in the form of knowledge or development of backward linkages. There is limited room for functional upgrading at branch plants as these higher-value functions remain at these headquarters. On the other hand, FDI plays an important role in entering GVCs because it provides market access to global buyers that can be difficult to ascertain, especially given the trend toward supplier consolidation. The challenge is in finding a balance in which the host economy does not become dependent on FDI, but is able to use the resources provided from it to eventually transition to a situation in which domestic firms have more control over higher-value activities (Kumar, Frederick, and Robertson 2016).

Second, textile production and apparel assembly have different requirements. Textile production is capital and energy intensive while apparel assembly is labor intensive. Textile production requires more workers that have knowledge of how to operate and repair machinery, perform finishing operations, and conduct quality assurance tests. There also are many types of textile inputs (for example, yarn types can be 100 percent cotton, man-made fiber, or various blends, which are produced on different types of machines). When setting up new textile facilities in a country, the types of textile facilities should complement the needs of the final products being produced.

Third, production complexity is fairly low for apparel, particularly in Vietnam. This means that the knowledge, capabilities, and technology required to produce apparel are simple (as well as industry-specific) and easy to learn compared with the requirements for other industries. While this is favorable for leveraging Vietnam's abundant low-cost labor force and provides vital opportunities to gain formal employment experience, particularly for women, it provides limited skills for chain upgrading (that is, the ability to take skills acquired in one industry and apply them to another).

Current Conditions and Challenges

In the Short Term, Weak Backward Linkages to Textiles

This is the primary challenge. Vietnam's textile production and the finishing function (for fashion garments) have not kept pace with the growth in apparel assembly. The development of a textile industry for exported apparel has been limited thus far for several reasons. First, the requirements to establish a textile industry are quite different than apparel (see previous section). Second, Vietnam is geographically close to key textile-producing countries, such as China, the largest global fabric supplier, with low barriers to importing textiles, and the import of inputs has not added much to lead times or product costs. Further, global brands provide apparel manufacturers with a list of specific fabric and yarn suppliers they can source from, and existing domestic textile manufacturers either do not have these relationships or do not produce products of export quality.

Vietnam has the chance to increase apparel exports in the short term in response to trade agreements if it develops strong textile production capabilities that meet quantity, quality, product type, and GVC linkage requirements needed.

Quantity

Data on the exact share of domestic versus imported textiles vary, but all indicate room for Vietnam to expand production. Quantity-wise, estimates suggest that less than half of what is needed for the export-oriented apparel industry is available. Further supporting this argument, Vietnam's share of domestic value-added content in gross exports in 2011 was among the lowest of major apparel-exporting countries. Vietnam is ahead of Cambodia, but behind other leading Asian exporters including China, India, Indonesia, Thailand, and Turkey.[3] Vietnam was the third-largest fabric importer in 2012, accounting for 6 percent of world imports (UNSD 2014). Textile machinery is another indicator of capacity, and in 2012, Vietnam had less than 2 percent of global installed capacity in weaving and spinning equipment. Knitted equipment capacity is higher, but this is primarily composed of semi-automatic, hand-knitting machines (Anson and Brocklehurst 2013a, 2013b).

Current capacity by stage in the textile supply chain is, in brief:

- *Fabric:* Existing production is primarily for domestic use with limited availability of export-quality fabrics.
- *Processing (dyeing and finishing; yarn, fabric, and apparel):* This is the most limited segment of the chain in Vietnam.
- *Cotton yarn:* Mills exist, but they primarily engage in exports. Chinese mills have set up in Vietnam to circumvent high domestic cotton tariffs.
- *Synthetic fiber and yarn:* With the new Petrochemical/Textile Fiber JSC facility (table 7.1) operating at full scale as of April 2014, there is adequate production capacity for the foreseeable future in synthetic yarn. Fabric and processing mills will be needed to convert the production of both cotton and synthetic yarn.
- *Cotton:* This is not a strategic area for Vietnam. China is the largest producer globally of cotton, so Vietnam already is geographically close to a major supply base. Further, trade agreements do not require raw materials to be produced in a constituent country to receive tariff preferences, but this is changing given the new trade agreements that will require textiles to be produced in Vietnam (or another country signing the agreement) to receive preferential tariffs.

Table 7.1 Textile Firms in Vietnam

Name	Ownership	Segments	Number of employees
Hoa Tho Corporation JSC	Domestic: Vinatex	Yarn, apparel	6,000
Phong Phu JSC	Domestic: Vinatex	Vertically-integrated, cotton	>4,000
Thanh Cong Textile-Garment Investment JSC	JV: non-Vinatex	Vertically-integrated	4,300
Nam Dinh Textile & Garment JSC	Domestic: Vinatex	Yarn, fabric (woven), dye	4,100
Tainan	Foreign: Taiwan, China	Yarn	3,400
Hue Textile Garment JSC	Domestic: Vinatex	Yarn, fabric (woven)	2,800
Texhong Textile Group	Foreign: Hong Kong SAR, China	Yarn, fabric	2,700
Hanoi Textile & Garment Co. JSC	Domestic: Vinatex	Yarn, fabric (woven, knit), dye	2,100
Dong Xuan Knitting Co. Ltd	Domestic: Vinatex	Fabric (woven)	2,000
Shenzhou International Group	Foreign: China	Fabric	–
Hualon/Recron/Reliance	Foreign: Malaysia/India	Fabric (synthetic)	–
Viet Thang Textile JSC	Domestic: Vinatex	Yarn, fabric (woven)	1,300
Bitexco Nam Long JSC	Domestic	Yarn	1,200
Dong Quang Knitwears Co., Ltd.	Domestic	Yarn	1,000
Ha Nam Textile Co.	Domestic	Yarn	1,000
Son Nam Textile and Garment JSC	Domestic	Yarn	1,000
Corporation 28 Co., Ltd.	Domestic	Yarn, fabric (woven)	800
Hanoi 19th May Textile Co.	Domestic	Yarn	700
Phu Bai Spinning JSC	Domestic: Vinatex	Yarn (cotton, polyester)	700
ChoongNam Vietnam Textile Co., Ltd.	Foreign: Korea, Rep.	Yarn (cotton; blends)	600
Dong Nam Textile JSC	Domestic	Yarn	600
Vinh Phu Textile JSC	Domestic	Yarn	600
Tra Ly Spinning JSC	Domestic: Vinatex	Yarn	500
Thien Nam JSC	Domestic: Vinatex	Yarn	300
Century Synthetic Fiber Corporation	Domestic	Yarn (polyester)	300
Petrochemical/Textile Fiber JSC (PVTEX)	Domestic: PetroVietnam	Fiber/yarn (polyester)	1,000
Formosa	Foreign: Taiwan, China	Fiber (polyester)	–
Hyosung	Foreign: Korea, Rep.	Fiber (spandex, export-oriented)	–

Source: Van Tot (2014), VITAS (2012), and company websites.

Quality, Product Type, and GVC Linkages

The larger issue for textile production is to produce the right mix of products in adequate quality and to target firms that have global supply relationships with key apparel exporters. As Vietnam prepares for these new trade agreements, it must remain cognizant of how buyers and MNCs interact in the GVC. For example, apparel buyers nominate textile suppliers, and apparel manufacturers are required to source from these firms. Buyers do this in order to maintain quality across products sourced in different countries and to assist with negotiations on purchases. Similar to apparel, there are MNCs in textiles that buyers have long-standing relationships with. It may therefore be difficult for domestic textile firms to enter these value chains without at least having a joint-venture relationship with an established, nominated textile firm. At present, the majority of textile companies are domestic (table 7.1).

A Domestic Rather Than Regional or Global Focus among Domestic Firms with Restricted Autonomy

Domestic firms are focused on vertically integrating within Vietnam and selling to the local market rather than understanding how the GVC works and identifying ways to become more engaged internationally. Domestic brands make up around 40 percent of formal apparel retail in Vietnam and have been around since at least the 1990s (Vietnamese Stakeholders 2015), but firms have little interest in exporting their brands or developing sales outlets in other countries. This inward perspective checks the potential for growth.

The domestic export-oriented firms that do exist are partly owned by Vinatex, a former SOE that is now partly owned by the government. Vinatex has about 120 companies which it either owns entirely or is a joint owner. Few new private, domestic firms have emerged since 2005 (though some new factories have been built), limiting attitudes that drive new upgrading strategies.

On functional upgrading, workforce gaps exist in:

- *Apparel:* Primarily soft skills (how to do business with global buyers), critical thinking, marketing (social and media), and technology (automated equipment, computer-aided design). Workers have had little interaction with global buyers. As such, apparel skill gaps are largely due to weak exposure and few education programs in these areas.
- *Textiles:* Mainly in chemistry-related areas (dyeing, finishing, synthetic production, and processing).
- *Educators:* Will be needed to develop a workforce with these skills in the above areas.

Vietnam should take advantage of the opportunities offered by trade agreements, but it must ensure that it does not lock itself into MNC-dominated export-oriented apparel assembly. The advantages afforded by trade preferences erode over time, as seen, and more sustainable development needs to be targeted in tandem. Expanding and increasing the capabilities of domestic firms for the export and domestic markets will be critical for long-term growth.

Concrete Actions

Expansion of textile capabilities should be pursued via targeted foreign investment or joint ventures with domestic firms, rather than focusing solely on domestic firms (Kumar, Frederick, and Robertson 2016). But before that, market analysis needs to look beyond aggregate statistics on consumption and production and also identify who current and potential buyers are and will be (buyers nominate suppliers, so the presence of domestic capabilities does not mean they will be used).

To secure its position and deepen integration with the global textile and apparel sector, Vietnam should aim to develop the capabilities to participate in higher value-added segments of the industry. This would involve tackling the workforce and education needs for functional upgrading.

The highest value-added segments of the apparel industry are based on knowledge-intensive human capital and require a labor pool with creative and critical thinking skills. Designers, along with industrial, chemical, and mechanical engineers and management and marketing positions, usually are workers with (industry-neutral) university degrees or shorter-term (less than two years) apparel-specific community college or vocational training degrees or certificates. Upward mobility related to skills acquired on the job is primarily limited to supervisor, line manager, and human resource positions. Vietnam lacks a supply base in these areas for two main reasons.[4] First, foreign firms perform these activities in their home countries and therefore have not generated an initial labor pool. Second, domestic firms have historically sold apparel indirectly to global brands by buying houses and agents, providing workers with limited exposure to the demands of global buyers and thus limited sales and marketing experience. Thus there is a lack of workers with skills in sourcing, supply chain coordination, and customer relationship management.

Vietnam will need to invest in educational programs to train future workers in these areas. For industry-specific skills, programs and research centers should be developed in conjunction with buyers and foreign apparel manufacturers (for example, ask MNCs or buyers to be advisors for university and vocational education curriculum development). For the existing workforce, attending classes at night to get associate degrees or international online classes could be pursued. Students can attend foreign universities or conduct internships with leading MNCs facilities abroad. In all cases, government or industry-sponsored funding schemes should be developed to help offset costs to workers and students (or at least top performers as an incentive scheme).

More widely in promoting domestic firm development, Vietnam can pursue several strategies. First, it should target new end markets and revitalize its branding efforts. The largest and the fastest-growing consumer market for apparel is in Asian countries, including Australia, China, Japan, Korea, and the Russian Federation. The retail sector in Asia presents more opportunities for growth in the higher value-added forward linkages because these markets do not have a long-standing domestic brand following and global brands have yet to fully tap these markets.

Global brands see the opportunities emerging in Asia, but also realize that the retail sector in these countries is quite different from that of their home countries, from store formats to sizing. Buyers will be more willing to form programs in which both parties have the potential to gain: buyers can tap the knowledge of locals in the domestic economy, while Vietnam builds a knowledge-driven workforce. Collaborative efforts could begin by establishing a multistakeholder design, production, and R&D center near an existing industrial park or cluster of textile and apparel activity. Such a center would be equipped with technology, equipment, and software used by leading MNCs in the apparel industry and would be a way to teach workforce skills.

Vietnam has a number of domestic dual-market firms, which have a comparatively long history in design and branding for the domestic market. These brands and skills can be used as a foundation to expand domestic brands and export these brands to nearby countries (often referred to as end-market diversification).[5]

Key Outcomes

In the short term, compliance with rules of origin will lead to increased exports, higher domestic value added, and greater manufacturing-related employment.

Longer term, pursuing export-oriented functional upgrading will lead to higher-paying, more skill-intensive jobs. Developing a more knowledge-intensive workforce for textiles and apparel with product development, design, and marketing skills will benefit not only the apparel industry, but also other industries due to the transferable nature of these skills.

Drivers and Enablers

The future of the Vietnamese textile and apparel industry will be supported by:

- Cost competitiveness (labor, electricity rates) and productivity.
- A supportive industrial environment. Vietnam's investment incentives and tariffs are competitive with other apparel producing countries.
- Trade preferences.
- Access to foreign markets (via MNCs).
- Connection (through trade and investment) and proximity to China.
- Product diversity and footprint in man-made fiber (synthetic) apparel.

Barriers, Threats, and Challenges

- Maintaining social and environmental compliance amid fast growth.
- A lack of skilled workers with experience in technology, marketing, and design, as well as middle managers for functional upgrading.
- Transitioning and finding a constructive balance between foreign and domestic, private ownership.

Notes

1. This analysis is based on a combination of secondary analysis and interviews with Vietnamese Stakeholders (2015). For a more detailed analysis of the industry in Vietnam, see also Frederick (2016) and the chapter on Vietnam in Frederick and Staritz (2012).

2. Or sourced from another constituent country of the trade agreement, but Vietnam's primary textile suppliers are not members (Hong Kong SAR, China, and the Republic of Korea).

3. This is based on OECD-WTO (2015) and includes textiles, textile products, leather, and footwear (ISIC 17, 18, and 19).

4. A third factor is that this situation is not unique to apparel, and there is not an ample supply base from other industries to draw on.

5. Skills exist in apparel design, but retail and apparel marketing, branding, and consumer market research are weaknesses.

Bibliography

Anson, R., and G. Brocklehurst. 2013a. "World Markets for Textile Machinery Part 1: Yarn Manufacture." *Textile Outlook International* 164: 118–56.

———. 2013b. "World Markets for Textile Machinery Part 2: Fabric Manufacture." *Textile Outlook International* 165: 96–145.

Frederick, S. 2016. "Benchmarking South Asia in the Global Apparel Industry." In *Stitches to Riches? Apparel Employment, Trade, and Economic Development in South Asia*, edited by G. Lopez-Acevedo and R. Robertson. Washington, DC: World Bank.

Frederick, S., and C. Staritz. 2012. "Developments in the Global Apparel Industry after the MFA Phaseout." In *Sewing Success? Employment, Wages and Poverty following the End of the Multi-Fibre Arrangment*, edited by G. Lopez-Acevedo and R. Robertson. Washington, DC: World Bank.

Kumar, A., S. Frederick, and R. Robertson. 2016. "Policies to Foster Apparel Exports and Jobs." In *Stitches to Riches? Apparel Employment, Trade, and Economic Development in South Asia*, edited by G. Lopez-Acevedo and R. Robertson. Washington, DC: World Bank.

OECD-WTO. 2015. Trade in Value-Added (TiVA). ttps://stats.oecd.org/index.aspx?queryid=66237.

UNSD (United Nations Statistics Division). 2014. "World Fabric and Yarn/Thread Exports (1990–2012) by Product Categories" (accessed April 1), from UNSD.

Van Tot, B. 2014. *Textile and Apparel Industry Report*. Hanoi:FPT Securities.

Vietnamese Stakeholders. 2015. *Interviews with Firms and National Stakeholders in Vietnam*. Interviewer: S. Frederick.

VITAS (Vietnam Textile and Apparel Association). 2012. *Vietnam's Textile and Apparel Directory 2012*. Hanoi: VITAS.

CHAPTER 8

Agribusiness in 2035
A Global Value Chains Perspective

Miles McKenna

Key Takeaways

Vietnam's agriculture sector has done an impressive job of entering and then strengthening its participation in global value chains (GVCs) over the last few decades. However, if the sector is to realize its full development potential by 2035, critical challenges must be overcome. A more competitive, more productive sector could help provide greater opportunities to the poorest segments of the population.

Arguably, the most important challenge for agribusinesses will be to improve the quality—and disprove the reputation for low quality—of Vietnam's agricultural products, both in domestic and international markets. Due in part to a failure to improve quality, productivity and sales are plateauing in key subsectors. So, unable to produce higher value-added, higher quality goods, many farmers, intermediaries, and national processors see unstable profits. Poor or often ill-advised agronomic practices have led to high rates of physical product loss and natural resource degradation. These problems are exacerbated by a lack of infrastructure and access to logistics services, inhibiting local and regional connectivity and overall competitiveness. Recent reports of human rights abuses of laborers in certain subsectors are also a serious concern and illustrate the immediate need for effective interventions in agri-GVCs.

A vision for Vietnamese agribusiness in 2035 should focus on upgrading at all levels—product, process, functional, and even intersectoral. Achieving this will require investment in necessary skills and capital to help agribusinesses overcome constraints in the domestic market and allow for increases in productivity and value-added growth. Success will drive structural transformation in the economy as farmers and agribusinesses become more efficient, productive, and profitable, while allowing the country to remain cost competitive as wages and living standards continue to rise.

Challenges Confronted

Vietnam's agriculture sector faces serious challenges to realizing its full development potential by 2035. These include improving agronomic practices through
climate-smart approaches to decrease high rates of physical product loss and
stop natural resource degradation, addressing land rights and reforms, building
infrastructure to improve connectivity, developing world-class logistics service
providers, increasing domestic value added, and preparing to compete in more
open global trade regimes.

A more productive, resilient, and connected sector would provide greater
opportunities for economic growth and social upgrading to the poorest segments
of the Vietnamese population.

Solutions Proposed

The government of Vietnam is already actively designing and implementing
targeted reforms to remove constraints on agricultural production. To increase
opportunities for and strengthen participation in GVCs, it will need to continue
to foster the absorptive capacity of farmers, agri-processors, and key services
providers in order to help each benefit from the tacit knowledge flows and technology spillovers inherent in GVC relationships. It should continue to pursue
two parallel tracks:

- *Pursuing traditional approaches to fostering GVC participation at the buyer/
  supplier level:* This would entail an initial focus on product and process
  upgrading (quality), in tandem with attracting strategic sector investment to
  facilitate functional upgrading. Vietnamese producers must also prepare for
  increased competition as the government proceeds with the reduction and
  eventual elimination of higher agricultural tariffs under current and potential
  trade agreements.
- *Improving logistics performance to facilitate stronger participation in agri-GVCs:* This
  would entail focusing on further developing necessary infrastructure, improving
  connectivity, and streamlining export procedures. By improving performance
  along its domestic supply chain, Vietnamese traders will be better able to meet
  the predictability, reliability, and time sensitivity demanded by global buyers.

Critically, with consolidation expected to be a primary feature of agricultural
development over the next 20 years, the government will also need to prepare
for the transition of low-skilled rural citizens out of agriculture while providing
the incentives and mechanisms to boost the efficiency of those who remain.
Policies targeting the following are recommended:

- *Education:* Further develop the knowledge and skills that will facilitate product
  and process upgrading for those who enter or choose to remain in the sector,
  envisioning the "future farmer."
- *Innovation via information and communication technology (ICT):* Better facilitate market information and improve productivity and efficiency through the

development or adoption of technological advances in agronomy and capabilities, especially in the more profitable and globally integrated subsectors.

- *Improved connectivity*: Create stronger buyer–supplier linkages domestically and globally through appropriate logistics and infrastructure.
- *Attracting strategic foreign investment:* Support the implementation and further development of policies that enable domestic suppliers to leverage knowledge and technology spillovers through foreign direct investment (FDI) and deeper integration and interaction with regional and global lead firms.
- *Standards:* Phase in stronger standards that address labor, quality, and sustainability issues, gradually improving natural resource management and sustainable farming techniques based on global good practice to allow Vietnam to boost its long-term competitiveness and to meet the future challenges of a changing climate.

Lessons to Be Learned

A strategic approach to upgrading in Vietnamese agriculture is warranted against a backdrop of GVCs. Targeting product and process upgrading in agri-GVCs will require supporting reforms and investment in connectivity, logistics, skills, quality infrastructure, and governance. What is good or necessary for agribusiness will likely be good for growth in other economic sectors.

Producers should concentrate on maximizing product quality while improving process efficiencies. Despite weak domestic price signaling, they should collaborate in learning about and exercising value-added techniques. This also involves reducing value-diminishing practices (such as over-fertilizing). Further, stronger public–private dialogue will provide the government with better information on what support is required for the industry as a whole to improve the reliability and value of goods produced.

The government should embrace value chain analysis when considering agriculture sector development, focusing on facilitating through regulation and incentivizing stronger buyer–supplier relationships. A good first step would be a comprehensive strategic segmentation analysis of a set of specific products or subsectors, identifying backward and forward linkages, critical tasks and capabilities, key success factors, and value-adding opportunities (and barriers). Vietnam's participation and position in regional and GVCs is likely to be fundamentally different by 2035, as the country embraces opportunities and confronts challenges of newly-signed and potential future trade agreements. Value chain analysis would help identify segments where appropriate regulatory reform and incentive systems should be built (or bolstered) and matched with appropriate compliance and enforcement capabilities to best position Vietnamese agricultural producers in an increasingly competitive global market.

The public sector also should focus on creating an enabling business environment for agribusiness. Beyond the hard infrastructure requirements for improving connectivity and market access, the government should identify and address key constraints to soft infrastructure, that is, the human capacity and institutions that deliver key services. This approach includes looking at processes specific to agribusiness, including seed registration, development and certification; quality infrastructure, including laboratories and skilled technicians; standards certification and accreditation; fertilizer and pesticide quality control and import permitting; access to finance; trader and transportation licensing; and contract enforcement and investment dispute mechanisms.

Common Lessons and Potential for Replication in Other Countries

Some of these lessons are:

- Strengthening participation and upgrading in GVCs requires national quality infrastructure and institutions in place to support the sector. The right balance of gradually introducing, incentivizing, and enforcing regulations is critical, but reforms will only be as effective as the government's capacity to implement and regulate them. A good framework is in place for technical regulations and voluntary standards, but enforcement is ad hoc at best and supplier buy-in and buyer confidence are low, and as a result noncompliant suppliers and low-quality products exacerbate vulnerabilities in markets.

- Making the most of comparative advantage in commodity markets requires developing a strong product and service reputation, and the ability to innovate. Where a commodity good is prone to global price fluctuations, and where many developing nations compete along the GVC, comparative advantage can be fleeting. It is essential to put in place the mechanisms and incentives to establish and continue to drive a reputation for quality, timeliness, and reliability.

- Enhancing the absorptive capacity and skills of producers is essential to support sustainable agriculture alongside appropriate government policies. Climate-smart agronomic practices are central to long-term sustainability. Without adequate producer education, extension services (whether private or public), and accessible high-quality inputs, the sustainability of the market and the sector's ability to adapt to climate change are questionable.

Current Conditions and Challenges

Volatile Global Commodity Prices

After nearly two decades of impressive GDP gains in Vietnam's agriculture sector, the effects of falling global commodity prices and the weak purchasing power of domestic consumers have raised concerns. Fishery and forestry products have continued to increase in value terms over the last decade, while other agricultural subsectors have stagnated. Many agricultural products are exported as commodities in raw, unprocessed form with minimal value added, such as bulk rice, coffee, tea, and rubber. These products are then processed and sold by downstream firms as packaged and branded goods in international markets for much higher prices. Vietnam has very few global brands, and downstream marketing and distribution are weak. These issues are not inherently negative, as many advanced economies also export agricultural commodities in primary form, but they merit serious attention given the volatility of commodity prices and their importance to the Vietnamese economy.

Concentration of Destinations for Major Agricultural Products

Vietnamese exports of major agricultural products tend to be concentrated in a few major destinations, illustrating both the power of large retail markets and the potential for Vietnamese agribusinesses to expand into emerging markets. The United States, China, the European Union, Japan, and the Republic of Korea are key destination markets for Vietnamese exports (table 8.1). Yet, with further integration of the Association of Southeast Asian Nations (ASEAN) Economic Community—and other potential regional free trade agreements (FTAs)—Vietnam is well positioned to play a larger role in regional and GVCs. As fast-growing economies in East and Southeast Asia continue expanding, it is likely that demand for higher-value products like coffee, shrimp, fresh fish, and other fresh produce will continue rising.

Underuse of Improved Seeds

Farmers' limited access to improved seeds and seedlings is a primary factor in the low quality of produce. Depending on soil and climate conditions, certain seeds and seedlings are more likely to produce higher yields, better varieties, and improve processing efficiency. However, a lack of supply and demand continues

Table 8.1 Geographic Dispersion of Major Vietnamese Agricultural Products, 2012

Product	Export value, 2012 US$	Global rank	Major destinations, 2012 (%)
Coffee	3.49 bn	2	Germany (16.8), United States (17.1), Spain (7.5), Italy (7.5), Japan (4.8)
Rice	3.25 bn	3	China (23.3), Indonesia (15.7), Malaysia (12), Philippines (11.2), Côte d'Ivoire (6.3)
Fish fillets	2.32 bn	3	United States (22.5), Korea, Rep. (5.8), Mexico (5.1), Spain (4.9), Japan (4.3)
Rubber	2.14 bn	5	China (35.3), Malaysia (21.8), India (8.7), Germany (4.7), Korea, Rep. (4.7)
Crustaceans	1.43 bn	4	Japan (28.4), United States (24.3), Korea, Rep. (8), China (5.4), Germany (4.5)
Coconut, Brazil nuts, and cashews	1.3 bn	1	United States (29.7), China (12.3), Netherlands (11.4), Australia (7.6), United Kingdom (3.7)
Pepper	734 mn	1	United States (17.1), Germany (16.8), Spain (7.5), Italy (7.5), Japan (4.8)
Cassava	585 mn	2	China (89.4), Korea, Rep. (7.6), Japan (1.1), Singapore and Malaysia <1 each
Molluscs	481 mn	6	Korea, Rep. (30.4), Japan (22.4), Italy (13.6), Thailand (7.6), Portugal (3.7)
Tea	200 mn	5	Taiwan, China (16.8), Other Asia (14.8), the Russian Federation (11), Pakistan (10.9), Indonesia (7.4)

Source: MIT Observatory of Economic Complexity 2012.
Note: Fish fillets includes non-fillet frozen fish, non-fillet fresh fish, and processed fish. Major export destinations based on fish fillets.

to keep their use in check. In rice, for example, nearly 70 percent of farmers use noncertified seeds, generally a mix of varieties saved from previous harvests. Registering new seeds is a lengthy and costly process.[1] Current regulatory requirements, such as pre-release testing before seed production can be scaled up for public distribution, should be reassessed based on global good practice.

Excessive Fertilizer Use

Excessive use of fertilizer is a major concern for the quality of agricultural products and long-term sustainability. Yields are not generally reduced if excess fertilizer is used and so many farmers overuse it as a precaution, leading to soil depletion and water contamination from nitrates and phosphates. Many farmers are not following good agricultural practice (GAP) to use the right types of fertilizer. In 2010, Vietnam's Ministry of Agriculture and Rural Development (MARD) issued Circular No. 36/2010/TT-BNNPTNT, which set strict rules for its production and use. It covered technical regulations and disclosures required for national certification, as well as regulations on fertilizer production, processing, importing, and trading. Yet inspections and enforcement are lax, in part due to a lack of coordination between government authorities.

Improper Use of Crop Protection Products

Inappropriate use of crop protection products, such as pesticides and herbicides, is harming the quality of agricultural products. A huge amount of unapproved, low-quality, spurious, and occasionally illegal products are sold to farmers, who rarely know how to use them properly. Pesticides are used in such abundance that they exceed the maximum residue levels allowed by some importing markets. Buyer rejections damage the reputation of individual suppliers and Vietnamese products as a whole. Although the government has laws in place,[2] again, the problem is enforcement.

Overuse of Water

Excessive and unregulated water use threatens the sustainability of some of Vietnam's most lucrative export crops. Inefficient irrigation systems, wasteful field application, and the cultivation of crops in unsuitable areas are all long-term concerns that require strict monitoring. Not only does excessive or irresponsible use lower the water table, it also acts to wash fertilizer, pesticide, and other pollutants, as well as loose sediment, into waterways, damaging freshwater ecosystems and creating problems downstream. For coffee and tea production in the Central Highlands in particular, falling water tables present a major problem. Farmers drill wells and are allowed to draw water from the local water table without any regulation and at no cost. Lead firms in the industry, like Nestlé, are working with farmers to try to improve practices.[3]

Farmer Groups and Cooperatives

Contractual, shareholder, and other cooperative models could help to replace the current and often inefficient smallholder production model, but attempts at these arrangements have thus far failed to provide large sector-wide gains. According to a recent World Bank Group study, most farmer groups in Vietnam are informal.[4] Cooperation, both within these groups and between these groups and government officials, is variable and only loosely involved in operations. Less than 3 percent of farmer groups identified in the study displayed any form of collaborative business linkages. Of those that did, collaboration consisted of jointly purchasing inputs, exchanging techniques and experiences, and sharing rented farm machinery. Almost none of the groups jointly sold products to inter-mediates or larger buyers. Other impediments in farmer groups included limited capacity of group leaders, lack of cooperation among group members, and little access to facilities and capital.

The government has encouraged a large field model in some decisions, including No. 62/2013-QD-TTg, which aims to deepen cooperation and create stronger linkages among farmers and facilitate centralized commodity production. Incentives in place for groups under this model include subsidized pesticide, labor, and machine rental; priority export contracts; temporary storage programs; training and technical guidance; and support for seedling costs. It seems, however, that farmers are reluctant to take advantage of these incentives.

The government also issued Decree No. 193/ND-CP to strengthen implemen-tation of the 2012 Law on Cooperatives. Elements include support for developing cooperatives, technical assistance, technology transfer, market development, trade promotion, and development projects in rural areas. Yet such support has not led to increases in the formation of cooperatives or to any great uptake by existing, weaker cooperatives.

Restrictions in Agricultural Associations

Agricultural associations are proponents of reform, and their role in facilitating it likely will grow stronger in the near future. Decrees No. 45/2010/ND-CP and No. 33/2012/ ND-CP provide a legal basis for organizing and running them. From a GVC perspective, many issues remain unresolved when it comes to asso-ciations deemed to have economic interests, those that seek to attract FDI, and those with foreign-invested firms as members. These foreign firms must fulfill all association obligations but are not allowed to vote or assume leadership positions within an association.

Weak Contract Enforcement

Weak execution and enforcement of contracts creates uncertainty for farmers and intermediaries. Contract farming arrangements in many subsectors, especially those between domestic small and medium enterprises and farmers, are not well developed. In addition, due to the large number of smallholder farms and the large number of intermediaries, both parties are left with many options when buying and selling in the market. Fluctuating commodity prices have led to numerous cases where parties that have signed production–purchase contracts have violated their agreements. Legal redress and mechanisms for dispute resolution are patchy, as local authorities do not prioritize contract enforcement. But with private investment and the leasing of agricultural land in developing countries rising since the food crisis of 2008, ensuring a strong domestic legal basis for contracts and their enforcement has become increasingly important for attracting FDI.

Continued Dominance of State-Owned Enterprises in Some Subsectors

Firms with majority or minority government ownership still play a major role in some agribusiness value chains. While that of state-owned enterprises (SOEs) has been drastically cut over the last decade, these firms are still major players, especially in input production. Wholly or partially owned SOEs dominate almost all fertilizer and seedling production, and are prominent as exporters of rice, coffee, and cashews. Rubber and wood products are also manufactured primarily by full or partial SOEs. A desire to maintain control and influence over strategic enterprises in key sectors (especially those related to food security) is not unique to Vietnam, but its implications should be carefully considered.

Vietnamese SOEs have the potential to emerge as lead firms in regional and GVCs, but they dissuade foreign firms from investing and operating in the country. Most foreign companies believe that the playing field will be skewed to these firms, with a comparative advantage through preferential access to finance, land, export licenses, and so on. Historically, SOEs have tended to be less effective in innovation and marketing, relying on large government-to-government commodity contracts. Such practices have weakened the country's reputation for quality and thwarted price-realization of exports.

Importance of Governance and Lead Firms

The government approved a comprehensive Agricultural Restructuring Plan (ARP) in 2013, shifting its priorities away from central planning and towards market-driven solutions for sustainable growth. The implementation of the ARP and other legislative efforts has been hindered by insufficient communication of policy, coordination of authorities, and enforcement of regulations. It is unclear, at the time of this report, whether MARD has developed a systematic approach to collaborate with other national and provincial authorities to improve how these policies are implemented and to achieve the goals of the ARP. Stronger laws (for example, banning small-scale slaughterhouses in residential areas) and stronger enforcement of standards are planned in the near term but will require careful consideration of the effects of such enforcement on very low income groups.

From a lead firm's perspective, tax incentives and subsidies are rarely enough without consistent, standardized regulations and effective enforcement. Two new laws, Decision No. 62/2013-QD-TTg and Decree No. 210/2013/ND-CP, attempt to balance these FDI incentives with mechanisms to support stronger linkages and greater potential for spillovers in the domestic market. Early returns on these policies have been less successful than desired but indicate a pragmatism that will be necessary to facilitate upgrading in agri-GVCs in the future.

Power dynamics have shifted in agri-GVCs to disproportionately favor lead firms and large retailers. Producers—and in Vietnam's case, smallholders—can find it very difficult to set the terms of trade and maximize gains in today's GVCs. Moreover, regulations prohibiting foreign firms from purchasing directly from farmers may limit extension services, technical assistance, technology transfer, and other support often provided by lead firms to suppliers.

Food Safety, Technical Regulations, and Quality Standards: Burden for Smallholders but a General Lack of Enforcement

Food safety, technical regulations, and quality standards are an integral aspect of participation in GVCs, but their implications for smallholders in Vietnam are uncertain. Beyond the technical regulations and sanitary and phytosanitary standards (SPS) of the international trade community, lead firms in GVCs continue to develop their own voluntary standards. These standards are often stricter than the technical or SPS regulations of an importing country's customs bureau, and they continue to evolve as firms attempt to cut costs, reduce risk, and preempt tightened food safety regulations in major developed economies. The scope and impact of these de facto standards continue to expand. For example, GlobalGAP originated as a set of standards developed by 13 European retailers in 1997; today it is the world's leading farm assurance program active in over 100 countries. Compliance with technical regulations, SPS, and voluntary standards can be costly for smallholders who do not enjoy economies of scale, creating barriers to market access and GVC participation, and forcing smallholders to downgrade activities or even leave the market (Lee, Gereffi, and Beauvais 2010).

Vietnam's value proposition for investors is diminished by poor enforcement of standards in many agricultural subsectors. Standards, even when they exist, are poorly monitored and enforced, leading to public health concerns and consumer distrust. Domestically, there is a belief among market forecasters that consumers are willing to pay a premium for higher-quality products, although given the relatively weak purchasing power of domestic consumers, this has thus far failed to send a strong market signal to farmers and investors. As a result, the market for higher-value products remains limited. Such products include hygienic fresh produce, and meat and dairy products, as well as safer, higher-quality inputs like certified seeds, better fertilizer, and better animal feed.

The government continues to expand VietGAP—its own national version of GlobalGAP—but more established international and private standards systems are outpacing it. Developed by MARD, VietGAP consists of 266 standards for medium to large production of agricultural, aquacultural, and forestry products at the time of writing this report. Decision No. 01/2012/QD-TTg established policies to support the adoption of VietGAP in agriculture, forestry, and fisheries. The cost of baseline surveys, topographical surveys, soil analysis, and analysis of water and air samples to determine ideal production areas, for example, is now fully covered by the government. The government states that its efforts in this area since 2008 have contributed to increased productivity and output, and accelerated change in agronomic practices, generating an increase of 30 percent of value added in agricultural production. Yet as small-scale production is still not covered by VietGAP standards, work remains to be done.

Vietnam at a Crossroads • http://dx.doi.org/10.1596/978-1-4648-0996-5

Concrete Actions

Vietnam is well positioned to remain competitive in agri-GVCs. Already a global leader in some product-specific value chains, the country has the natural endowments and capacity to maintain these positions and upgrade in GVCs. Much of this potential is captured in an updated study from the Ministry of Industry and Trade's Export Promotion Agency on export potential, encapsulated in table 8.2, which takes a brief look at the potential of some of the products identified, which could be achieved through upgrading, value addition, and investment by lead firms and large buyers.

Table 8.3 provides a further breakdown into product-specific activities where value added could be increased through greater investment.

Table 8.2 Export Potential by Product

Product	Export potential
Coffee	Coffee is one of Vietnam's most important agricultural exports, and is of particular importance to the Central and Central Highlands areas. The sector is almost entirely export oriented, with 95 percent of manufacturing productivity going as exports. Coffee export output reached over 1.5 million tons in 2012, with total export turnover of $3.5 billion, an increase of 25.7 percent in quantity and 19 percent in value from 2011. Vietnam is the biggest Robusta coffee exporter in the world. The country's favorable environment, climatic conditions, and low production costs make it one of the most competitive producers in the world. However, Vietnamese coffee suffers from relatively low quality due to poor processing, a lack of modern drying equipment, and outdated harvesting technologies. Exporters have patchy marketing skills, and the country does not have trademarks. According to MARD, 90 percent of coffee is exported in raw form with little value added, and so Vietnamese coffee is sold below average global market prices. Still, having established a dominant position in the world market and still having the opportunity to upgrade post-harvest processing and handling, the export potential of the Vietnamese coffee sector remains high. To maximize this potential, changes in production, processing, and promotion are required to further improve the value added of the Vietnamese coffee brand. **Potential types of upgrading: Process, product, and functional**
Rubber	Vietnam is one of the largest natural rubber exporters in the world. Ninety percent of rubber output is for export, and rubber's future export potential is high. Vietnam is one of the world's top three countries by yield which, according to the Rubber Research Institute of Viet Nam, has more than doubled since 1990, reaching roughly 1,720 kg/ha, equal to that of Thailand and trailing only India. Export turnover reached $2.52 billion in 2013, according to the General Department of Vietnam Customs. Rubber exports are not, however, maximizing their potential due to poor processing technologies and lack of developed rubber-product industries in Vietnam. The export turnover of rubber products is low. In fact, the country remains a net importer of almost all rubber products. Improvements in efficiency and the development of a domestic processing industry will be key in developing the sector. **Potential types of upgrading: Process, product, functional, and intersectoral**

table continues next page

Table 8.2 Export Potential by Product *(continued)*

Product	Export potential
Catfish	Vietnam holds a more than 90 percent share of the world catfish market, including roughly 70 percent of global sushi catfish, which is now exported to more than 130 countries. Primary markets include the United States, Europe, and Southeast Asia. Total exports have decreased to the European Union, but exports to the United States are increasing. Sushi catfish is raised mainly in the Mekong River Delta, employing about 10 percent of the labor force in this region. Cultivation in Vietnam enjoys advantages over competitors due to favorable natural conditions and high export potential.
	Poor sectoral linkages and unhealthy price competition have, however, negatively affected the quality of sushi catfish exports and hurt the product's reputation. In addition, the potential for expanding aquaculture land production and output is low. The sushi catfish sector should therefore focus on improving the quality and sustainability of sushi catfish farming and processing.
	Potential types of upgrading: Process and product
Tuna	Vietnam exported an estimated $520 million of tuna in 2013. Tuna catching and processing also create many jobs for fishers and low-skilled laborers.
	Long-term sustainability of tuna production faces challenges. The average size of fishing vessels is small, and the fleet lacks modern post-catch preservation technologies. Poor techniques, including hand fishing and use of improper fishing lights, is also very likely to deplete tuna resources and reduce quality. More recently, concerns over labor and human rights have been cause for concern. Due to high global demand, however, export potential is still high.
	Potential types of upgrading: Process
Shrimp	In 2012, Vietnam exported shrimp to 92 markets with a total estimated value of $2.25 billion. This was a slight decrease from 2011, largely caused by epidemics that increased the price of Vietnamese finished products by 15–20 percent relative to Ecuador, India, and Indonesia. Shrimp exports to Japan have decreased since Japan applied a new regulation to check 100 percent of imported Vietnamese shrimp. Poor processing is a concern, with little value added. Loose linkages in the production chain and the large role played by intermediaries are other issues. As quality is not closely controlled, the sector's reputation has been knocked.
	Even with more consolidation, concentrated production, and improved linkages in the production chain, competition will be very tight, especially with Ecuador, India, and Thailand. But as global demand for shrimp is high, the sector's long-term potential also remains high.
	Potential types of upgrading: Process, product, and functional
Cassava	Cassava is a kind of plant easily adaptable to different soil conditions and is grown widely, in the North Central Coast, Central Coast, Central Highlands, Northern Midlands, and Southeastern regions. According to the General Department of Vietnamese Customs, the export value of cassava and cassava products in 2012 was $1.37 billion and $1.1 billion in 2013, giving Vietnam a combined global market share of 27.3 percent. However, the number of cassava-exporting countries and territories has expanded rapidly, from 59 in 2009 to nearly 100 in 2012. Vietnam's exports are reliant on Chinese imports, which make up 85 percent of the total export value of Vietnam's cassava sector. The sector will also need to mitigate the high risks of pollution and soil erosion in cassava production.
	Export potential is high, but Vietnam needs to diversify its export markets and gradually decrease reliance on China. Trade promotion efforts will be critical, as will enhanced support in infrastructure and the application of science and technology, especially for processing starch and cassava products. Further, to ensure the sector's sustainable development, the government and private sector need to pay attention to environmental protection.
	Potential types of upgrading: Process and functional

table continues next page

Table 8.2 Export Potential by Product *(continued)*

Product	Export potential
Pepper/spices	Vietnam is the world's leading exporter of pepper, and most of its pepper production is for export. In 2012, export turnover climbed by 10.4 percent from 2011, to $687.2 million. The total land area for pepper production has increased as pepper prices have risen. According to the Vietnam Pepper Association, global demand is stable and is likely to rise in the coming years, bolstering pepper prices.
	Vietnam's pepper-processing technology has not received enough attention. Pepper-processing activities for export focus on two main products, unground black pepper and unground white pepper. Almost all exporting enterprises buy pepper from merchants, accounting for about 80 percent of the total pepper volume traded, causing difficulties in controlling quality, origin, growing processes, and differentiation of pepper types. Better application of science and technology to pepper processing is needed to develop the sector further and to improve valued added. Among other spices, some higher value-added products are manufactured in small quantities and have the potential to expand, for example, mixed spice combinations, cinnamon, and ginger. The export potential of these products should be further researched.
	Potential types of upgrading: Process, product, and functional
Rattan, bamboo, and leaf products	Products made of rattan, bamboo, and leaf are traditional Vietnamese products. Vietnam is also one of the countries with comparative advantage in materials and weaving craft. Bamboo and rattan commodities are found across the country. The Northern and Central regions have a higher concentration of bamboo, rattan, and rush products, the Southern region of water hyacinth and palm leaf products. According to the General Statistics Office of Vietnam, the export value of bamboo, rattan, and leaf products was $231.7 million in 2012, or about 16.3 percent of the national export turnover of the arts and crafts sector, and roughly 3.7 percent of the global market. These products also create employment for participants in value chains, especially poor rural women and ethnic minorities.
	According to ITC Trademap, the main export markets are the United States, Germany, Japan, and France, with the United States accounting for 23.8 percent of total export values. Emerging export markets for Vietnam's bamboo and rattan in recent years include Australia, China, the Russian Federation, and Spain. As long as demand for these products continues to rise globally, export potential will be high.
	Potential types of upgrading: Process, product, functional, and intersectoral
Wooden and wood art products	Wooden products and wooden items such as mosaic wooden products, faux antique items, and picture frames make up one of the country's export strengths. Mosaic wooden products are produced mainly in Northern craft villages, while faux antique items, picture frames, handicraft boxes, and other products are manufactured mainly in industrial parks in Ho Chi Minh City, Binh Duong, and Vinh Long. In the Central region, there are also some small wood art villages with export potential. According to the General Statistics Office of Vietnam, the national export value of wooden products in 2012 was $133 million, accounting for about 9.43 percent of the national export turnover of the arts and crafts sector, and just over 2 percent of the global market.
	Since 2008, Vietnam's wooden exporting market has expanded to many economies, including Malaysia, Sweden, and Taiwan, China, and registered a strong increase in export turnover. The export potential of this group is high.
	Potential types of upgrading: Process, product, and intersectoral

Source: Ministry of Industry and Trade Export Promotion Agency; authors.

Table 8.3 Potential Activities for Investment to Raise Value Added

Activity/Investment	Reasons for potential
Specialty rice mills	• Little need for investment in general rice mills: local investors continue to expand mills and seem to have access to requisite capital, technology, and skills. • Sufficient general rice grades from local mills for current buyers. • Investors are very interested in building specialty rice mills (fragrant, glutinous, and others), if local authorities and farmer groups are ready to work with them to organize farmers to grow these rice varieties. • Investors see rising demand and prices and want to secure supply. • These investments offer potential to increase higher-value rice exports, raise farmer incomes, and reduce costs (as investors will want to work with farmers to introduce new varieties, minimize fertilizer and pesticide use, and improve agronomy).
Rice products manufacturing	• The local market for rice flour, noodles, and other rice products is well supplied. • However, growing demand for gluten-free products is raising global demand for rice-based products. • Lead firms or investors with the latest gluten-free technologies and market intelligence can help tap into this market. • The usual limitations on shipping bulky or fragile items may restrict some opportunities, but for global food companies seeking to tap into this growth trend, Vietnam could be a natural choice.
Specialty (Arabica) coffee mills	• Investors see little value in investing in Robusta processing mills: professional wet or dry milling does not add sufficient value to beans over standard farmer-processed beans. • Investors are interested in building mills for Arabica in suitable areas, if local authorities and farmer groups are ready to work with them to organize farmers to grow more Arabica. • Investments offer potential to increase higher-value coffee exports, raise farmer incomes, and reduce costs (with improved varieties, fertilizer and pesticide use, and agronomy). • Suitable Arabica areas are in remote parts of the Central and Northern Highlands, where farmers have fewer income opportunities.
Fruits, vegetables, and flower farms—storage, grading, and packing	• Relative to other agri-export leaders, Vietnam exports low volumes of fresh fruits, vegetables, and flowers. • Even for the domestic market, modern chilled warehousing, transport, and packing operations are underdeveloped. • Attracting lead firms to help establish state-of-the-art fresh produce handling centers near Hanoi and Ho Chi Minh City airports, both for domestic and export markets, would create increased income opportunities for Vietnam's fruit, vegetable, and flower farmers.
Fruits and vegetables—secondary processing	• Similarly, development of fruit and vegetable processing facilities (juicing, drying, canning, freezing) will help expand exports and enable farmers to generate revenues beyond fresh sales during harvest season.
Aquaculture—primary processing	• Numerous local firms are already going well and are quickly expanding. • The sector could benefit from new investment in the latest technologies, market access, and branding, among other innovations. • Opportunities are in new areas where Vietnam has not yet developed significant expertise, including marine farming and seaweed farming.
Aquaculture—secondary processing	• There are opportunities to attract investors with technology and know-how to tap into underdeveloped high-value segments, such as smoked fish, as well as to develop improved fish oil and fish meal processing facilities. • Feed producers complain that fish meal quality in Vietnam is inferior and they still need to import fish meal.

Source: IFC.

Vietnam at a Crossroads • http://dx.doi.org/10.1596/978-1-4648-0996-5

Absorptive Capacity

The degree to which domestic producers and traders benefit from participation in GVCs—by improving productivity, increasing value addition, and upgrading—ultimately depends on their absorptive capacity. Investments must be made in developing human capital and skills, improving research and development collaboration, and aligning education and vocational training with local economic activities, which should be prepared to diversify.

Key Outcomes

By analyzing the future direction of agribusiness through a GVC framework, the government will be able to pinpoint activities within product-specific value chains where targeted reforms will best develop comparative advantage and boost competitiveness. Entering GVCs, expanding and strengthening participation within them, and turning that participation into sustainable development each poses strategic questions that must be met with carefully tailored policy approaches. The evolution of regional and megaregional FTAs, as well the rising capacity of regional low-cost competitors like Cambodia, the Lao People's Democratic Republic, and Myanmar will present new opportunities and new threats to Vietnamese agribusinesses over the next two decades. A better understanding the nature of GVC participation, governance, and power relationships—and the agriculture–manufacturing–services linkages along product-specific production chains—will help the government target reforms that boost performance and competitiveness not only in agriculture, but economywide.

The government should seek to strike a balance between supporting domestic producers as they seek to develop new and stronger backward and forward linkages in GVCs, and attracting investment from large foreign firms. The latter will require continued effort to improve the investment climate and business regulations, especially institutional reforms that increase predictability of investment, transparency, and accountability. These reforms are likely to improve overall sectoral performance and competitiveness in all agri-GVCs. Attracting FDI also will require further investment in infrastructure to improve connectivity.[5]

Beyond these broad horizontal needs, the more difficult question will be in developing the proper tools to effectively attract the *right* foreign investors—those willing to strengthen forward and backward linkages with domestic suppliers, transfer knowledge and technology, and support social upgrading—while ensuring a level playing field for domestic and foreign actors. The government has a critical role to play in helping to organize domestic value chains, strengthen linkages between firms, and provide innovative programs to enable local entrepreneurs to find and exploit niches.

Investment attraction policies should be tailored to enable domestic producers to leverage the knowledge and technology spillovers provided through closer integration and interaction with regional and global lead firms. This approach will entail a shift away from direct support to farmers and agribusinesses for inputs and income, which can have distortionary effects. This is not to say the government should withdraw support for farmers. Rather, programs should focus investment on developing world-class skills, absorptive capacity, innovation, export promotion, and investment attraction. The government will need to allow the market to dictate the contraction and consolidation of firms based on market competition.

The government should consider new mechanisms for individuals and firms to accumulate larger quantities of production land. It should not, of course, rescind its Revised Land Law or renege on the culturally anchored decisions of past land distribution. However, under certain conditions, it should consider new measures to facilitate easier transfer of land use rights, mitigating the risks of informal agreements common to the current market. This issue can be addressed through strengthening contract law and contract enforcement. Price-sharing formulas and equity or profit share systems may work to incentivize stronger linkages between farmers, intermediaries, and exporters if each party deems the contract to be legally binding and enforceable.

Vietnam should continue to expand VietGAP and encourage the private sector to embrace international and voluntary standards. The simple reality is that these standards are voluntary only in name—failing to meet standards means failing to reach market. Vietnamese producers are slowly embracing them, but the pace of progress and willingness across subsectors varies. By meeting international standards, producers will improve the quality of their products, reduce waste and inefficiencies in the production process, and create opportunities to sell to new buyers and new markets. There are multiple roles for the government to ensure that the country takes a carefully planned and phased approach to best position its private sector to meet increasingly stringent requirements, whether via technical regulations in new trade agreements and through voluntary standards driven by large buyers. Incrementally increasing and strengthening enforcement of existing regulations is paramount. Developing robust traceability systems will also be critical, especially with the expectation that new trade deals will strengthen rules-of-origin requirements.

On ensuring that inputs meet global standards, the government can revise tariff codes and eliminate nontariff barriers to ensure access to quality inputs—recognizing the importance of importing to export in GVCs. Strengthening border management systems can help to ensure that poor quality and illegal products do not reach local markets. Where poverty dimensions make it difficult for producers to adopt standards, policymakers can develop a menu of green agricultural policy options and allow farmers to choose the options best suited to their circumstances (Lovo, Bezabih, and Singer 2015).

The government should continue to support climate-smart innovation and entrepreneurship, leveraging the country's experience and talent in ICT and other high-tech sectors to provide new and improved services to the agricultural sector. The provision of improved cold chain and logistics services will be a first step. But over the next two decades, the service industry in Vietnam has the potential to provide high-tech climate-smart extension services and more effective marketing and branding services to agricultural producers and traders. Such services will help to increase domestic value added embedded in exports, and boost competitiveness as producers move toward precision agriculture. Lead firms likely will play a critical role by providing access to improved technology, market information, and global good practice, as well as through support mechanisms to help suppliers meet standards. Pre-competitive cooperation and coordination, as well as stronger public–private dialogue mechanisms, can help to speed this process.

The government will need to redefine its role in the sector, and this will create new human resource challenges. As more efficient, better informed investors move into agriculture, the governance structure within and across agri-GVCs will become increasingly driven by lead firms and large buyers. International flows of know-how and related spillovers will mean that the government is less likely to play a central role in advisory services and technology transfer and upgrading. Beyond the traditional areas of planning and technical subjects (irrigation management, disease surveillance, among others), government officials may not be well equipped to take on some of the new facilitative roles required for a restructured agriculture sector. These include those requiring deeper expertise in enforcing environmental standards and food safety regulations, attracting investment, and incubating innovation. Programs will be needed to bridge this skills gap.

As key demographic and economic structural changes reshape the country, the government will need to develop stronger plans for human capacity development. A core feature of the GVC framework is the focus on building absorptive capacity, developing skills, and creating the conditions to develop a world-class workforce over the long term. The education system will need to provide the skills for a more technologically driven, ICT-enabled, services-reliant agriculture sector. As the market matures and evolves, extension activities likely will be performed increasingly by the private sector. A competitive services sector will be a comparative advantage, and attractive for deeper investment. Services can also provide opportunities for employment and business development in rural and peri-urban areas. Citizens will need the skills necessary for these new professions. The government should continue to improve and broaden programs designed to strengthen linkages between universities, research centers, the private sector, and domestic producers.

Drivers and Enablers

The future of Vietnamese agribusiness will be driven by demographic changes, agricultural restructuring efforts, the future of regional and global trade, and the governance of lead firms in GVCs. (The last three are discussed in more detail just below.) Younger generations increasingly seek new, nonagrarian sources of income in cities and peri-urban centers. Developing the skills for those that transition to off-farm and nonfarm activities will be essential in achieving socioeconomic development and stability. Those who remain in farming will need to increase productivity and improve quality. As GDP is forecast to continue growing, resulting in a larger middle class, domestic consumption patterns are also likely to change (Westcott and Trostle 2013). Higher consumption of meat and processed foods will provide new opportunities in the domestic market for Vietnamese agribusinesses to develop the skills and capacities to become effective, competitive regional and global traders—skills and capacities that can further benefit from the positive spillovers of GVC participation.

Barriers, Threats, and Challenges

Agricultural Restructuring and the Importance of ICT, Connectivity, and Services

Government officials acknowledge the challenges of structural transformation in agriculture, as well as the need for a market-driven approach to agriculture, for higher-quality goods, for more sustainable practices, and for adaptation to climate change. These goals have been translated into broad targets—expansion of cultivated land by product, specific per head increases in livestock, and increases in practically all outputs—yet they do not fully take into account the structure of global industries vis-à-vis GVCs. MARD recognizes this problem and has called for more coherence between plans on regional and industry linkages.[6]

High-tech farming techniques and tools, ICT-enabled services, and advanced logistics are the major drivers of what is now termed precision agriculture. Most Vietnamese smallholders will lack the capacity in 2035 to invest in high-tech, web-enabled farm equipment such as automated sensor-based irrigation systems and satellite-based precision applications of fertilizer and pesticides. In Vietnam's more lucrative subsectors (for example, aquaculture) or subsectors where environmental degradation will force the need for technological solutions sooner rather than later (such as coffee), precision agriculture likely will come online over the next decade, and increasingly quick as the country approaches 2035. (Decree No. 210/2013/ND-CP already has dedicated financing for research and technology development—as much as 70 percent of the cost for new research and 30 percent of the cost of piloting applications.)

As rural citizens increasingly seek new off-farm and nonfarm employment, the need for higher productivity among remaining farmers coupled with new ICT-enabled services will produce new employment opportunities along value chains. Logistics performance, in particular, will need to continue improving, as it is a key input linking segments of large value chains.[7]

Bilateral, Regional, and Megaregional Free Trade Agreements

The future of the trade landscape in Southeast Asia likely will be drastically altered by bilateral, regional, and megaregional FTAs. The government not only has to meet its World Trade Organization (WTO) obligations, but will likely have to meet additional obligations as it continues to pursue bilateral trade agreements (such as with Korea) and deeper integration into the ASEAN Economic Community. New trade agreements likely will further liberalize market access and remove nontariff barriers, no doubt leading to stronger competition for Vietnamese agribusinesses and smallholders in domestic and international markets (Arita and Dyck 2014). Megaregional FTAs may contain stronger regulatory and quality standards, reaffirming the need to improve quality. The likelihood of strict rules of origin for goods to receive preferential treatment under these new agreements also will increase the need for improved traceability and stronger regulation.

Greater regional and global integration will make it hard for Vietnamese agribusinesses to compete in some agri-GVCs, so policies should be designed to help producers shift into activities where they enjoy stronger comparative advantage. The government has encouraged firms to increase value addition by closing the value chain, or pursuing vertical integration strategies. Given that Vietnam's comparative advantage in agriculture is its low-cost production, and in view of the likely evolution of the trade landscape over the next 20 years, a traditional approach to vertical integration would appear to be difficult for even the largest Vietnamese firms. In some cases, vertical integration may be the best strategy. In others, it may be better for firms to embrace the philosophical approach of GVCs: seek their comparative advantage in segment-specific activities, specialize, and create closer linkages with global suppliers of inputs and downstream buyers. The government should carry out thorough, product-specific value chain analyses to better understand which activities, along which segments of agri-GVCs, present the most opportunity for job creation, increased labor productivity, and value addition.

Sustainable Governance in GVCs

Agri-GVCs are likely to continue to transform farm-to-fork relationships, as large buyers consolidate power, drive standards, and allow quality-based competition to restructure production systems. Food safety and quality concerns will be paramount, but the global trade landscape is trending toward more environmentally friendly international standards, human rights protections, and mandatory sustainability reporting regimes. As a member of the ASEAN Economic Community, Vietnam likely will have to adapt—and quickly—to more rigorous standards. Issues being addressed by regional bodies include wildlife trafficking, illegal logging, sustainable management of ocean and coastal resources, energy efficiency, infrastructure for electric vehicles, responsible mining practices, chemical health and safety cooperation, trade in environmental goods, and aviation emissions.

While national and voluntary standards have occasionally been seen as, or acted as, disguised protectionism, it is critical for the government to better understand the likelihood of negative effects and the potential future costs of addressing these effects reactively rather than proactively. Increased participation in GVCs can have a procompetitive effect, leading to increased competition for limited or vulnerable resources. Raising the scale of production can amplify this effect, requiring carefully planned investments in infrastructure (Taglioni and Winkler 2014). Climate-smart policy prescriptions can strengthen global competitiveness. With an effective strategic vision, Vietnam can strengthen the abilities of its firms to sustain GVC participation. Recent research has shown that the benefits of environmental regulation often vastly outweigh the costs, helping to induce innovation in clean technologies that produce economywide benefits (Eccles, Ioannou, and Serafeim 2014; Marchi, Maria, and Micelli 2013).

Improved natural resource management and sustainable agronomic practices based on global good practice will allow Vietnam to boost long-term competitiveness while positioning itself to prepare for the challenges of a changing climate. Vietnam is one of the world's most vulnerable countries to climate change.[8] A high proportion of the country's population and economic assets (including irrigated agriculture) are in coastal lowlands and deltas, meaning that crucial economic sectors such as agriculture, energy, and infrastructure, are exposed to climate risks that could influence the country's long-term development prospects. Current rates of environmental degradation in the country are a serious concern. Reacting to a depleted natural environment and the changing climate will create new challenges for firms as they seek to ensure the long-term predictability, reliability, and time-sensitive delivery of goods necessary to participate in GVCs. Climatic disruption can impair these firms' ability to access inputs and deliver products, for which reason the world's most successful firms already are embracing a culture of disruptive thinking when envisaging how best to meet these challenges.

Mitigation, resilience, and adaptation present critical policy questions affecting the public and private sectors, and decisions today will have implications and impacts well beyond 2035. The government has taken action to limit the country's greenhouse gas emissions, as well as other mitigation measures with direct implications for the long-term sustainability of agricultural subsectors. Decision No. 799/QD-TTg lays out a national action program for reducing GHG emissions by limiting deforestation and forest degradation, sustainably managing forest resources, and conserving and enhancing forest carbon. From an adaptation standpoint, the government has taken action. Decision No. 142/2009/QD-TTg and Decision No. 49/2012/QD-TTg will help pay for new inputs in agricultural cultivation, livestock, and aquaculture production in the event of disease or natural disasters. Decision No. 315/2011/QD-TTg expanded on a pilot agricultural insurance scheme in 21 provinces under which the government subsidizes up to 90 percent of the premium. The program has attracted over 300,000 households to participate, but the lack of cooperation from large insurance companies—due to the high risk of agricultural insurance—means the scheme may never be scaled up nationwide.

While recent government decisions evidence awareness of these risks, it is unclear how much technical work is being done to monitor and mitigate them. The potential effects of business-as-usual farming techniques and climate change could affect soil fertility, soil erosion, watershed patterns, rainfall patterns, coastal erosion, salinity intrusion, and resilience to drought, flooding, and tropical storms. While these issues are unlikely to present catastrophic challenges over the next 20 years, failure to acknowledge them now and build mitigation and adaptation strategies into current policy could have major intergenerational consequences. This is an issue of key importance to coastal aquaculture, rice production in low-elevation areas, and potential infrastructure investment to facilitate greater trade from agricultural hubs. Strengthening data collection systems, communicating across government ministries, and enhancing collaboration with international partners on climate issues will help ensure that Vietnam is well placed to tackle future climate challenges.

Notes

The author would like to thank Steven Jaffee, Van Hoang Pham, and Tim Sturgeon for their guidance and excellent contributions in preparing this chapter.

1. Based on interviews with multiple public and private stakeholders.
2. Resolution No. 27/2009/NQ-CP, for example, allocates funds for treatment and disposal of expired plant protection products, the treatment of sites contaminated by pesticide residue materials, and measures to reduce (illegal) repositories of plant protection chemicals that pollute the environment.
3. See http://www.nestle.com/csv/case-studies/AllCaseStudies/coffee-water-vietnam.
4. The World Bank Group carried out a study of farmer groups across Vietnam—spanning Northern, Central Coastal, Central Highlands, and Mekong Delta provinces—in July 2014.
5. More information on specific policies to target the development of modern ICT-enabled services and improved connectivity can be found in the *Vietnam 2035* Background Note on ICT.
6. For a more detailed analysis of agricultural policy in Vietnam, including an in-depth discussion of the pros and cons of the Agricultural Restructuring Plan, see Kummritz et al. (2016).
7. Vietnam ranks 48th of 159 countries in the World Bank Group's Logistics Performance Index. See http://lpi.worldbank.org/international/global.
8. For a full analysis of Vietnam's climate-related vulnerabilities and risks, see http://sdwebx.worldbank.org/climateportalb/doc/GFDRRCountryProfiles/wb_gfdrr_climate_change_country_profile_for_VNM.pdf.

Bibliography

Arita, S., and J. Dyck. 2014. "Vietnam's Agri-Food Sector and the Trans-Pacific Partnership." Economic Information Bulletin Number 130, United States Department of Agriculture, Washington, DC. http://www.ers.usda.gov/media/1692699/eib130.pdf.

Eccles, R. G., I. Ioannou, and G. Serafeim. 2014. "The Impact of Corporate Sustainability on Organizational Processes and Performance." *Management Science* 60 (11): 2835–57.

Kummritz, K., G. Santoni, D. Taglioni, and D. Winkler. 2016. "Vietnam's Integration in Global Value Chains." Background Note to the World Bank's *Vietnam 2035* Report, World Bank, Washington, DC.

Lee, J., G. Gereffi, and J. Beauvais. 2010. "Global Value Chains and Agrifood Standards: Challenges and Possibilities for Smallholders in Developing Countries." *Proceedings of the National Academy of Sciences* 109 (31): 12326–31.

Lovo, S., M. Bezabih, and G. Singer. 2015. "Green Agricultural Policies and Poverty Reduction." Grantham Research Institute Policy Brief. Grantham Research Institute on Climate Change and the Environment, London. http://www.lse.ac.uk/Grantham Institute/wp-content/uploads/2015/01/2087_GRI_LSE-Agriculture-GGGI-policy _lores_51.pdf.

Marchi, V. D., E. D. Maria, and S. Micelli. 2013. "Environmental Strategies, Upgrading, and Competitive Advantage in Global Value Chains." *Business Strategy and the Environment* 22 (1): 62–72.

MIT Observatory of Economic Complexity. 2012. *Vietnam Country Profile*. http://atlas .media.mit.edu/en/profile/country/vnm/.

Taglioni, D., and D. Winkler. 2014. *Making Global Value Chains Work for Development*. Washington, DC: World Bank. https://openknowledge.worldbank.org/handle/10986 /18421.

Westcott, P., and R. Trostle. 2013. "USDA Agricultural Projections to 2022." United States Department of Agriculture, Economic Research Service, Washington, DC. http:// www.ers.usda.gov/publications/oce-usda-agricultural-projections/oce131.aspx.

CHAPTER 9

Vietnam's Evolving Role in ICT Global Value Chains

Timothy Sturgeon and Ezequiel Zylberberg

Key Takeaways

Vietnam's information and communications technology (ICT) sector is booming. While most employment growth has been in low-skilled assembly jobs in electronic hardware (mainly final assembly of smartphones), a small, dynamic set of knowledge-intensive business services has emerged and is showing strong growth—software services and business process outsourcing (BPO), mainly for export. Both these subsectors are poised to grow rapidly in the near future, but face bottlenecks that will require general improvement in the business climate and some urgent, focused policy measures.

Vietnam is at a crossroads. It can grow as an enclaved export platform specializing in low value-added assembly functions; or it can leverage the current wave of growth to move into higher value-added functions in ICT global value chains (GVCs). Perhaps even more ambitious, it could work to create an ecosystem to support a nascent set of dynamic and innovative domestic ICT hardware, software, and ICT-enabled services firms that can drive the adoption of ICT in local, regional, and even global markets with their own "invented in Vietnam" products.

While the creation of tens or even hundreds of thousands of new production jobs will be a welcome facilitator of the country's structural transformation, the benefits of this mode of growth can be short lived as incomes and wages rise. Moreover, with Vietnam's Association of Southeast Asian Nations (ASEAN) trade agreements maturing, the Trans-Pacific Partnership (TPP) on its way, and the likely entry of even lower-cost countries such as Myanmar into regional trade and investment flows, the window of opportunity for Vietnam in labor-intensive GVC functions could be relatively brief.

Challenges Confronted
A Poor Business Climate

There is a lack of transparency in the vendor selection process for government contracts, and bureaucracy is cumbersome. Local private companies, state-connected companies, and foreign-invested enterprises operate according to different sets of rules, explicit and implicit. Rules tend to work against local private companies, a set of firms that could contribute most to developing a dynamic domestic industry. Intellectual property rights protection is poor, creating unacceptable levels of risk for firms of all sizes. Finally, the education system is poorly suited to the modern international business environment.

Numerous Industry-Specific Barriers among Startups and Small and Medium Enterprises (SMEs)

Access to reliable sources of risk capital is tight, although there are a few globally connected venture capital firms in the country. Current accelerator and incubator programs are limited in size and scope and lack partners who understand both local and global markets.

Little Incentive for Diaspora Returnees to Enter the ICT Sector

Returnees face bureaucratic hurdles that restrict deep economic integration and mobilization of connections to foreign capital markets and management teams. Returnees can bring technical expertise, management experience, market linkages, and financial support, all of which are urgently needed in Vietnam.

Lack of Success in Increasing Foreign Firms' Research and Development

Vietnam views foreign firms as potential catalysts of technological upgrading. But strategies to increase research and development (R&D) activities of such firms have been unsuccessful. The Law on High Technologies, for example, has a narrow view of what constitutes high tech, deterring participation by innovative firms that would benefit from the fiscal incentives on offer. Further, links between universities and the private sector are weak and ill-suited to fruitful technology transfer.

Sector-Specific Challenges

Although the government understands the importance of developing backward linkages from foreign lead firms to local suppliers, it has been largely unsuccessful in its efforts to build supplier capabilities and match potential partners. Some policymakers remain optimistic about Vietnam's potential role in semiconductor fabrication. However, this is likely to be beyond the country's reach because of high technical, capital, energy, and water requirements, as well as low global prices and transport costs from well-established global centers of fabrication (Europe; Singapore; Taiwan, China; and the United States). Finally, software and services firms are hampered by the scarcity of professionals with appropriate language, technical, and managerial skills.

Solutions Proposed

Recommendations fall into two broad categories: horizontal (general, economy-wide) and vertical (specific to the ICT sector).

Horizontal

Focus on improving the business climate. Elements include reducing bureaucracy and corruption, improving vendor selection transparency, streamlining government processes, equalizing incentives between local and foreign-invested companies, strengthening IP protections, and mainstreaming soft business skills into the education system.

Build a vibrant startup ecosystem by making it easier to start and scale up a company. This could include improving access to capital, bolstering the existing base of accelerators and incubators, and leveraging diaspora returnees as a resource.

Reimagine high tech and prioritize innovation. Steps here would include amending the Law on High Technologies to adopt broader definitions of R&D and high-tech enterprises. Participation by universities in industry-related projects should be encouraged.

Vertical

Better implementation of existing local content development programs and matching Vietnamese suppliers to foreign-invested firms. A National Support Industry Fund should be set up and administered by an inter-agency committee to support local suppliers that want to engage with foreign-invested lead firms. This would help to bring local firms up to global standards and best practices.

Do not direct resources to semiconductor manufacturing. If Vietnam wants to participate in the now-fragmented semiconductor GVC, it should focus on integrated circuit design and back-end assembly, packaging, and testing, not on fabrication.

Prioritize capacity building in the software and ICT-enabled services industries. Vietnam has a real opportunity to develop globally competitive ICT and ICT-enabled services firms, especially startups with their own branded products and services. Foreign language, managerial, and technical training programs should be enhanced to aid in the development of viable product-based firms.

Current Conditions and Challenges

This chapter examines Vietnam's evolving role in ICT GVCs, providing an overview of how the country's ICT industry first emerged post liberalization and the position it occupies in GVCs today.[1] Key trade and foreign direct investment (FDI) statistics reveal Vietnam's emerging role as an export-oriented final assembly hub, especially for mobile phone handsets. ICT services firms hold a great deal of promise and could provide most of the opportunities for future development. The chapter ends with an examination of the sector's legal and policy framework.

The ICT sector has several important features. First, it is extremely dynamic and fiercely competitive. Innovation is so rapid that new products and services are regularly disruptive to longtime incumbents. For policymakers, simply keeping up to date with trends in the sector can be daunting.

Second, ICT is increasingly pervasive, and is an example of what Hirschman (1958) calls a propulsive sector. The adoption of ICT is likely to have driven vast improvements in economic efficiency (Mann and Kirkegaard 2006). In business and institutional environments, ICT systems have moved beyond their earlier role as labor-saving tools to become core platforms on which work takes place, products are built, and services are delivered. Because it is both pervasive and propulsive, the sector demands the attention of policymakers.

Third, as in many other sectors, ICT goods and services increasingly are produced in highly fragmented GVCs, with value often added in a slew of countries before goods and services make their way to end users. Famously, Apple's product packaging includes the label "Designed in Cupertino and assembled in China." But fragmentation is not confined to hardware. An enterprise software information technology (IT) consultancy might rely on platform software from Oracle, Microsoft, or SAP to build systems customized for particular vertical applications, such as taxation or the capture, storage, search, and analysis of medical records.

Fragmentation in GVCs can mean that companies and even entire countries and regions sometimes participate in the industry yet remain walled off from higher value-added activities, from innovation, and from the processes of new industry creation (Linden, Kraemer, and Dedrick 2007). For policymakers, the focus is shifting to capturing high value-added niches in GVCs and away from attempting to create fully vertically integrated national industries, which is an increasingly anachronistic approach in today's world.

Vietnam's ICT Sector: Overview

Vietnam's hardware sector has expanded dramatically in the last few years with large investments from lead firms (such as Samsung and LG), contract manufacturers (Foxconn and Jabil Circuit), and platform leaders (Intel and Microsoft). Box 9.1 briefly describes the main actors in ICT GVCs. These firms' investments—made largely due to the Vietnam's low cost of labor, proximity to regional suppliers, and relatively stable investment climate—have helped transform the country's industrial landscape in a very short period.

While the number of software and services firms in Vietnam has grown considerably, employment and revenue are, on aggregate, a fraction of what they are in hardware manufacturing, and foreign firms are less visible. The software and services sector includes a few large software and IT services firms and many small and medium software outsourcing and ICT-enabled services firms (often referred to in Vietnam as BPO or digital content providers), many of which are oriented toward the global market.

Notebook computers, mobile phones, software, and ICT-enabled services are now among Vietnam's most important exports. Global lead firms are some of the

---

Box 9.1 Key Private Actors in ICT GVCs

The fragmentation and globalization of the ICT sector has resulted in the creation of several actors that collectively bring products and services to market.

Lead Firms

Lead firms coordinate GVCs and often earn the lion's share of profits through the sale of branded products and systems to end-users. In ICT, they are often present in various market segments, and are recognizable due to their global branding efforts. Because of these efforts and their technological leadership, these firms can exert power over all but a few of their suppliers through their purchasing practices (Sturgeon and Kawakami 2011).

Contract Manufacturers

The modular nature of ICT hardware has allowed lead firms to delegate an increasing range of functions to contract manufacturers, whether they be electronics manufacturing services firms, which furnish manufacturing and ancillary services, or original design manufacturers, which provide manufacturing plus nonstrategic (iterative) product design services (Sturgeon and Kawakami 2011). These global suppliers serve a range of lead firms around the world.

Platform Leaders

Platform leaders are companies that have been successful in implanting their technology (in the form of software, hardware, or a combination) in the products of other companies (Gawer and Cusumano 2002; Sturgeon and Kawakami 2011). In extreme cases, platform leaders can capture the bulk of industry profits and retain tight control over the innovative trajectory of the industry.

IT Services Firms and ICT-Enabled Service Providers

Almost all the defining features of services—that they are nontradable, nonstorable, customized, and insensitive to price competition—are changing in ways that enable and motivate international sourcing. With standardization, commodification, and increasing scale, labor inputs to services have become more sensitive to costs, providing enterprises with the motivation to take advantage of the new sourcing options for a wide range of services and business functions. IT services firms do anything from system maintenance to software development and IT consulting. ICT-enabled service providers specialize in back office administrative tasks, sales, customer service, elements of R&D, and other services that can be delivered remotely.

Source: Sturgeon and Kawakami 2011.

---

county's largest employers—Samsung alone employed 75,000 in the country when the fieldwork for this study was carried out (January 2015). But apart from significant job creation, much of the growth in hardware exports has been hollow from a technological learning and industrial upgrading standpoint. Specifically, backward linkages to the domestic supply base—or supporting industry, as it is referred to in Vietnam—remain weak or nonexistent.

On the services side, Vietnamese software firms have found success at home and abroad. Companies like TMS Solutions and FPT Software have expanded their base of operations and deliver services in multiple locations around the world. However, they occupy a fairly low-value niche with limited upgrading prospects, as they do not have successful products of their own and are unlikely to be supported by their clients if they choose to develop their own consumer brands.

The ICT Hardware Sector

Vietnam's hardware trade is concentrated in a few narrow product groups (figure 9.1). Eighty-one percent of imports are in intermediate electronic components such as integrated circuits and light emitting diodes, while final goods imports are concentrated in communications equipment such as the base stations needed for rapid expansion of Vietnam's mobile communications infrastructure. (China's Huawei, a leader in low-cost mobile telephony infrastructure, is a major vendor.)

Exports are even more concentrated, with 75 percent of exports in communications equipment, mainly mobile handsets, which account for 88 percent of communications equipment exports. In reality, however, ICT hardware exports are even more concentrated than these figures suggest. According to the General Statistics Office of Vietnam, Samsung Electronics Vietnam is responsible for 98 percent of the country's mobile handset and component exports. Other product groups important to Vietnam's ICT goods export basket are computers and storage devices (12 percent of ICT hardware exports) and automotive electronics (6 percent). Vietnam is also an important producer and exporter of automotive wire harnesses, with $1.9 million in exports in 2013.

Figure 9.1 Vietnam Hardware Trade by Subsector, 2013

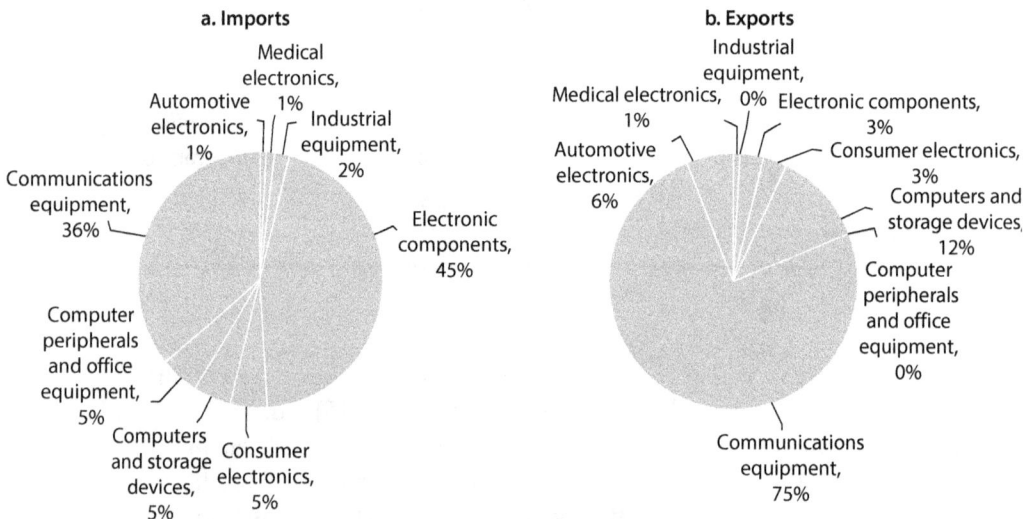

Source: UN Comtrade database.

Figure 9.2 Electronics Domestic Value Added as a Percentage of Exports, 2009

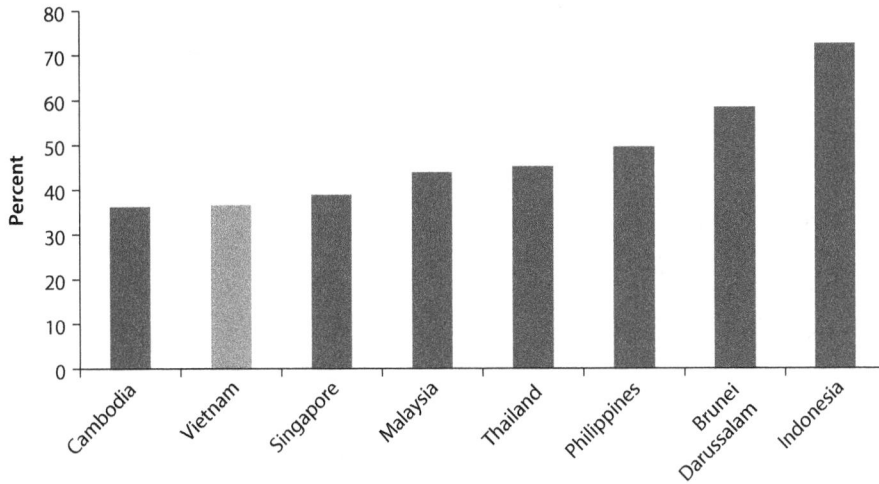

Source: OECD–WTO TiVA dataset.
Note: Myanmar and the Lao People's Democratic Republic are not included in the TiVA dataset.

A large percentage of Vietnam's hardware exports can be linked to foreign investors, and production consists mainly of assembly of imported intermediate inputs. According to estimates from the Organisation for Economic Co-operation and Development–World Trade Organization Trade in Value Added (TiVA) dataset, only 36 percent of Vietnam's electronics exports[2] in 2009 comprised local value added.[3] Vietnam ranks low relative to its ASEAN counterparts on this metric: it is next to last among the eight ASEAN countries for which TiVA data are available (figure 9.2). Thus, while ICT hardware export growth in recent years has been impressive, it has depended heavily on imported components.

In fact, the foreign content of Vietnam's hardware exports has grown relative to domestic content since 1995 (figure 9.3). While TiVA data are only available from 2009, our field research suggests that local content remains a small portion of Vietnam's electronics hardware exports, and that TiVA estimates exaggerate local value added. The consensus among respondents interviewed in Vietnam was that FDI has grown markedly since liberalization, but that linkages between foreign investors and local Vietnamese firms remain very weak.

Global Lead Firms

Several global lead firms are active in Vietnam, prominently Samsung, LG, Panasonic, and Microsoft (Nokia). Samsung is one of the largest foreign investors in the country with $9 billion invested, and an additional $3 billion smartphone factory under development. Its existing investments include a smartphone production facility in Bac Ninh province, a smartphone and tablet display assembly facility, an electromechanical assembly operation for camera modules, and the Samsung Vietnam Mobile R&D Center.

Figure 9.3 Vietnam's Electronics Exports and Inward FDI, 1995–2009

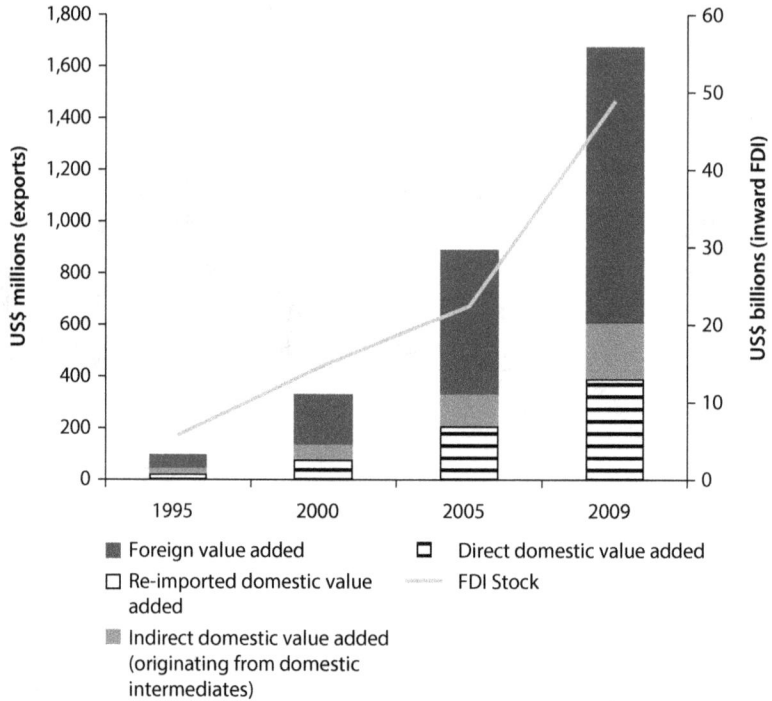

Source: OECD–WTO TiVA Dataset; UNCTAD FDI database.

The Bac Ninh facility is the largest smartphone factory in the world, producing 120 million units a year (Bloomberg News 2012). The new smartphone production facility will be set up in the Saigon Hi-Tech Park just outside Ho Chi Minh City. Samsung employs 75,000 production workers and software engineers, hiring an average of 2,000 people a week for its production facilities. Vietnam is responsible for one-third of Samsung's global output.

Samsung relies heavily on suppliers in the Republic of Korea that have co-located in Vietnam to produce intermediate inputs. Of the company's 67 suppliers in the country, only four are Vietnamese.[4] The prominence of packing companies is no accident, because packaging is one of the lowest value-added inputs to any manufacturing operation. In all, 53 of Samsung's suppliers are from Korea, seven from Japan, and one each from Malaysia, Singapore, and the United Kingdom (Viet Nam News 2014a, 2014b). Vietnamese suppliers, in short, make up a negligible portion of local content.

Efforts to increase local content have largely failed. In 2014, the Ministry of Industry and Trade announced that Samsung would source 91 parts for its Galaxy handsets and 53 parts for tablets from local suppliers. Targeted components included relatively simple parts, including batteries, earphones, USB storage devices, insulation tape, and parts of data transmission cables. In July 2014, Samsung held a workshop with the Vietnamese government and 200 local firms to see which of these components could be sourced locally. Samsung presented its purchasing policy for different components and had individual meetings with interested potential suppliers. Given that the phones and tablets produced in Vietnam are in Samsung's high-end range, parts are complex and quality requirements are high (for example, phone cases are now made of precision-machined aluminum, not plastic). None of the 200 local firms were able to meet Samsung's requirements. Interviews suggest that government efforts to create a support industry have been ineffective, and that companies have had to develop the supply base on their own.

A new player in the handset market, Microsoft recently acquired Nokia's Lumia smartphone factory in Bac Ninh (11,000 employees). Assembly of Nokia's smartphones was moved from China because of rising labor costs, and is now concentrated in Brazil, Mexico, and Vietnam. Vietnam is Microsoft's second-largest employment base after the United States. There are only a few local suppliers, but a company manager interviewed for this study expected the support industry to grow as more lead firms entered the country.

Other global lead firms with investments in Vietnam include LG and Panasonic, which have set up production facilities in the north to manufacture white goods (for example refrigerators, washing machines, and air conditioners). Many of these products are heavy and difficult to transport, and so are produced mainly for sale in the domestic market.

Local Lead Firms
The cost and time associated with launching a successful product brand as well as competition from established global firms have long made it difficult for firms in developing countries to start at the front of the value chain. While large emerging market lead firms like Huawei and Xiaomi have succeeded in challenging incumbents at home and abroad, it is far more common for firms in developing countries to seek engagement with GVC as suppliers. Some Vietnamese firms have sought to create their own brands from the beginning, leveraging the global supply base and existing platforms to quickly develop and launch products in Vietnam and beyond.

One such firm is BKAV, a company started by three students at the Hanoi University of Technology in 1995. The founders saw antivirus software as an emerging area of need in the market, and believed that Vietnam had the capacity to build an effective solution locally. They licensed their antivirus software for free until 2006, at which point they developed and began to distribute a commercial version. Around the same time, they started developing general software solutions for e-government, but as the company lacks both the relationships and the scale necessary to win contracts with the central government, it has focused on serving government at the provincial and municipal levels. As soon as the antivirus product began to sell (they now have 17 million users in the country), the company began to push revenues into their budding hardware area. BKAV now offers 60 hardware products and employs 500 hardware and software engineers in their R&D division. One of their products is a smartphone, which they developed by leveraging relationships with global suppliers and platform leaders. They source their chipsets from Qualcomm, which introduced them to other international suppliers for printed circuit boards, batteries, camera modules, and other key components. Their operating system is adapted from Google's Android.

Another local lead hardware firm is Tosy, a humanoid robot manufacturer that has been successful worldwide, garnering awards in consumer electronics and toy exhibitions around the world and selling its products in over 60 countries.

Finally, Dinhviso has successfully scaled up from an entrepreneurial startup focused on digital GPS product development to a maker of its own brand of hardware black boxes that can be mounted to taxis and motorbikes to track their location, and retrieve them in case of theft.

These examples suggest that, while it is difficult for Vietnamese firms to lead value chains, access to the global supply base as well as to existing platforms allows them to bootstrap and grow more quickly than if they developed all tools and components internally.

Global Contract Manufacturers

It is becoming unusual for lead firms making high volume consumer electronics to do all their own final assembly, or any of it at all. In Vietnam, some lead firms like HP and Apple produce though contract manufacturers. Given Vietnam's emerging role as a low-cost manufacturing hub, the number of global contract manufacturers setting up in the country will likely increase in the future. The country already hosts a number of global contract manufacturers including Foxconn (Hon Hai Precision Industry) and Jabil Circuit, as well as some smaller local firms like the Mechatronics Engineering Group.

Jabil Circuit (United States) set up its 273,00 square foot facility in the Saigon Hi-Tech Park in 2007, and uses it for medium- to high-volume manufacturing of industrial, energy, and health care goods. The facility traditionally has depended heavily on Hewlett Packard, for which it dedicates 70,000 square feet for the production of 1 million inkjet printers a year. Company documents suggest that Jabil has diversified its client base since entering the country. Jabil, much like other contract manufacturers, will often make new investments if it has at least one anchor client on board. Once the initial investment has been made, the firm begins to seek out new clients to fill capacity.

Foxconn (Taiwan, China) established two $80 million production facilities in 2007, one in Bac Ninh province and the other in Bac Giang province. These facilities initially focused on producing digital camera modules, computer motherboards, and cable connectors. Foxconn made written commitments to establish plants in another four cities and provinces when it first signed an agreement with the Ministry of Planning and Investment in 2007, but many of these factories have yet to be built. Compal—an original design manufacturer, also from Taiwan, China—invested $500 million in a laptop production facility in 2007. However, the factory, which started production in 2010, remains underutilized. Yet despite delays and difficulties, Foxconn and Compal likely will remain important players

in Vietnam's ICT industry for years to come, given the country's growing importance as a low-cost manufacturing hub, and its likely emergence as a consumer
electronics market as well.

Contract manufacturers provide certain advantages for policymakers. First,
they work for a range of end customers, while the captive operations of a lead
firm such as Samsung work only for the parent company. Working for a diverse
set of customers requires additional competencies (materials management,
design, frequent line changes), accelerates learning, and offers the possibility that
local lead firms can take advantage of world-class manufacturing services nearby.
Contract manufacturers can also provide a conduit for the local assembly of final
products that may have otherwise been imported. The contract manufacturers in
Vietnam, now and in the future, constitute a valuable resource for policymakers:
world-class manufacturing services for hire.

Platform Leaders

One of the most powerful platform leaders in the global ICT industry, Intel, was
one of the first electronics firms to invest in Vietnam. Intel first announced that
it would be investing $300 million in an assembly and testing facility in Vietnam
in January 2006. Within 10 months, the estimated figure had risen to $1 billion.
Intel received large investment incentives from the start, including a four-year
corporate tax holiday followed by a nine-year period paying only half the country's 28 percent corporate tax rate (Atkinson and Ezell 2012). The facility has
been operational since 2010, and is still the company's largest assembly and testing facility outside the United States. The plant assembles two of Intel's core
products: the system on chip for tablets and smartphones and the Haswell CPU,
the fourth-generation Intel Core Processor.

While the plant is packaging cutting-edge chips for the global market, linkages to local suppliers remain weak. When the facility came online in 2010,
Intel had only three Vietnamese suppliers. That number is up to 16, and Intel
hopes to reach higher levels of local content in the future, although the quality
of local suppliers remains too low for sourcing of core inputs (Tuoi Tre News
2014). It is unclear whether the company has a supplier upgrading program
in place.

The IT Services and ICT-Enabled Services Sectors in Vietnam

While IT services and ICT-enabled services are promising sources of growth and
competitiveness for the country, detailed international comparator statistics on
these subsectors are not readily available. There is no harmonized and internationally agreed upon definition of what constitutes ICT-enabled services, nor
does the Vietnamese government collect systematic data on services. Thus data
on IT services for Vietnam vary by source. The General Statistics Office of
Vietnam, the Ministry of Information and Communication (MIC), and key
industry associations offer different figures for number of firms, revenue, and
employment. An executive at a software outsourcing firm interviewed for this
study claimed that none of these data sources are accurate.

Nevertheless, from the disparate sources, we can surmise that Vietnam's role in these segments of the ICT GVC has expanded considerably. According to the Vietnam Software Association (VINASA), which publishes data from the MIC and other sources, the software sector generated $2.7 billion in 2013, with $1.3 billion from software and $1.4 billion from digital content.[5] Employment stood at 88,820 in software and 67,680 in digital content the same year. As table 9.1 suggests, revenue from exports has grown faster than revenue from domestic sales. Exports made up just 29 percent of total revenues in 2005, but grew to 43 percent by 2010. Software exports grew at 45 percent a year, while domestic sales grew by 28 percent annually. VINASA representatives estimate that software exports in 2014 amounted to about $500 million.[6]

An important reason for Vietnam's growth as an export base is its cost advantage over competitors in the region. Its workforce is far less expensive than China's or India's (figure 9.4). Entry-level computer programmers in Vietnam earn just 54 percent of what their Chinese counterparts earn, and 36 percent of their Indian peers. According to data collected by the MIC, ICT workers in Vietnam have a lower annual attrition rate (5–7 percent) than workers in China (10–30 percent) and India (50 percent). In 2014, Vietnam surpassed India to become the second-largest exporter of software services to Japan, after China (Viet Nam News 2013). While Vietnam will not compete on cost forever, it should leverage its low-cost labor force to build human capital and drive upgrading efforts in the near term.

Cost-competitive wages have driven growth in industry segments like software outsourcing and BPO. Software outsourcing is generally less capital-intensive than hardware manufacturing, creating opportunities for domestic firms to enter the market and grow quickly. Most of the larger software outsourcing firms in Vietnam are local companies serving the global market, and most have their production sites in Vietnam and small sales and marketing presences in key markets around the world, especially the United States and Japan.

Interviews with BPO firms confirm that Vietnam has attracted a great deal of work that was previously done in places like China, India, and Eastern Europe.

Table 9.1 Vietnam Software Industry and Export Revenue, 2005–10

Year	Domestic revenue		Export revenue		Total revenue
	Value (US$ million)	Share of total revenue (%)	Value (US$ million)	Share of total revenue (%)	Value (US$ million)
2005	169	72	68	29	236
2006	219	68	101	31	321
2007	285	66	147	34	432
2008	371	64	213	36	584
2009	463	60	309	40	772
2010	579	57	432	43	1,011
Annual growth (%)	28		45		34

Source: Jang, Lee, and Ko 2010. Data and forecasts from Ho Chi Minh City Computer Association.
Note: Data for years 2008, 2009, and 2010 are projections.

Figure 9.4 Average Monthly Salary for Software Engineers, Selected Countries, 2012

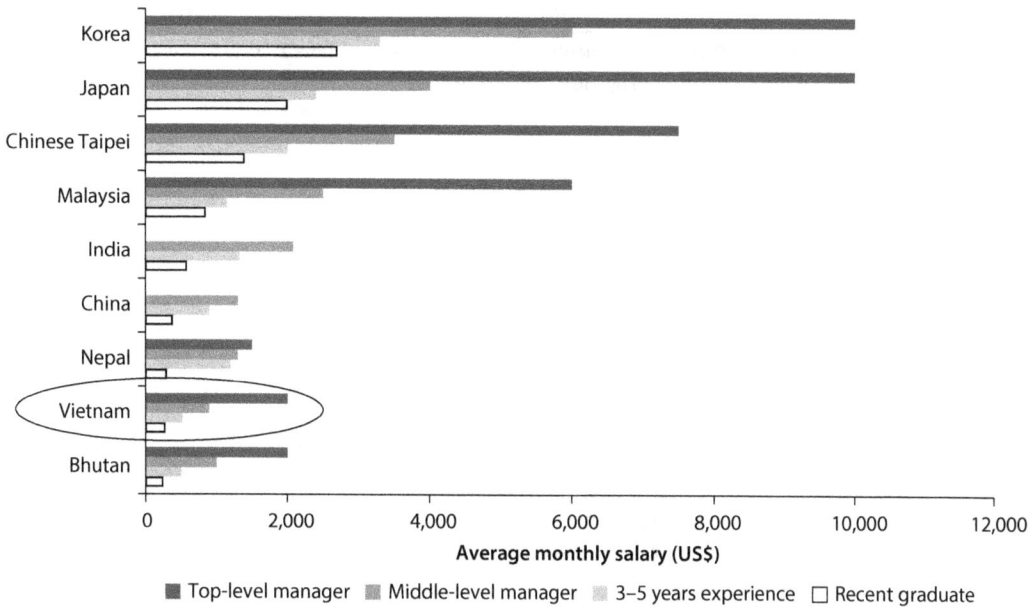

Average monthly salary (US$)

■ Top-level manager   ▨ Middle-level manager   ▨ 3–5 years experience   ☐ Recent graduate

Source: ASOCIO and KPMG 2009. Country and territory industry associations: Bhutan (BICTTA), Taiwan, China (CISA), the Republic of Korea (FKII), Japan (JISA), the MIC for India and China, Nepal (NCA), Malaysia (PIKOM), and Vietnam (VINASA).
Note: Data for India and China compiled separately. Data for top-level management are unavailable from the MIC.

However, this niche is primarily occupied by foreign firms taking advantage of Vietnam's cheap labor force. Upgrading opportunities in the BPO space remain limited given the low complexity of the work and not enough skilled personnel to shift into higher value-added ICT-enabled services.

Four Types of IT Services and ICT-Enabled Services Firms, and Entrepreneurial Firms, in Vietnam

While large, multinational corporations (MNCs) dominate the hardware manufacturing industry in the country, Vietnam's IT services and ICT-enabled services sectors have foreign and domestic firms of varying sizes. ICT firms in Vietnam typically fall into one of four types (table 9.2). There are a number of small but growing entrepreneurial firms developing products for the local, regional, and global markets. Table 9.3 lists the top 15 IT services and ICT-enabled services firms by revenue in Vietnam, some of which are discussed in more detail below.

Type 1: State-Oriented IT Services Firms Producing for the Local Market

The Financing and Promoting Technology Corporation (FPT) is one of the largest and most important former state-owned enterprises (SOEs) in the country. In 2003, the government restructured the organization, dividing it into three nominally independent firms: FPT Information System Company (a state-owned systems-integrator and software developer), FPT Distribution

Table 9.2 Four Types of IT Services Firms in Vietnam by Ownership and Market Orientation

	Local market (65% of output)	*Export market (35% of output)*
Locally owned	**Type 1: State-oriented**	**Type 2: Local SME exporters**
	Dominated by a few medium- to large locally owned firms that are state owned or formerly state owned with good connections to government (such as FPT, CMC). They generally sell customized solutions based on platforms offered by firms like Microsoft and SAP.	Many small to medium locally owned software development firms producing for export, several with connections to overseas Vietnamese (for example, TMA Solutions, KMS Technology).
Foreign owned	**Type 3: MNCs focused on the local market**	**Type 4: MNC exporters**
	Many MNC IT services and system integration firms, the only firms qualified for large systems, often with consultants onsite for support, customization and maintenance (such as IBM). Some of these firms also sell customized solutions based on global platforms. The main clients are other MNCs operating in Vietnam.	A few MNC branch operations providing software development and ICT-enabled series (digital content and BPO) for export (such as Harvey Nash, Robert Bosch). Some of this work is for external clients and some for parent companies (captive operations).

Source: VINASA (export shares); authors.

Table 9.3 Top 15 IT Services and ICT-Enabled Services Firms by Ownership and Market Orientation, 2013

Rank by revenue	*Name*	*Ownership*	*Main markets*	*Number of employees*	*Revenue (US$ million)*	*Key competencies*	*Type*
1	Joint Stock Company for Telecoms and Informatics	Vietnam	Vietnam	502	168	Software application development, renting telecommunications infrastructure, IT consulting	1
2	FPT Software Company	Vietnam	Japan, United States, EU, Vietnam	6,000	101	BPO, cloud computing, mobility, integrated circuit design	1
3	FPT Information System	Vietnam	Vietnam	5,000	34	Enterprise resource planning, e-government	1
4	TMA Solutions	Vietnam	United States, Canada, EU, Australia, Japan	1,700	27	Cloud computing, big data & analytics, mobile	2
5	HiPT Group	Vietnam	Vietnam	262	25	Systems integration, software development, IT equipment	1

table continues next page

Table 9.3 Top 15 IT Services and ICT-Enabled Services Firms by Ownership and Market Orientation, 2013 (continued)

Rank by revenue	Name	Ownership	Main markets	Number of employees	Revenue (US$ million)	Key competencies	Type
6	Harvey Nash	United Kingdom	United States, United Kingdom, EU, Vietnam	945	20	Software development, BPO	3
7	Elcom Corp.	Vietnam	Vietnam	335	20	Software development, R&D, systems integration	1
8	Tinhvan Technologies	Vietnam	Vietnam	363	14	Software development, digital content, IT consulting	1
9	Global Cybersoft (Hitachi Consulting)	United States	United States, Japan, EU, Vietnam	850	12	Enterprise application integration, testing, software development	3
10	KMS Technology	Vietnam	United States	459	9	Product development, software testing	2
11	MK Smart	Vietnam	Vietnam, Japan, Southern Africa, Latin America	409	8	Card printing, payment card security, automatic payment	2
12	NTT Data	Japan	Japan, Vietnam	190	8	Software development, IT consulting, manufacturing and logistics	4
13	Technology and Media Investment Development	Vietnam	Vietnam	90	6	BPO, cloud computing	1
14	SPi	Philippines	United States, EU	800	4	Digitization services, content solutions	4
15	Fuji Computer Network	Japan	Japan	350	4	Software development, systems integration, computer aided design	4

Source: VINASA 30 Leading IT Companies 2014.

(the firm that owned the master distribution contracts with IBM, HP, Cisco, Microsoft, Oracle, and other large firms), and FPT Internet (controlled Internet activities in Hanoi and Ho Chi Minh City) (Phan 2008).[7] Today FPT counts on seven member companies across four business sectors, including: technology, communications, retail, and distribution and education.

The most important of these firms, FPT Information System, employs 5,000 people and provides 40 percent of the government's outsourced IT services. In 2013, the company was awarded contracts to implement treasury and budget management information systems for the Ministry of Finance, to manage the personal income tax system for the General Department of Taxation, and to build and run an enterprise resource planning system for Vietnam National Petroleum Corporation. Other government agencies and SOEs that have relied on FPT for enterprise resource planning systems include the Sai Gon Paper Corporation, Vinamilk, and the Cables and Telecommunication Materials Corporation.

Another important member company is FPT Software, which focuses primarily on the internal market, but has expanded to 17 countries in recent years. It has 300 Vietnamese employees based in Japan and another 30 Japanese employees based in Vietnam. Much of this work was initially for Hitachi, with which FTP has had a relationship for 10 years. Originally, the firm was doing basic coding and testing in Vietnam. Over time, it captured higher-value segments of the GVC, namely software engineering and architecture. Operating as a global supplier, FPT Software recently set up an outsourcing hub in Myanmar to service 40 of its largest Japanese clients. As a director of Quang Trung Software City indicated in an interview, switching costs in software outsourcing are higher than one might imagine. This, along with the tendency of Japanese lead firms to pursue long-term relationships with suppliers, helps explain the firm's progression up the value chain.

Type 2: Locally Owned IT Services Firms Producing for the Export Market

Another leading Vietnamese IT services firm is TMA Solutions, a private firm started by six engineers in 1997. It expanded abroad in the following years, opening sales offices in Canada, the United States, Australia, and Ireland. All of TMA's work in the early days was in telecommunications software (mostly for Nortel). With Nortel's bankruptcy in 2009, business fell by 50 percent and the firm started to diversify into finance, health care, logistics, education, and e-commerce software services. Its core sectors are now telecommunications (700 employees), finance and insurance (150 employees), and e-commerce (250 employees). In 2010, it established an R&D center in Vietnam's most important software development zone, Quang Trung Software City. The aim of this 30-person team is to develop TMA-branded products to commercialize overseas. While software outsourcing remains TMA's main line of business and source of revenue, the company has staged efforts to develop proprietary products, albeit with patchy results to date.

The case of KMS Technologies further illustrates the difficulties associated with product development. Much like FPT Software and TMA Solutions, the company's main line of business is software outsourcing. The company generally provides software architecture, design, development, and testing services for clients. The work is highly collaborative, with daily virtual meetings and trips of two or three months by software engineers to the United States to meet with clients at their facilities. KMS has developed a few of its own products in recent years. Its 12- to 15-person R&D group has been separated from KMS to avoid conflicts of interest with outsourcing clients. One spinoff, QASymphony.com, licenses KMS's software testing tool. The company now has a U.S.–based executive team and has raised $2.5 million in investment capital. KMS also spun off SuperBrightyStudio, a gaming studio that develops games for domestic and regional markets. Company executives indicate that upgrading from software outsourcing to product development is complex because of the difficulty associated with finding good Vietnamese managers, as well as limited access to risk capital in the country. Management indicates that having an international management team and access to capital abroad are keys to success.

Type 3: Global IT Services Firms Producing for the Local Market

There are very few global IT services firms operating in Vietnam with the purpose of serving the local market. Generally, serving the public sector requires strong links to government. However, IBM is an exception. IBM left Vietnam in, but returned in 1994, setting up offices in Hanoi and Ho Chi Minh City. Today, it focuses on the public sector as well as banking and telecommunications. It has set up a number of industry-specific centers in the country, including a Banking Center of Excellence, a Cloud Computing Center, and a Global Delivery Center.

Another example is Microsoft, which has a small software operation (140 employees evenly split between Hanoi and Ho Chi Minh City) that provides support to local clients. The team includes a group of 10 engineers that help developers use the MS enterprise platform, Azure. Software piracy is an issue in Vietnam. To combat this, Microsoft runs a program that provides 800,000 students and teachers with free access to cloud-based software (Office), in the hope that they will buy the software once they are working in companies, or starting firms of their own.

Type 4: Foreign-Owned IT Services Firms Producing for Export

Export-oriented, foreign-owned IT services firms typically are multinational affiliates using Vietnam as a base to provide software outsourcing and ICT-enabled services (BPO, for example) to clients around the world. For these firms, the cost of labor is a key driver of investment and expansion. SPi is a Philippines-based content solutions BPO company with some 20,000 employees around the world. The Vietnam branch employs 800 people to provide global clients with non-voice BPO services (such as PDF conversion) for the publishing, health care, and entertainment industries. The company earns 40 percent of its revenues from contracts with postal services in Europe, to which they provide real-time data entry services, collecting and processing images of scanned packages, letters, and postcards. The Vietnam branch has 500 clients, all of which are foreign.

Similar to SPi, Digi-Texx was started in Vietnam in 2003 with German capital. It began by offering library indexing services to European libraries, and has since expanded its range of services to include invoice processing, eBook development, scanning services, software development and IT solutions, and image processing. While most of its work is for export (90 percent), it is developing local clients.

Harvey Nash is a United Kingdom–based executive search, professional recruitment, and IT outsourcing company with 1,000 employees in Vietnam, the company's low-cost production platform.

Other foreign firms exporting software and services to clients around the world include Hitachi Consulting Services (United States, formerly Global Cybersoft), Fuji Computer Network (Japan), and Luvina Software (Japan).

While opportunities for upgrading remain scarce in ICT-enabled services, the BPO firms interviewed for this project have demonstrated that they do exist. For example, SPi began by offering simple digitization services, but has since begun hiring people with Chinese, Korean, Japanese, Dutch, and German language skills, increasing the range of markets they can reach with more complex service offerings. Digi-Texx has developed its own software tools to help its employees process handwritten documents quickly.

Yet the local market for BPO services has not yet developed. Companies interviewed indicate that they can offer quality services to multinational clients abroad, but that such services are not yet in demand in Vietnam. Further, multinational firms may face difficulties breaking into the local market, given their limited access to government.

Entrepreneurial IT Services Firms in Vietnam

Despite the difficulties associated with establishing an IT startup in Vietnam, various entrepreneurs have found success in the local, regional, and even global markets. Mobivi, for example, is an innovative firm started by a successful overseas Vietnamese entrepreneur who returned to Vietnam to start a mobile payment platform similar to the successful Kenyan product M-Pesa. In 2011, the company pivoted from mobile money—given the low margins and opacity of the banking sector—to develop iCare, an employee benefit program for factory workers in Vietnam. It allows factory workers making between $200 and $250 a month to buy consumer products on an interest-free installment basis. The service has been successful, and is now being rolled out in Cambodia, India, Indonesia, and the Lao People's Democratic Republic. The company uses existing local e-commerce firms, local distributors, and enterprise resource planning tools to provide, sell, and deliver products to an underserved segment of these populations.

Other examples are VNG, which began in game development and shifted into social networking, and Appota, which began in 2011 by licensing games from China and has since created its own mobile platform for digital content.

While there is no shortage of success stories, these cases read more like anomalies than products of a carefully calibrated startup ecosystem. Sources with knowledge of Vietnam's startup ecosystem argue that the technical talent exists, but that managerial skills are difficult to find. Further, venture capital firms like IDG Ventures (United States) and Cyber Agent Ventures (Japan) are active in the country, but the venture capital network is not robust enough to support the volume of activity in the country. Exit strategies in Vietnam are limited to larger venture capital firms or an initial public offering abroad. The only ICT firms listed on the Vietnamese stock market are large SOEs.

Legal and Policy Framework

The policy choices made by the government in recent years have had profound effects on the country's industrial structure. In the 1990s, most industrial output came from either SOEs or foreign firms. The Enterprise Laws of 2000 and 2005 facilitated the development of many new private businesses. Further, WTO accession and greater regional integration forced the government to withdraw some support from SOEs. More than 160,000 new domestic firms were established between 2000 and 2005. During this period, SOE industrial output declined as a share of total industrial output, from 32 percent to 18 percent (Perkins and Anh 2010). FDI remained relatively stable, however. Domestic private firms grew despite continued difficulties tied to access to capital and land. While SOEs and private enterprises are now nominally on equal legal footing, sources indicate that private firms are at a considerable disadvantage in accessing land, capital, and government contracts.

While the space for industrial policy has shrunk in recent years due to WTO accession and regional agreements, the government continues to influence the trajectory of ICT development in various ways. The Law on Investment (2005) has helped to attract new foreign investors, many of whom have fueled the tremendous growth in electronics exports in recent years. The Law on High Technologies (2008) uses fiscal incentives to drive innovation in ICT and a number of other advanced technology areas. The government has focused a great deal on supporting the development of IT services and ICT-enabled services, beginning with the first national five-year ICT plan (1993) and the first resolution on the development of the software industry (2000). These efforts continue with increases in public sector outsourcing of IT services. But real barriers to local development remain.

Law on Investment

Vietnam's inward stock of FDI reached $22.4 billion in 2013. Japan is the largest investor, with $8.4 billion invested as of 2012. Other large investors include Korea ($5.8 billion), Malaysia ($2.8 billion) and Singapore ($2.6 billion).[8] While foreign firms have been active in Vietnam for quite some time, regulatory clarity, attractive incentives, and the establishment of economic, industrial, high-tech, and export processing zones have accelerated the rate of investment since the early 2000s.

The Law on Investment has been an important driver of such investment. Incentives for new investors include import duty exemptions for equipment, materials, means of transportation, reduction in corporate tax, an exemption from tax on technology transfer activities, the ability to carry losses for up to five years for tax purposes, accelerated depreciation of fixed assets, and preferential access to and tax reduction on land. A government decree passed in 2006 defined key areas eligible for investment incentives, including biotechnology, advanced manufacturing, ICT, agriculture, labor-intensive factories, infrastructure development, and social services. The law outlines investor rights and obligations, and reinforces the notion that investments and intellectual property are protected from expropriation and theft. It defines the four types of zones, and outlines investment procedures for companies wanting to invest in one of these areas.

Law on High Technologies

The Law on High Technologies was passed in 2008 with the aim of driving industrial development in a range of areas, including biotechnology, automation, materials, and information technologies. Although it has been marginally effective to date, the law remains one of the few policy instruments aimed at accelerating the process of local technological upgrading. Companies that manufacture high-tech products and have a presence in Vietnam are eligible for a range of fiscal incentives in exchange for spending on local R&D.[9] Firms must obtain a certificate from the Ministry of Science and Technology to certify that they are high-tech enterprises, are working on high-tech projects, and are engaged in R&D that follows the contours of the state's priorities (Decision No. 55/2010/QD-TTg). Technologies eligible for promotion include visualization, cloud computing, and high-definition display and image identification software.

Companies that establish R&D facilities or high-tech business incubators are exempt from land use levies and benefit from steep reductions in enterprise income tax, value-added tax, and import and export duties. They also are eligible for funding from the National Hi-Tech Development Program, a Vietnamese D 1 trillion fund earmarked for high-tech enterprise development. In exchange for these incentives, companies must spend at least 1 percent of annual revenues in Vietnam on R&D in the country. Researchers' salaries, conference travel, and other professional development activities, facility and equipment rental, material purchasing and transportation are all admissible expenses (Circular No. 32/2011/TT-BKHCN).

According to the Law on High Technologies, at least 5 percent of the workforce conducting R&D projects must have at least a university degree. Herein lies the law's principal limitation: Vietnam does not have the human capital necessary for firms to embark on large R&D projects. The development of highly skilled IT professionals has largely been left to the private sector (box 9.2).

Box 9.2 Examples of Private Workforce Development Initiatives

The Samsung Vietnam Mobile R&D Center (SVMC) was established in 2012, and remains the company's largest R&D facility in Southeast Asia. To remove the talent bottleneck, Samsung has channeled $2.5 million toward grants and scholarships at the Hanoi University of Science and Technology. It has also agreed to provide $1.4 million in scholarships and laboratory equipment for students at the Posts and Telecommunications Institute of Technology in Ho Chi Minh City. While Samsung has invested heavily in university-led

box continues next page

workforce development programs, one company executive claims that students leave universities unprepared to work at the SVMC. Thus the company trains its new hires extensively to get them up to speed.

Much like Samsung, Intel found the lack of technical and managerial human resources a serious problem. Since launching the Intel Study Abroad Program in 2009, the company has invested $7 million to sponsor 73 Vietnamese students' bachelor degrees at Portland State University, United States. The program has been successful in that it has created the foundation of engineering talent that Intel sorely needed. Intel has also developed and sustained a partnership with Arizona State University in which Vietnamese students and teachers are sent to study abroad. A few thousand Vietnamese have been sent to the United States since the partnership began in 2010. Given that the Intel factory has now successfully trained and hired the managers and engineers it needs, future workforce development efforts will focus on training students at local institutions like the Royal Melbourne Institute of Technology in Ho Chi Minh City.

FPT started an IT university in 2006 with the aim of training the next generation of IT professionals. The university has 16,000 students who choose from 10 to 15 programs and learn either English or Japanese during their studies (Jang, Lee, and Ko 2010). FPT uses the university to meet its own human resource needs. Together, FPT Information Systems and FPT Software hire around 60 percent of graduates.

Such private initiatives, along with IT-focused degree programs run by Vietnamese colleges and universities, will be critical if the government is to reach its goal of training 600,000 IT professionals by 2020.

Laws Supporting IT Services and ICT-Enabled Services

The first five-year ICT plan (1995–2000) focused on computerizing the public sector to improve Vietnam's standing versus neighboring countries on the United Nations annual E-Government Survey. However, before long the government began to see ICT as a potential leading economic sector. The 2002–05 ICT Master Plan reflected the importance of developing ICT outside the public sphere. The 2006 Law on Information Technology and subsequent decrees reinforced the state's emphasis on ICT, particularly software and digital content.

While Vietnam first exported software in 1997, only in 2000 did the government set out to establish a domestic software industry with an outward orientation (Hong 2005). Prime Minister Phan Van Khai put the first five-year plan for software development into effect in June 2000. The plan sought to create the human capital necessary for a viable software industry. Between 2000 and 2005, the Ministry of Science Technology and Environment and the Ministry of Education and Training coordinated efforts to train 25,000 IT specialists and computer programmers. They have since revised their target upwards considerably, aiming to train 600,000 IT professionals by 2020.

The government has a range of incentives for IT services firms. Software companies benefit from exemptions on value-added tax and export taxes, a reduced corporate income tax rate of 10 percent in accordance with the Law on Domestic

Investment Encouragement and the Law on Foreign Investment, an allowance of 10 percent of pretax revenue for R&D spending, accelerated visa procedures for foreigners, and a reduced personal income tax rate for ICT professionals. Software firms are granted preferential access to credit and land. Interviews suggest that these incentives have been instrumental to industry growth in both domestic and foreign markets. By 2013, software turnover in Vietnam surpassed $1 billion, half of which was exported (VINASA).

In 2014, Prime Minister Nguyen Tan Dung decreed that government agencies could outsource IT services to the private sector in an effort to cut down on labor costs and increase productivity. This decision could have a profound effect on the domestic IT services sector, although it remains to be seen whether smaller firms will be able to take advantage. The state has also created seven IT development zones,[10] which now account for a large proportion of IT services and ICT-enabled services companies. The 300 companies in these zones employ 46,000 people.

The Vietnamese government clearly believes that ICT has the potential to transform the economy. But for this goal to be realized, certain policy-related issues need to be addressed, including the country's misguided push into semiconductor fabrication, its relegation of training to the private sector, and its lackluster support for domestic suppliers wanting to engage with global lead firms in Vietnam.

Concluding Remarks

The single most important lesson from this study is that ICT GVCs show continuous change and opportunity. Assumptions about industry life cycles—where product segments stabilize as the industry matures and then shift to developing countries—do not seem to apply to the ICT sector. Long exposure to the industry's rapid but volatile growth and the sudden emergence of huge new market opportunities (for example, the personal computer, the mobile phone, and the Internet) has allowed ICT companies in the developing world to quickly build up extraordinary capabilities.

We need to ask not how emerging economies can repeat the experiences of successful recent developers like Singapore and Taiwan, China, but rather what roles might be available in ICT GVCs in the future. Newcomers should seek to avoid the pitfalls and limits of GVC engagement and supplier-led upgrading, for example becoming trapped in low value-added GVC segments such as assembly. However, in an integrated global industry this has proven to be exceedingly difficult, even for firms with established roles in the industry and deep expertise in their GVC niche.

Forward-looking policymakers and entrepreneurs in Vietnam must instead consider the possibilities of tapping into the same palette of globally distributed capabilities that global firms in the industry see, as well as acknowledging the expanding potential for new combinations. Capabilities in the ICT sector are now widely distributed across the globe, and these will continue to create huge opportunities for suppliers and lead firms in ICT GVCs. New industries and value chain combinations inevitably will include more firms—lead firms, contract manufacturers, component suppliers, and even platform leaders—based in newly developed and developing countries such as Vietnam.

We can anticipate, given the right conditions, a spate of new lead firms born in developing countries without the expectation that they will need to move up the supply chain ladder in their efforts to become branded companies. More ICT platforms, functions, and services are available than ever before, either for sale or for hire, and it is only a matter of time before one, and then several new, world-beating ICT companies from Vietnam find a way to combine these elements and come to dominate some as-yet unknown product or market area in the always-exciting ICT industry.

Notes

This chapter draws on a World Bank working paper, Sturgeon and Zylberberg (2016), and on Sturgeon and Kawakami (2011).

1. Material outlining key GVC actors, including lead firms, contract manufacturers, platform leaders and ICT and ICT-enabled service providers, at the global level originates from Sturgeon and Kawakami (2011).

2. The TiVA dataset defines industries using the International Standard Industrial Classification (ISIC) system, revision 3. The electronics category is titled electronics and optical equipment and includes manufacturing codes for office, accounting, and computing machinery; electrical machinery and apparatus; radio, television, and communication equipment and apparatus; medical, precision, and optical instruments; and watches and clocks. Thus, the definition of the electronics industry used by TiVA differs from the definition we are using for the UN Comtrade data presented above. The two data sources have not been harmonized and therefore should not be compared directly.

3. TiVA describes a statistical approach used to estimate the source(s) of value (by country and industry) that is added in producing goods and services for export (and import). For more information, see http://www.oecd.org/sti/ind/TIVA_FAQ_Final .pdf.

4. Goldsun Packaging and Printing JSC (corrugated paper packaging materials), the Thang Long Packaging Production Export–Import JSC (thin-film packaging), Viet Hung Packaging Company Ltd (corrugated paper packaging), and Nam A Company Ltd (packaging).

5. VINASA counts on 240 member companies that account for 70 percent of Vietnam's software production and 60 percent of its software workforce. Data available from http://goglobal.jisa.or.jp/Portals/0/data/library/20120718_000042/VINASA _Vietnam.pdf.

6. According to one software outsourcing executive, when VINASA was asked from whence its export statistics came, it indicated the Ho Chi Minh City Computer Association (HCA). When HCA was asked the same question, it said the export data came from VINASA.

7. The government retains a small ownership stake in the company.

8. Data come from UNCTAD Bilateral FDI Statistics. Data from the Republic of Korea were last updated in 2010. As of 2014, the Republic of Korea passed Japan as the largest investor in Vietnam.

9. Average turnover from high-tech products must be 60 percent for three consecutive years and 70 percent for the fourth year.

10. Saigon Hi-Tech Park, Saigon Software Park, Quang Trung Software Park, Hanoi IT Trading Center, Da Nang ICT Infrastructure Development Center, National University of Ho Chi Minh City's IT Park, and Can Tho University Software Center.

Bibliography

ASOCIO (Asian-Oceanic Computing Industry Association) and KPMG India. 2009. "Asia-Oceania Vision 2020: Enabling IT Leadership through Collaboration." ASOCIO report.

Atkinson, Robert, and Stephen Ezell. 2012. *Innovation Economics: The Race for Global Advantage.* New Haven, CT: Yale University Press.

Bloomberg News. 2012. "Vietnam Tech Exports Overtaking Garments Eases Trade Gap." November 8. http://www.bloomberg.com/news/articles/2012-11-07/vietnam-luring -tech-companies-narrows-trade-gap-southeast-asia.

Fernandez-Stark, Karina, Penny Bamber, and Gary Gereffi. 2011. "The Offshore Services Value Chain: Upgrading Trajectories in Developing Countries." *International Journal of Technological Learning, Innovation and Development* 4 (1–3): 206–34.

Gawer, Annabelle, and Michael Cusumano. 2002. *Platform Leadership: How Intel, Microsoft, and Cisco Drive Industry Innovation.* Cambridge, MA: Harvard Business School Press.

Hirschman, Albert. 1958. *The Strategy of Economic Development.* New Haven, CT: Yale University Press.

Hong, Tran Lae. 2005. *Overview of Vietnamese Software Enterprises in 2005.* Ho Chi Minh City: Ho Chi Minh City Computer Association.

Jang, Seungkwon, Heejin Lee, and Kyungmin Ko. 2010. "Becoming a Fast Learner in Offshore Software Outsourcing: The Case of Vietnam's FPT Software." *International Area Review* 13 (1): 183–203.

Linden, Greg, Kenneth Kraemer, and Jason Dedrick. 2007. "Who Captures Value in a Global Innovation System? The Case of Apple's iPod." Working Paper, University of California at Irvine, Personal Computing Industry Center (PCIC), Irvine, CA.

Mann, Catherine, and Jacob Kirkegaard. 2006. *Accelerating the Globalization of America: The Next Wave of Information Technology.* Washington, DC: Institute for International Economics.

OECD (Organisation for Economic Co-operation and Development) and WTO (World Trade Organization). 2015. "TiVA (Trade in Value Added) Database." https://stats .oecd.org/index.aspx?queryid=66237.

Perkins, Dwight, and Vu Thanh Tu Anh. 2010. "Vietnam's Industrial Policy: Designing Policies for Sustainable Development." UNDP—Harvard Policy Dialogue Paper 3, Series on Vietnam's WTO Accession and International Competitiveness Research, Ash Institute for Democratic Governance at the John F. Kennedy School of Government at Harvard University, Cambridge, MA.

Phan, Chau. 2008. "Vietnam as an IT Outsourcing Destination." Capstone Project for Business, Policy, and Strategy Course, Washington Research Library Consortium. http://aladinrc.wrlc.org/handle/1961/4778.

Sturgeon, Timothy, and Momoko Kawakami. 2011. "Global Value Chains in the Electronics Industry: Characteristics, Crisis, and Upgrading Opportunities for Firms from Developing Countries." *International Journal of Technological Learning, Innovation and Development* 4 (1): 120–47.

Sturgeon, Timothy, and Ezequiel Zylberberg. 2016. "Vietnam's Current and Future Role in Information and Communications Technology Global Value Chains." Policy Research Working Paper, World Bank, Washington, DC.

Tuoi Tre News. 2014. "80% of the World's Computer Chips Will Be Made by Vietnam by 2015: CEO." August 30. http://tuoitrenews.vn/business/21324/80-of-worlds-computer -chips-will-be-made-by-intel-vietnam-by-2015-ceo.

United Nations. 2016. "UN Comtrade (Database)." http://comtrade.un.org/.

Viet Nam News. 2013. "Viet Nam Climbs IT Software Exports Ladder." September 30. http://vietnamnews.vn/economy/245585/viet-nam-climbs-it-software-exports -ladder.html#KmmWp8feA6zp6olj.97.

———. 2014a. "Samsung Chooses Few Vietnamese Suppliers." October 17. http:// vietnamnews.vn/economy/261534/samsung-chooses-few-vietnamese-suppliers .html#M7qJrmvKQOuikk2X.97.

———. 2014b. "Local Firms to Make 144 Samsung Components." December 18. http:// vietnamnews.vn/economy/264165/local-firms-to-make-144-samsung-components .html#0G1sPJFy6UMP2xJH.97.

CHAPTER 10

The Role of Vietnam's Services Regulation in the ICT Sector

Martín Molinuevo

Key Takeaways

Upgrading Vietnam's information and communications technology (ICT) industries is a quest to incorporate more and higher value-added services in the value chain. This progress toward servicification is needed in Vietnam's existing electronic manufacturing industry and its nascent information technology (IT)–enabled business services. For the former, adding value requires moving beyond the current contract manufacturing niche and expanding services related to research and product development, testing and analysis, as well as establishing local brands and developing factory-less startups. For the latter, Vietnam needs to expand business services related to knowledge outsourcing, especially in the IT sector.

Challenges Confronted
These processes are, however, hindered by the restrictive regulatory and institutional framework for domestic and foreign firms; weak telecommunications infrastructure; and the poor availability of skills and supporting professions such as accounting and legal services.

In the last two decades, Vietnam has, though, made huge strides in all three areas, reducing barriers to trade and investment, expanding telecoms coverage and reducing its costs, and revamping education and promoting programs for developing technical skills. Still, complementary measures are needed to reap the full benefits of Vietnam's Đổi Mới policies.

Solutions Proposed
In the business environment, mandatory procedures for domestic and foreign firms, such as company registration, licensing, and mergers and acquisitions, would benefit from a more transparent, streamlined, and efficient business environment.

Greater transparency and capacity in dispute resolution, particularly in enforcing court and arbitration decisions, are essential.

The telecoms sector would benefit from greater capacity and transparency more generally, too, as well as the removal of caps to foreign participation, which would help attract foreign capital for the sector's equitization program. In addition, as a sector dominated by state-owned enterprises (SOEs), a stronger competition policy with increased capacity, clear mandates, and the ability to enforce antitrust decisions is needed to ensure a level playing field for all operators and to attract private participation.

Vietnam has made solid progress in reducing barriers to establishing skilled personnel and individual services providers. The implementation of the Association of Southeast Asian Nations (ASEAN) Mutual Recognition Arrangements for professional services—in particular for architecture, engineering, accounting, and medical professionals—will help facilitate movement of skills into the country.

Lessons to Be Learned

This chapter suggests the following for the public sector and private firms:

- The public sector should ensure a conducive regulatory and institutional environment that reduces formal and de facto barriers to domestic and foreign business by providing a transparent and effective regulatory environment. The government should also support the ICT industry by expanding market opportunities through deeper progress in market integration with its ASEAN and ASEAN+ partners.
- While enacting transparent regulations and establishing solid institutions remains an essential task for the government, stakeholders should seek active participation in the regulatory process to increase transparency, promote greater understanding of the industry by regulators, and establish official rapid-response mechanisms for regulatory challenges.

Common Lessons and Potential for Replication in Other Countries

- The quality of regulation and institutions is one of the main components for expanding and upgrading the services sector. Transparency, streamlined processes, predictability, and reliability are key features of an attractive business environment. Clear and enforceable competition rules can reduce distortions and the abuse of dominance in the services sector (such as telecoms). Moreover, tighter regulatory cooperation between countries in the region can reduce any one nation's regulatory burden through mutually beneficial trade facilitation measures.
- Deeper regional integration can expand and increase value added of services. Stronger integration generates larger labor, consumer, and producer markets, increasing domestic expertise and allowing for the expansion of services to regional markets.

Current Conditions and Challenges

Changes in technology have increased the tradability of services in recent years. IT allows services to be digitized, facilitating storability and transmission across borders and reducing the need for producers to be near consumers. IT-enabled services refer to individual business processes that can be delocated and delivered through digital means. A firm can identify and separate these services from its main business line and source it from another firm specialized in such activities. (Outsourcing refers to the acquisition of such services from another, locally established firm, while offshoring points to services traded internationally.)

Two services play a central role in the entry and upgrading in the offshoring market: telecom connectivity and education services. Based on a review of the cost structure of offshoring services firms, Sudan et al. (2010) observe that the existence of competitive telecom markets, especially for broadband, and the availability of employee skills are the most important factor in the growth of the IT-enabled services sector. The costs of basic offshoring services suggest that skills and infrastructure account for around 60 percent of the primary costs of operations.

The unbundling of business processing to an increasing differentiation of goods and, especially, services, also affects electronic manufacturing. The electronics global value chain (GVC) consists of raw materials and inputs to electronic components, electronic components themselves, subassemblies, final product assembly for a variety of end market segments, and the ultimate buyers of final products. Complementing the manufacturing process are services related to research, product and process development, design, marketing and aftersales services that add value to the final product. These services, particularly those linked to research and development (R&D), are those that support the main value-adding activities in the value chain, such as new product development, circuitry and semiconductor design, software integration, and product architecture development (Frederick and Gereffi 2013).

Vietnam is at an early stage of maturity in its contribution to the electronics value chain, which leaves ample room for adding value. The technological level of a nation can be evaluated on the basis of many elements such as total expenditure on R&D, creativity in science and technology, and the system of technological development. Sturgeon and Kawakami (2010) identify four channels used by developing-country firms to upgrade their position in the electronics GVC: acquiring global brands; developing own-branded products separately from contract manufacturing businesses, so as to avoid competing directly with their own clients; developing own brands from contract manufacturing, where the clients is not involved in retailing hardware; and developing factory-less startups, which rely on existing design and manufacturing firms for production.

Most business services in Vietnam that serve as inputs in the value chain usually are unregulated, and are affected mainly by horizontal laws and regulations, institutions, and procedures, that is, those that broadly affect all services sectors.

Services in telecoms, finance, the professions, and transport are key backbone services usually covered by a specific sectoral regulation and often their own regulatory body. Business-oriented services, like business process outsourcing (BPO) and IT-enabled services, technical testing and analysis, and R&D, are not usually the focus of sectoral regulation, but are covered by general laws related to business regulation. These latter activities are often linked to foreign participation not only in terms of invested capital, but also the need to attract skills and access knowledge from abroad through, for example, patents or partnerships with foreign institutions. Thus these business-oriented, high value-added services tend to be sensitive to domestic regulations and practices that affect the establishment and operation of foreign investments, and to measures that regulate the movement of capital and skills across borders. Examples of such horizontal laws and regulations are now discussed.

A Restrictive Foreign Investment Regulatory Environment
Foreign Investment Laws

Laws on foreign investment can restrict Vietnam's ICT services growth unnecessarily. Manufacturing remains the primary draw for foreign investors, accounting for 70 percent of registered FDI. International investors are attracted by Vietnam's political stability, competitive wages, a relatively skilled (for labor-intensive manufacturing) and disciplined workforce, and proximity to Chinese supply chains (World Bank 2014b). However, foreign participation in some service companies is capped by law or regulation, at 49 percent or 65 percent for example in some telecoms services. In addition, while foreign investors are allowed to buy shares in many domestic companies without facing restrictions, ownership limitations apply to some companies: foreign ownership cannot exceed 49 percent of companies listed on the Vietnam stock exchange and 30 percent of listed companies in the financial sector, for example. Individual foreign investors usually are limited to 15 percent ownership, though a single foreign investor may increase ownership to 20 percent through a strategic alliance with a local partner (EIU 2014).

Vietnam's licensing regime is influenced by a planned economy approach (UNCTAD 2008). All foreign investment projects must be formally approved by the administration under a certification procedure that entails judging whether a proposed investment is in Vietnam's interest, even if it falls within the parameters of sector, size, and permitted level of foreign ownership. Rules and conditions for certification of the investment vary depending on the size of investment and whether it is has majority participation of foreign capital (figure 10.1). The information requested for investment registration is partly for statistical purposes, but also for the authorities to make a full evaluation and assess whether it fits into the regional or national development policy—the Master Plans. The latter requirement is quite open-ended and potentially a hurdle to foreign or domestic private investors. Master Plans are detailed and numerous, and can potentially be used to refuse the issuance of an investment certificate for otherwise valid projects (UNCTAD 2008).

Figure 10.1 Investment Certification Requirements

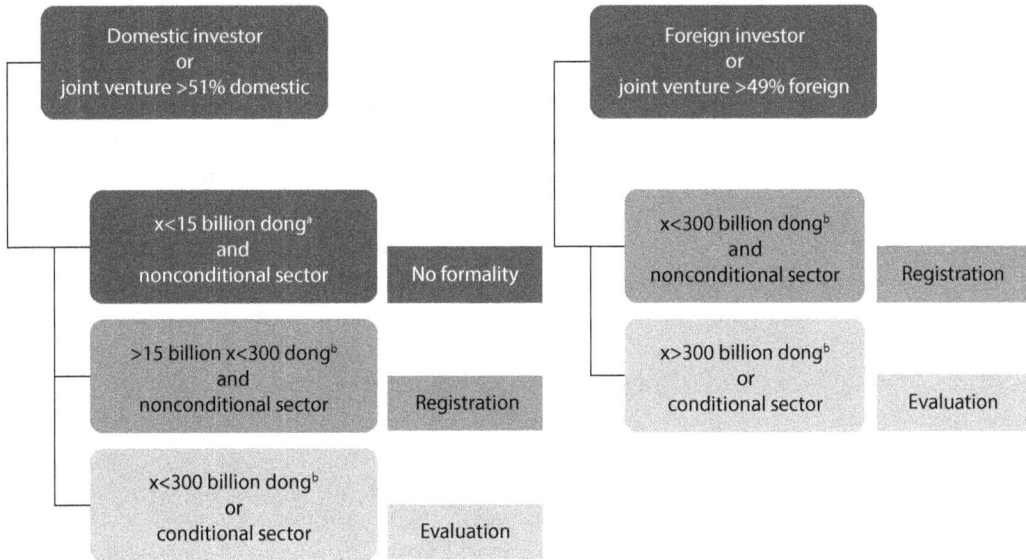

Source: UNCTAD 2008.
a. $938,000.
b. $19 million.

Procedures to obtain investment certification tend to be complex and lengthy. Investment may require approval from several ministries or agencies (or both), depending on ownership (foreign or domestic), size, and sector. Investments in conditional sectors (which means that screening procedures are in place), such as broadcasting, mining, telecoms, banking and finance, ports and airports, and education are subject to a more complex licensing process (US Commercial Services 2014). It may take 30–45 days to obtain an investment certificate and even longer—up to six months—to get an amendment to the certificate approved. These delays often relate to the need for the Ministry of Planning and Investment to obtain the opinions of various government agencies for certain projects (EIU 2014).

The complexity of the procedure makes the assistance of a local expert (Vietnamese or foreign) extremely useful in seeking investment approval. Lack of in-country experience can result in drawbacks like the choice of the wrong partner, acceptance of verbal promises at face value, escalation of costs after signing a contract, or misunderstandings with local authorities (EIU 2014).

The government is aware of these shortcomings and has taken some important measures to address matters. In 2014, it issued Resolution 19 (March 18), which prioritizes shortening the time for processing and completion of administrative procedures, reducing administrative costs, and strengthening transparency and accountability of state administrative agencies. The revised Law on Bankruptcy, passed in July 2014, was another effort to improve the legal framework for businesses. The Enterprise Law and the Investment Law, expected to improve corporate governance in enterprises and SOEs in particular, were approved by the National Assembly in November 2014 (World Bank 2014b).

While the Investment Law and Enterprise Law generally set out an invest-ment-friendly regulatory environment, they maintain important formal and informal restrictions including, on the formal side, the 49 percent limit to foreign participation in listed Vietnamese companies, which is one of the main hurdles (EuroCham 2015). Informal limitations could be addressed through more trans-parent and streamlined procedures for investment registration and certification. In particular, greater clarity in the criteria for approval of conditional investments would bring needed transparency to the system. In addition, the establishment of a one-stop shop for business registration and investment licensing could help address inconsistencies and uncoordinated implementation of laws and regula-tions by government agencies (WTO Secretariat 2013).

Competition Policy

Competition policy lacks clarity and suffers from weak enforcement capacity, though competition regulation moved a step forward when the Law on Competition came into force in 2004. Notably, the law prohibits enterprises with significant market power from taking measures that would limit competition. The law also grants the competition authorities (the Viet Nam Competition Administration Department and the Viet Nam Competition Council) the ability to monitor prices set out by companies that, alone or as a member of a group, could be in a dominant position in a market. These companies must submit any proposal to change the retail tariff to the Ministry of Information and Communication (MIC) before issuing the tariff.

Some commentators have noted that the law lacks clarity in the tasks and jurisdictions between the MIC and the competition authorities (Lee 2011). The resulting gaps result in limited independence of these authorities and weak capacity to enforce competition rules, particularly when they involve state-owned companies (Long and Walker 2012).

The government should seek to reduce distortions in competition and the abuse of dominance in the services sector, such as telecoms, through clear policy guide-lines and a strong independent competition institution (Long and Walker 2012).

Currency Exchange and Fund Transfers

Foreign exchange regulations may also impede foreign investment. The Investment Law and other foreign exchange regulations set out provisions on remitting for-eign currencies earned by foreign firms on their investment in Vietnam as invest-ment protection. Foreign investors, subject to meeting their tax and other financial obligations to the government, are allowed to purchase foreign curren-cies from licensed credit institutions to meet their noncapital transactions and other permitted transactions (such as repayment of offshore loans and remittance of dividends abroad). The law sets out a broad range of permitted transactions. The banks are in charge of foreign exchange compliance and will guide customers. As long as the proper documentation is provided to the bank, including proof of the source of the funds, offshore remittances are not a problem. There is no prof-its remittance tax (Mayer Brown 2013).

Access to Dispute Settlement

Conditions for dispute resolution and enforcement of rights are a weak link in the regulatory and institutional framework. Commercial and economic disputes are settled by the courts pursuant to the 2004 Civil Procedure Code and the Law on Enforcement of Civil Judgments of November 14, 2008. The time limit for initiating a lawsuit is two years from the date of infringement. The first instance court's decision may be appealed to the next level within 15 days of the publica-tion of the judgment. The settlement of economic disputes by arbitration is governed by the Law on Commercial Arbitration of June 17, 2010 (WTO Secretariat 2013).

Although substantial progress has been made in the commercial judicial system in the last 20 years, much remains to be done on courts' transparency and effi-ciency. Foreign investors tend to avoid settling business disputes in the Vietnamese court system and often in their contracts provide for disputes to be settled through arbitration, often in Singapore. The main reasons why foreign investors avoid Vietnamese courts seem to relate to judges' independence (Eurocham 2015) and to challenges and delays in enforcement (Mayer Brown 2013).

Weak Telecommunications Infrastructure

A solid telecoms infrastructure is key for attaining economic competitiveness and necessary for increasing value added. Offshoring services rely on telecoms as a means of delivery, especially as value chains are increasingly divided into tasks that can be performed in different locations, entailing fluid coordination and heavy load-sharing of digital information.

While consumer-oriented telecoms have expanded in recent years, business-grade infrastructure needs further strengthening. Telecoms services as inputs to other industries, in particular ICT, need reliability to ensure constant communi-cation, and speed to support the transmission of massive amounts of data, often in real time. But broadband speeds in Vietnam have been increasing more slowly than in similar countries in the region. Other indicators, such as the availability of secure Internet servers, also suggest that telecoms services oriented to other businesses lag in Vietnam.

Weak independence of Vietnam's telecoms regulatory body stifles efficient market development, service prices, and foreign and domestic firm participa-tion. The MIC is the sector's policymaking and regulatory body. Among other things it sets consumer tariffs for telecoms services and interconnection charges between operators. There is no independent regulatory authority (WTO Secretariat 2013). The government retains control over fixed telephone service charges but operators have the freedom to determine retail tariffs for other services. Yet for important services, such as mobile services and the Internet, operators need to pre register their proposed tariffs with the MIC before apply-ing the charges (Lee 2011). In this way, the MIC controls the retail tariff of significant market power operators in each segment, such as the Vietnam Posts and Telecommunications Group (VNPT) and Viettel. All other operators set their own retail tariff based on market forces, but the MIC decides on the basic and important interconnection charges. In 2010, for instance the MIC required all mobile service providers to apply no more than a 15 percent discount (WTO Secretariat 2013).

The 2009 Law on Telecommunications and Radio Frequency, which entered into force in July 2010, constitutes a framework for telecoms regulations and marks the first time that such regulations were combined in a single comprehensive law. It contains provisions for a pro-competition regulatory regime, covering abuse of market power regulation, interconnection rules, and access to essential facilities; it is expected to open up potential new opportunities for trade and investment by foreign firms and control the aggressive promotional campaigns by mobile operators (WTO Secretariat 2013).

The law has many regulatory items to be developed by implementation rules and regulations in the future. For example, it divides telecoms services into two categories—basic and value-added—without defining the scope of each. It also offers a legal basis for foreign and domestic investors to participate in the sector. Specifically, Article 18 stipulates that the forms and conditions for investment in telecoms services applicable to foreign investors must comply with Vietnamese laws and Vietnam's WTO commitments, without further specifying the maximum foreign investment ceilings for each of the service categories (Lee 2011).

Decree 25 provides the minimum capital requirements and investment commitments needed to offer telecoms services. In addition to the basic licenses required by telecoms legislation, foreign investors who intend to provide telecoms services must first obtain an investment certificate issued by the licensing authorities. If the project is not covered by a plan approved by the prime minister, the licensing authority must seek opinions on the project from the Ministry of Planning and Investment, the MIC, and any other relevant organizations. They must then request that the prime minister render a decision on the investment policy, adjust the national plan, or open the investment market further to foreign investment (Russin and Vecchi 2013).

Limitations on foreign ownership apply to telecoms companies, as set out in Vietnam's WTO commitments. On its accession to WTO in January 2007, Vietnam made commitments in certain areas (Russin and Vecchi 2013):

- *Facilities-based telecoms services:* Joint ventures with telecoms service suppliers licensed in Vietnam are allowed. Foreign investors may hold a maximum stake of 49 percent of legal capital.
- *Non–facilities-based telecoms services:* Joint ventures with telecoms service suppliers licensed in Vietnam are allowed. Foreign investors may hold a maximum stake of 51 percent of the legal capital of a joint venture. Beginning January 2010, three years after accession, joint ventures have been allowed without any restrictions on choice of partners. The stake of foreign investors, however,

may not exceed 65 percent of legal capital. For virtual private networks and value-added services (except Internet access services), joint ventures have been allowed since accession, but foreign participation may not exceed 70 percent of legal capital. To obtain majority control, approval is required.

Despite Vietnam's success in telecoms structural reform, the expansion and increased quality of the telecoms infrastructure remains a priority to ensure good services to ICT industries, as does a stronger regulatory body independent from the market operators and policymaking institutions (Lee 2011; WTO Secretariat 2013).

Poor Availability of Skills

Availability of skills and talent is a key determinant of innovation-related industries, including IT industries. IT-enabled services, as well as services that serve the electronics industry, depend critically on skills related to engineering and informatics. Professional skills are critical in supporting the development of local firms and in attracting foreign investment. Accounting, for example, generates information on the financial position and profitability of operations—essential for good financial management and accountability—providing the foundation of a country's fiscal system and playing a key role in corporate governance (Trolliet and Hegarty 2003). In recent years, the government has adopted policies to strengthen education. Updated curricula and a focus on education have led to a literacy rate above 98 percent, and results from the Programme for International Student Assessment are comparable to some high-income countries (Bodewig et al. 2014).

An open regulatory framework for movement of persons can support skills development. By attracting qualified personnel, Vietnam can help bridge the current gap in technical and managerial talent. Foreign experts would also help increase spillovers into domestic capacity, particularly in professional services or other highly specialized technical positions.

Restrictions on labor movement may be limiting skills attraction and development in Vietnam. The country's labor market-needs test, which permits the hiring of foreigners only to those areas where no comparator domestic skills exist, while restrictive, is found in some countries at all levels of development. The condition is inherently discretionary and leaves ample space for the authorities to decide whether domestic skills exist. In an effort to attract skills, the government should apply this test conservatively, allowing in a greater number and diversity of experts. Even more, the government may consider implementing a skills attraction program for areas of interest, in particular for business services.

In accordance to the Labor Code and implementing regulations, foreigners must obtain a work permit to be employed in Vietnam. While this principle is also common practice, in Vietnam the rule applies to foreigners in the country, regardless of the intended duration, and so captures, for example, intracorporate transferees coming for just a few days or those on training or conducting maintenance. This entails an additional cost and does not bring major benefits (Eurocham 2015).

ASEAN's seven mutual recognition agreements (MRAs) should be prioritized to coordinate mobility of professionals among party nations. The MRAs offer mutual recognition of authorization, licensing, or certification. The agreements on architecture and engineering are perhaps the most advanced, drawing on internationally recognized standards, and provide for the recognition of titles from any ASEAN country and the creation of an ASEAN registry. ASEAN MRAs can help Vietnam attract professionals and incentivize domestic students to continue into higher education.

Concrete Actions

Integrating Regionally

Regional integration is important for expanding and upgrading services. A recent study by the ASEAN Secretariat and the World Bank finds that regional trade in services lags well behind potential, and below that with non-ASEAN countries. Further, ASEAN members are exporting primarily traditional services such as transportation and travel/tourism, and have been generally less successful in tapping into the new services opportunities such as IT and business-related services. The ASEAN Economic Community offers a market of more than 600 million people and $2.3 trillion GDP. Services integration would foster competition and productivity given its size and the need for intermediate services for manufacturing (ASEC and World Bank, forthcoming), and is particularly relevant for Vietnam, as a middle-income economy wanting to increase local value added in goods and services.

One of the main reason for the generally disappointing services trade performance and integration in ASEAN is the lack of services market openness and the presence of regulatory barriers. Regulatory regimes in most ASEAN members are more restrictive than in comparator countries outside Asia, and only minor progress has been made in reducing restrictiveness since the adoption of the ASEAN Economic Community Blueprint in November 2007.

Thus a true single market remains a distant goal. And even removing quantitative and discriminatory limitations or formal restrictions will not be enough for regional services integration due to regulatory restrictions that fall outside current negotiations. Thus far the region has focused on eliminating formal barriers to trade and investment in services, but ASEAN countries have done little to complement the reduction of formal barriers with positive actions such as coordinated regulatory policies in services. Still, to expand its services market and integrate further in the region, advancing regulatory cooperation within ASEAN remains a priority for Vietnam.

Strengthening Regulatory Cooperation

Regulatory cooperation may be more important for ASEAN countries than nonmembers because of their uneven quality of regulations. For all ASEAN members except Singapore, regulatory weaknesses have remained since the entry into force in 1995 of the ASEAN Framework Agreement on Services, especially among low-income members, despite some regulatory improvements.

The empirical literature identifies regulatory heterogeneity as a significant impediment to trade. Kox and Lejour (2005), for example, find a negative and significant effect of the level of regulations, as well as heterogeneity, on services trade. Kox, Lejour, and Montizaan (2005) find that such heterogeneity hampers bilateral service trade in the EU, as well as bilateral direct investment. They also assess the impact of the EU services directive on lowering the intra-EU heterogeneity in product market regulation for services, and its effect on bilateral trade and investment in the internal market for services. They find that commercial services trade in the EU could increase by 30–60 percent and foreign direct investment stock in services by 20–35 percent. These findings point to the huge benefits of harmonizing regulations.

Regional trade agreements are also an opportunity to build optimal regulatory areas for services. Such areas are composed of a set of countries whose welfare can potentially be maximized by regulatory convergence (Mattoo and Sauvé 2011). An optimal regulatory area implies not only regulatory convergence, but the adoption of similar regulatory principles to enhance regulatory governance. In this context, the optimal regulatory area would imply cooperation in three areas:

- Regulatory convergence, through harmonization or mutual recognition.
- Convergence of regulatory principles, in particular regarding the design, adoption, and application of regulations.
- Convergence of regulatory capacity, which includes cooperation among regulatory bodies, exchanging information for regulatory purposes and experiences on regulatory reforms and identifying and adopting good regulatory practices in new areas.

In ASEAN, one example of services integration to be pursued through regulatory cooperation is company law. Following the EU experience, ASEAN member states should evaluate the basic requirements for setting up companies, including areas like compulsory disclosure of information, and power of representation of company organs. Requirements on disclosure, in particular, may include the harmonization of information requirements and the establishment of an official company register accessible by all member states. Another example is harmonizing disclosure requirements for capital markets so as to facilitate capital flows. Work has already started in providing common guidelines and standards.

Key Outcomes

In the last two decades, Vietnam has made strides in all three major areas considered—regulatory and institutional framework, telecommunications infrastructure, and skills availability. However, complementary measures are needed:

- In the business environment, procedures for domestic and foreign firms, such as company registration, licensing, and mergers and acquisitions, need more transparency and streamlining, especially in dispute resolution and enforcement of court and arbitration decisions.

- The telecoms sector would benefit from greater capacity and transparency, removal of caps to foreign participation, and a stronger competition framework to ensure a level playing field among all operators.
- Vietnam should push to implement ASEAN's MRAs, in particular for the architecture, engineering, accounting, and medical professions.
- The government should strive to advance the removal of the remaining formal restrictions to trade and investment in services among ASEAN partners, such as foreign equity limits, and to enhance regulatory cooperation in services.

Bibliography

Akamai. 2014. *Akamai's State of the Internet Report*. http://www.akamai.com/stateofthe internet/index.html?WT.mc_id=soti_banner.

ASEC and World Bank. Forthcoming. *ASEAN Services Integration Report: A Joint Report by the ASEAN Secretariat and the World Bank*. Washington, DC.

Baldwin, Richard. 2012. "Global Supply Chains: Why They Emerged, Why They Matter, and Where They Are Going?" CEPR Discussion Paper 9103, Center for Economic Policy and Research, Washington, DC.

Bodewig, Christian, Reena Badiani -Magnusson, Kevin Macdonald, David Newhouse, and Jan Rutkowski. 2014. *Skilling Up Vietnam: Preparing the Workforce for a Modern Market Economy*. Directions in Development. Washington, DC: World Bank.

Cattaneo, Olivier, G. Gereffi, S. Miroudot, and D. Taglioni, 2013. "Joining, Upgrading, and Being Competitive in Global Value Chains: A Strategic Framework." Policy Research Working Paper Series 6406, World Bank, Washington, DC.

Cattaneo, Olivier, and Peter Walkerhorst. 2012. "Legal Services: Does More Trade Rhyme with Better Justice?" In *Exporting Services: A Developing Country Perspective*, edited by Arti Grover Goswami, Aaditya Mattoo, and Sebastián Sáez. Washington, DC: World Bank.

EIU (Economist Intelligence Unit). 2014. *Industry Report: Telecommunications*. London.

Eurocham. 2015. "Whitebook 2015: Trade/Investment Issues and Recommendations." European Chamber of Commerce in Vietnam. www.eurochamvn.org.

Frederick, Stacy, and Gary Gereffi. 2013. "Costa Rica in the Electronics Global Value Chain Opportunities for Upgrading." Center on Globalization, Governance and Competitiveness, Duke University.

Gereffi, Gary, and Karina Fernandez-Stark. 2010a. "The Offshore Services Industry: A Global Value Chain Approach." Center on Globalization Governance and Competitiveness at Duke University Durham, NC.

———. 2010b. "Chile's Offshore Services Value Chain." Center on Globalization Governance and Competitiveness at Duke University, Durham, NC.

Goswami, Arti Grover, Aaditya Mattoo, and Sebastián Sáez. 2012. *Exporting Services: A Developing Country Perspective*. Washington, DC: World Bank.

Humphrey, John, and Hubert Schmitz. 2002. "How Does Insertion in Global Value Chains Affect Upgrading in Industrial Clusters?" *Regional Studies* 36 (9): 1017–27.

Kox, Henk, and Anne Lejour. 2005. "Regulatory Heterogeneity as an Obstacle for International Services Trade." CPB Discussion Paper 49, CPB Netherlands Bureau for Economic Policy Analysis, The Hague.

Kox, Henk, A. Lejour, and R. Montizaan. 2005. "The Free Movement of Services within the EU." CPB Document 69, CPB Netherlands Bureau for Economic Policy Analysis, The Hague. http://www.cpb.nl/eng/pub/cpbreeksen/document/69/doc69.pdf.

Lee, Roy Chun. 2011. "Telecommunications in Viet Nam." APEC document 2011/SOM2/SYM/012.

Mayer Brown. 2013. *Guide to Doing Business in Vietnam.* https://www.mayerbrown.com/files/Publication/d50296ec-1a78-426f-bb80-19f26d82e709/Presentation/PublicationAttachment/a733e0f7-4d69-4032-aa19-662ebda028c1/GuideToDoingBusinessInVietnam.pdf.

Long, Tran Thang, and Gordon Walker. 2012. "Abuse of Market Dominance by State Monopolies in Vietnam." *Houston Journal of International Law* 34 (2).

Mattoo, Aaditya, and Pierre Sauvé. 2003. "Domestic Regulation and Trade in Services: Key Issues." In *Domestic Regulation and Service Trade Liberalization*, edited by Aaditya Mattoo and Pierre Sauvé. Washington, DC: World Bank.

MIC (Ministry of Information and Communications). 2011. *Viet Nam Information and Communication Technology.* MIC.

Russin and Vecchi. 2004. *Setting Up an Operation in Vietnam.* Hanoi and Ho Chi Minh City: Russin and Vecchi.

———. 2013. *Telecommunications in Vietnam.* Hanoi and Ho Chi Minh City: Russin and Vecchi.

Sturgeon, Timothy, and Momoko Kawakami. 2010. "Global Value Chains in the Electronics Industry: Was the Crisis a Window of Opportunity for Developing Countries?" Policy Research Working Paper, World Bank, Washington, DC.

Sturgeon, Timothy, and Olga Memedovic. 2011. "Mapping Global Value Chains: Intermediate Goods Trade and Structural Change in the World Economy." Working Paper 05/2010. United Nations Industrial Development Organization, Development Policy and Strategic Research Branch, Vienna.

Sudan, Randeep, Seth Ayers, Philippe Dongier, Arturo Muente-Kunigami, and Christine Zhen-Wei Qiang. 2010. *The Global Opportunity in IT-Based Services: Assessing and Enhancing Country Competitiveness.* Washington, DC: World Bank.

Trolliet, C., and J. Hegarty. 2003. "Regulatory Reform and Trade Liberalization in Accountancy Services." In *Domestic Regulation and Services Trade Liberalization*, edited by A. Mattoo and P. Sauve. Washington, DC: World Bank and Oxford University Press.

UNCTAD (United Nations Conference on Trade and Development). 2008. "Investment Policy Review Viet Nam." New York and Geneva: UNCTAD.

US Commercial Services. 2014. "Vietnam Market for Telecommunications Equipment and Services." http://2016.export.gov/vietnam/build/groups/public/@eg_vn/documents/webcontent/eg_vn_076819.pdf.

World Bank. 2014a. *The Little Data Book on Information and Communication Technology 2014.* Washington, DC: World Bank.

———. 2014b. *Taking Stock: An Update on Vietnam's Recent Economic Development.* Washington, DC: World Bank. http://documents.worldbank.org/curated/en/2014/07/19791861/taking-stock-update-vietnams-recent-economic-development.

WTO Secretariat. 2013. "Trade Policy Review: Vietnam." WTO Document WT/TPR/S/287/Rev.1. Geneva.

CHAPTER 11

Vietnam in the ASEAN Motor Vehicle Industry

Guillermo Arenas with contributions from Timothy Sturgeon

Key Takeaways

The automobile industry in Vietnam is small and underdeveloped by regional standards: its size in terms of unit sales is one-fiftieth of Thailand's and less than one-twentieth of Indonesia's. The assembly segment is heavily reliant on imported parts and focused on serving the domestic market, given the high cost of competing regionally. The domestic market is, however, severely constrained by high population densities, sparse road networks, and current traffic congestion (largely motorcycles).

Market upgrading requires demand- and supply-side approaches. On the demand side, a shift is required from mobility of vehicles to mobility of people. The government should invest in road infrastructure and simultaneously in public transport to create a networked, multimodal urban mobility system, which will require multiple components to design, operate, and monitor the system. On the supply side, efforts should be concentrated on producing two-wheelers for the domestic and regional markets, with the ultimate aim to upgrade through servicification (the role of services, not only as inputs into the economy but as a mean of changing the way value is created).

Challenges Confronted

The stage of development of Vietnam's motor vehicle industry varies across the three most important segments: two-wheelers, passenger cars, and commercial vehicles. The two-wheeler industry is well developed and has a very strong supplier base. About 90 percent of value added in this segment is domestic, with only some of the most advanced electronic components imported from Japan or Thailand. The added value in passenger cars is seen at several stages: welding, painting, and attaching bulky items or low value-added parts fit for local sourcing. Buses and trucks have a higher local content, with 30 percent of engines, gearboxes, and transmission systems, and 70 percent of electrical components, produced domestically. Truck frames and trunks are all domestically produced.

Vietnam's cities, including its largest cities, still have relatively good mobility, due in large part to the predominance of motorcycles as the main mode of transportation. However, high population densities and sparse road networks in large cities like Ho Chi Minh City and Hanoi are simply incompatible with adoption of private cars as a major means of transport. One of these cities' main challenges is already traffic congestion and impaired mobility. The annual economic costs of road traffic congestion were recently put at $272 million for Bangkok, $68 million for Jakarta, and $51 million for Manila (2.1 percent, 0.9 percent, and 0.7 percent of GDP) (Dahiya 2015). The key issue is how to enable mobility without worsening traffic congestion and pollution problems

Vietnam has two main options:

- Focus on maximizing gains achieved from domestic value-added activities within the motor vehicle segments (product and process upgrading). This approach is a traditional global value chain strategy for development but is constrained by domestic demand and regional producer competitiveness. Efforts should be concentrated on two-wheelers for both the domestic and regional markets with the aim of eventual servicification.
- Enhance transport infrastructure including investment in public transport systems. This approach would expand the need for related services, creating new jobs, while alleviating environmental, densification, and congestion pressures. It would create new opportunities for moving large groups of people, quickly, freeing road space for commercial and remaining vehicle traffic.

Solutions Proposed
No city in Vietnam has a well-functioning urban transport system and even regular bus services are heavily underdeveloped in Ho Chi Minh City and Hanoi. In the short to medium term, this chapter suggests that motorcycles should not be neglected, as an effective means of urban transport, while car use should be discouraged by accurately passing on its costs, including social costs such as congestion, to car drivers. In the longer term—the timescale for construction of new transport infrastructure—Vietnam should prepare for motorization by investing in metropolitan urban infrastructure and urban transport systems.

Investing in knowledge, capacity, and management is also vital. Institutional fragmentation abounds in the sector and should be an area of focus, as should integrating transport and land use planning and development.

Lessons to Be Learned
The automobile is just one element of a mobility system—an element governed by extensive regulations, constrained by the need for fuel and dependent on a network of roadways and parking spaces. There is considerable sector development opportunity in pursuing infrastructure upgrades, public transit systems, mobility connectivity, and advances in manufacturing technology, such as robotics.

This chapter suggests the following interconnected roles for private firms and the public sector:

- Private manufacturing firms and service providers can deepen market integration at higher value-added stages. Manufacturing firms shift labor from low-skilled activities to more service-like tasks such as design and prototyping. This would require them to take advantage of advanced manufacturing techniques like robotics and additive manufacturing, while ensuring any unproductive labor loss is offset by capacity development in design and engineering.
- The public sector can support private firms by itself investing in—or incentivizing investment by private firms, universities, and trade schools—in research and development (R&D) of mobile connectivity and new manufacturing technologies. In addition, land use planning and transport development should be more closely integrated, aimed at alleviating environmental issues, densification, and traffic congestion.

Common Lessons and Potential for Replication in Other Countries

Developing countries facing the same auto sector challenges as Vietnam can similarly pursue higher value-added activities in vehicle development, alongside improvements in transport infrastructure and public transit. Replicable lessons include:

- Expanding industrial policy beyond product-centric models presents new opportunities in sector value addition. By focusing on mobility of people rather than of vehicles, new opportunities in infrastructure development, sector servicification, and public transit networks open up. This approach can be replicated in many developing countries that face the same urban transport issues as Vietnam. Encouraging innovation in technologies and the integration of third party software into government-run transport services provides opportunities for efficiency, growth, and exports. There are also three wider lessons, however, from this solution.

- Effective industrial policy requires a change of approach. To start with, it requires a move from sectors to tasks and competencies of comparative advantage. Then it requires policymakers to identify whether specific regulatory barriers hinder the full potential in these tasks and competencies. It also suggests prioritizing the development of skills and technologies that can be redeployed to other sectors, and the financing of public goods in education and infrastructure that are informed by a forward approach to development in technology and emerging business models. And support to creating local markets, particularly for services, and to clustering firms in a well-integrated ecosystem, may support upgrading and leapfrogging in GVCs. This alternative approach to industrial policy is likely to be less expensive than traditional approaches.

- A country's biggest problems can be the biggest source of comparative advantage. Managing domestic urban mobility problems through solutions that are innovative and informed by the latest advances in technology, Vietnam can gather valuable expertise and skills that can be deployed in any country with similar issues. It can also create a domestic market for goods (small commercial vehicles and buses) that have favorable export prospects.

- Support to data and information gathering, and use of open-source systems, can contribute to upgrading and leapfrogging. Data and information are important assets nowadays, as most industries evolve toward an ever-more intensive use of big data infrastructure and content. Interesting datasets and open source information and communications technology (ICT) systems allow a sector to attract the best technology, skills, and leading expertise and a country to identify problems and simulate effects of alternative remedies. These can create innovative solutions that can become a source of comparative advantage and support exports of high value-added services, goods, and technology.

Current Conditions and Challenges

Domestic Tier 1 and 2 Suppliers

Vietnam has about 200–300 auto part manufacturing enterprises, most of which are small and medium enterprises (SMEs) with low production capacity and low technology. The number is just one-fifth of that in Indonesia and one-fiftieth of that in Thailand.

Although some simple and labor-intensive parts like seats have been localized, original equipment manufacturers depend on imports for the majority of their parts and components. Although multinational companies in the automotive sector entered the market nearly two decades ago, the most important parts, such as engines and gearboxes, are still imported from branches of parent companies or from foreign suppliers.

With an underdeveloped local supply base, localization levels are very low with some sources putting local content use at around 10–20 percent. In comparison, local parts used in the dominant light pickup industry in Thailand average 80 percent, passenger cars 45 percent, and motorcycles 90 percent. Without a major parts industry, car production costs are higher than elsewhere in the region because of taxes on imported components.

Employment, Wages, and Human Resource Requirements

This chapter proposes the deployment of intelligent transportation systems (ITS) and shared-use mobility to reach a double goal of helping Vietnam upgrade its participation in the motor vehicle GVC and open opportunities in new target sectors (ICT); and improve urban mobility in Vietnam. The proposal would lead to technological, skills, and environmental upgrading, and requires a shift in emphasis to a different market segment in the auto sector, one that has the potential for fostering functional and intersectoral upgrading. Such a shift, however, will come with new human resource requirements and demands for training to produce a highly skilled labor force that eventually can be redeployed to other sectors of the economy.

The skills acquired in the conception, development, and implementation of software transport solutions and those possibly originating from new opportunities for ancillary services can be redeployed to provide solutions to industries such as logistics, transport, tourism, and health care. The expertise gathered by Vietnam's firms in establishing and managing a modern system of urban mobility can become the basis for exporting services of urban mobility management internationally.

The added value in the passenger car segment is currently in labor-intensive stages like assembly, welding, painting, and attaching bulky items or low value-added parts fit for local sourcing, such as tires, batteries, and wire harnesses. The average compensation for the main tasks in which Vietnam specializes is among the lowest in the auto sector.

Tax Policies

Import duty on passenger cars is high but was reduced from 60 percent to 50 percent in 2014. Under the Association of Southeast Asian Nations (ASEAN) Free Trade Area (AFTA) all tariff on fully assembled cars imported into Vietnam from other ASEAN countries will be eliminated by 2018. However, it is still to be determined to what extent the ASEAN auto trade will be completely liberalized after that date. Countries like Malaysia have been able to protect their domestic markets with the use of strict import licensing, special domestic tax rebates for preferred national brands, and other measures that go beyond custom tariffs.

The local industry imports most components, which are subject to a tariff of 20 percent. Automakers operating locally must be able to compete with Thailand, where many vehicles are made in free-trade zones and parts are sourced locally or imported without duties.

Besides high import tariffs, Vietnam imposes high taxes on automobiles: special consumption tax of 45–60 percent, value-added tax (VAT) of 10 percent, and locally imposed registration fees of 2–10 percent (table 11.1). The special consumption tax applies different rates of tax according to engine size and the

Table 11.1 Domestic Tax Percentage for Automobiles by Capacity, 2014

	1–9 Seats	10–15 Seats	Others (trucks, buses)
Special consumption tax	45–60	30	15
Less than 2,000 cc	45	–	–
2,000–3,000 cc	50	–	–
More than 3,000 cc	60	–	–
VAT	10	10	10
Other	10–15	2	2
Registration fees	10–15	10–15	10–15

Source: IPSI 2015.

number of seats in vehicles, to encourage use of vehicles with smaller, less pollut-ing engines. The high taxes are also used to discourage car ownership.

The Ministry of Industry and Trade has submitted a proposal favoring multi-use cars that seat six to nine people with a cylinder capacity of less than 1.5 liters, and meeting EU emission standards, to be main product of Vietnam's automotive industry. The special consumption tax for this type of car has been reduced to 30 percent, with a 2 percent registration fee and 5 percent VAT.[1]

Air Pollution

A report from the Ministry of Environment and Natural Resource shows that most big cities in Vietnam are facing worsening air pollution (Vietnam Investment Review 2014). For several years, the air quality in Hanoi has been poor 4 days out of 10 and vehicular traffic has been responsible for 70 percent of air pollution nationally. Statistics from the Ministry of Transport show that 2.5 million patients spend an estimated $66.8 million a year for examinations and treatment for respi-ratory diseases in Hanoi, and 5.6 million patients spend $70.9 million a year for similar treatment in Ho Chi Minh City (Viet Nam News 2014).

Increased Urban Density

Ho Chi Minh City (9,450 people per km^2) is the 20th most densely populated city in the world. Private automobiles create major traffic congestion even when only a small proportion of the resident population own cars, lengthening com-muting times. The road space area in Hanoi is also small. In many neighborhoods, road space represents no more than about 20 percent of the total built-up area, at the average built-up density of Hanoi, this translates into a road area of 11 m^2 per person. Cars use a very large amount of road space for on-road parking and when moving (14 m^2 for a car parked on street and 40 m^2 for a car running at 30 km/hour) (World Bank 2011).

The current road network and the high density will be simply incompatible with the demand for road space created by a shift to individual cars for even a small fraction of the current trips made by motorcycles. For instance, at the cur-rent average Hanoi density (188 person/ha), a car ownership of 250 per 1,000 people (similar to the average for Malaysia but much less than in Kuala Lumpur) would require a vehicular street area occupying 19 percent of the total built-up area—practically the entire current street rights of way in Hanoi—just to allow half the cars owned to run at 30 km/h. As the centrally located districts have densities close to 400 p/ha, a car ownership of 250/1,000 would guarantee total gridlock in the central part of Hanoi (World Bank 2011).

Advances in Manufacturing Technology and Implications for Labor

Advances in manufacturing technology have the potential to erode the labor cost advantage that low-wage countries have in auto assembly. Advanced robotics, which create much more flexibility in the way automation can work in a factory, and additive manufacturing (3D printing) have the potential to reduce the demand for unskilled labor for some tasks, decisions about location, and more importantly, change were the value added is created (from pure manufacturing to more service-like task like design and prototyping).

The high precision, consistency, and ability to perform repeated task with little supervision allow car manufacturers to increase output levels, reduce production lead times and provide a consistent high quality of their products. Robots are frequently used in the automotive sector for welding, cutting, grinding, polishing, and painting. Some of the tasks currently done in Vietnam could easily be replaced by robotics, which will reduce the need for unskilled labor. For example, the Changan Ford factory in China has reached near complete automation of the body-in-white assembly process (KUKA Robotics 2014).

Concrete Actions

Sustainability

As the adverse consequences of climate change and higher pollution levels materialize, countries will introduce more restrictions on vehicle emissions, to which the auto industry could respond in three main ways: improve the efficiency of the internal combustion engine, increase the use of lightweight materials, and encourage a shift in the modes of transport, especially in dense urban areas.

Automakers are turning to smaller engines fitted with turbochargers and fuel injection systems that achieve better mileage without a loss of performance. They are hedging their bets by investing in several powertrains that include hybrids, battery electric vehicles, and fuel cell vehicles powered by hydrogen. At the moment none looks like the outright winner. By 2050, the world's car fleet is likely to be propelled by a broad mix of powertrains (The Economist 2013).

Increasing the use of lightweight materials (high strength steel, plastics, aluminum, and carbon fiber) is another approach. Different manufacturers are pursuing their own ways to reduce their cars' weight. Jaguar Land Rover is backing aluminum, BMW carbon-fiber composites, and Hyundai is working on replacing ordinary steel with smaller quantities of advanced high-strength steel. According to AlixPartners, the proportion of conventional steel in a typical car will fall from two-thirds today to about one-fifth in the future.

Finally, many urban areas around the world are introducing restrictions on the use of internal combustion engines in designated city zones while encouraging a shift to mass public transport systems as a more efficient and less polluting form of transport. In Bogota, Curitiba, and Santiago (Chile), the introduction of bus rapid transit systems have improved urban mobility while reducing emission by a wide margin. In Beijing, a driver wanting to purchase a vehicle with an internal combustion engine must first enter a lottery and may wait two years before receiving a license plate. Licenses are much easier to get for people who buy state-approved electric vehicles. In the future, vehicle-use restrictions are likely to grow more stringent as urbanization increases (McKinsey 2014).

From a user perspective, a shared-use mobility model would function to increase transport accessibility while reducing private ownership/use and related pollution levels. Shared-use mobility enables users to access transport on an as-needed basis and plays an important connection function in multimodal trips. This model has taken off in many countries thanks to private sector involvement; key to maximizing gains is first-to-market advantage in any particular jurisdiction.

Increased Connectivity

McKinsey (2014) estimates that the dramatic increase in vehicle connectivity will increase the value of the global market for connectivity components and services to €170 billion by 2020 from €30 billion while the total cost of ownership of vehicles will remain stable for consumers, which raise the relative importance of electronic components in the auto industry.

To develop the complex new connected vehicle, the auto industry will not only have to develop IT or hardware capabilities to allow connectivity but also software, content, and customization. Although the majority of this added value is connectivity hardware, this leaves a large market for apps, entertainment, and navigation software. Connectivity is already altering the competitive landscape: companies from the software and telecommunications sectors are already entering the automotive market, such as Google and Apple.

The key for the auto industry will be to look at the recurring revenues accruing from connectivity features, for example subscription fees or in-app purchases, subscription-based content, and services from in-car users that can be monetized. The new revenue and profit streams will create a niche for developing specialized software and services-based business models. For example, Amazon generates $41 in revenue per Kindle Fire tablet with advertising and services. Connectivity services and content—and the software development that enables it—will flourish as automobiles become more digitally enabled.

McKinsey (2014) estimates that after 2020 self-driving cars will trigger the next wave of disruption in the automotive industry. On average, semi-autonomous drive will free up one hour every day for drivers and, thus, further fuel connectivity-related business models, in particular with respect to media and content. When the demands of driving are lifted, when the interiors of vehicles may give automakers opportunities to generate revenue from the occupants' connectivity and car time.

Advances in Manufacturing Technology

As cars use more electronics, larger and more complex wire harnesses are needed for in-vehicle connectivity and Vietnam already produces some of this. The presence of Tier 1 suppliers like Yazaki, Sumi Hanel, and Sumidenso have extensive operation in the country, one area of focus for Vietnam would be the backward integration into drawn and coated wire and connectors. Another area would be to create local digital content and services for private and public transport.

Robotics and additive manufacturing are changing the composition of the industrial workforce. In the future, new technologies will generate job opportunities for engineers to work with advanced robots and robotic operation systems as well as programming and maintenance and repair. This should be viewed as an opportunity to move up to better paying jobs and upgrade skills. The net result (once accounting for certain losses) will be complex and vary by industry but nevertheless will create opportunities in other areas such as services, program, maintenance, and so on. In particular, service and maintenance for both robotics and AM machines is often an overlooked but promising field for Vietnam.

Robotics-intensive sectors demand more skilled workers and pay higher wages. According to an analysis based on data from the U.S. Bureau of Labor Statistics, manufacturing sectors with the highest robotic use—automotive, electronics, and metals—employ about 20 percent more mechanical and industrial engineers than less robotic-intensive sectors do. These industries also employ a higher proportion of installation maintenance and repair workers, due to their need to program, operate and service robots. Surprisingly, production-line workers in these sectors also tend to earn higher wages than less robotic-intensive industries (PwC 2014).

While there is a wealth of knowledge around design for manufacturing, much less is available on design for 3D printing. Additive manufacturing techniques also involves technical challenges, which include setting environmental parameters to prevent shape distortion, optimizing the speed of printing, and adjusting the properties of novel materials. The design know-how needed to successfully develop 3D printing operations is already in Vietnam as Honda inaugurated a sintering workshop to 3D print motorcycle parts in its Vinh Duc plant in 2015. The creation of centers of excellence and training of engineers to develop strong experience in additive manufacturing should be the next step if Vietnam is to strengthen and deploy its 3D printing capabilities to other sectors.

As robotics and additive manufacturing become cheaper and applications widen they will be adopted by more industries, allowing experienced workers from the automotive sector to be redeployed. AM can be redeployed to other industries outside of auto and the potential is huge.

Success will largely depend on reshaping and building a workforce that can exploit these technological advances. The increased demand for more capabilities needed from the design and engineering skills for additive manufacturing will differ from simple assembly or welding—activities that currently dominate the auto industry in Vietnam. Because robotics and additive manufacturing skills can be easily redeployed to other manufacturing industries, investing in developing these skills can benefit most of the manufacturing industries in the country.

Key Outcomes

The renewed emphasis on public transport as the core of the new multimodal mobility model will increase demand for buses, which should create new manufacturing jobs and export opportunities. By 2030, Vietnam will need 38,285 buses in circulation to meet demand, if it were to switch to the proposed model of urban mobility (IPTE 2015). Assuming a standard replacement rate of buses after 12–15 years and that the majority of buses are produced locally, this could translate into 300–500 jobs by 2030.

Further, because the local bus industry is in a position to develop more capabilities beyond assembly, the type of jobs created will be better and wages will be higher. For instance, by successfully integrating into mold making and testing, the local bus industry could pay a wage premium of over 25 percent in relation to wages in the basic activities that are currently being undertaken like interior assembly, seats, and wiring. An intelligent bus system in big cities like Hanoi and Ho Chi Minh City will create an additional, but modest, number of jobs. A bus operations control center with typical responsibilities (coordinating bus operations, responding to mechanical breakdowns, managing on-time performance) could provide an additional 30–40 jobs in each major city.[2]

The biggest potential benefit of switching to a multimodal system will be on the software development side. An ITS system provides many opportunities for local engineers to develop software for bus scheduling, maintenance scheduling, integrated ticketing systems, and real-time passenger information for smartphones, in addition to services needed to integrate third-party software into the public transport system. Further, ITS always need adjustments and upgrades, and so provides opportunities for long-term maintenance services contracts for local firms. In the United States, three occupations with higher than average wages (software developer, hardware developer, and engineer) account for 32 percent of the jobs needed in the ITS industry.

Vietnam could also see the digital transport services ecosystem blossom by developing transport applications. Besides developing software directly linked to transport intelligent systems, local developers will find opportunities to develop smartphone applications that respond to locality-specific transport issues. For instance, if a significant percentage of traffic congestion is directly linked to searching for a parking space, this will provide incentives to develop applications that, relying on sensors installed at each parking space, allow users to use GPS to find empty parking spaces in the city. Again, these skills—and the hardware/infrastructure investments needed to bring these solutions to market—could be transferred to develop services and solutions for other advanced industries like logistics, transport, and health care.

Besides the potential benefits for value added, export, and upgrading in GVCs, the shift from motorcycles and other private vehicles to public transport will help the environment. Public transport has the potential to transport more people than individual cars for a given amount of road space (articulated buses can replace around 100 cars and occupy only 5 percent of the road space needed by the latter) reducing congestion and emissions at the same time. The renewed emphasis on public transport systems will also help reduce travel time and improve accessibility to commercial areas. For instance, it is estimated that the new bus rapid transit system in Ho Chi Minh City will reduce travel time by public transport along the project corridor by a third and increase by 13 percent the number of users that can access the Thu Thiem development area within 45 minutes. Additionally, Ho Chi Minh City's bus rapid transit project will reduce greenhouse gas emissions by 23,000 tons a year relative to a business-as-usual case.

Drivers and Enablers

The deployment of an ITS and associated technologies will require heavy investment in hardware and software. Although hardware investment (in cameras, sensors, radar) must be done before the operational phase, the real new solutions to urban traffic problems will demand even more complex software platforms. For example, the city of Pittsburgh is piloting a new initiative to install a network of smart traffic signals that use radar sensors and cameras to monitor traffic, and sophisticated algorithms to instantly adjust signals based on real-time conditions without human assistance. Each intersection in the pilot is fitted with a computer that formulates a plan based on traffic observations and communicates it to neighboring intersections, and it can instantly adjust to accommodate surges caused by disabled vehicles, crashes, street closures, or event traffic (Pittsburgh Post-Gazette 2014).

The availability of advanced local cloud computing infrastructure and programming capabilities will be key to the functioning of a modern ITS. The pilot described for the city of Pittsburgh operates in real-time, as each control box re-computes its traffic allocation plan and re-communicates projected outflows as frequently as once per second in rolling horizon fashion, but demands heavy technological resources. Vietnam should aim at this opportunity and improve its cloud computing and other ICT infrastructure and by investing heavily in workforce programming skills. The deployment of a modern ITS should be used as a catalyst to create positive spillovers of skills and capabilities into other sectors of the economy.

The multimodal nature of the new mobility model will demand close collaboration between the public and private sectors and academia. Realizing that most local governments do not have the resources or skills to solve the urban mobility problems by themselves, a growing number of cities are entering into partnerships with the private sector to address these issues. For instance, the city of Boston is using real-time data from Waze, the world's largest community-based traffic and navigation app, to improve traffic signal timing and ease congestion (Daily Free Press 2015). In similar fashion, the pilot undertaken by the city of Pittsburgh to deploy a network of high-tech traffic signals was a result of collaboration with Carnegie Mellon University, and this collaboration will likely expand in the future.

The government should create an enabling environment for startup firms that encourages private–public collaboration. There are significant barriers to starting and growing ICT companies in Vietnam, including weak access to finance, poor access to internationally effective managerial talent, limited infrastructure (incubators, accelerators), and a general lack of support and encouragement for private entrepreneurship. By removing barriers to innovation and developing and e-commerce framework that harmonized with global platforms, Vietnam could create regionally and globally competitive firms that can expand to other markets.

Barriers, Threats, and Challenges

The main challenge facing this new model of urban mobility is to convince motorcycle users to switch to public transport as their main mode of transport. Motorcycles provide affordable and flexible door-to-door mobility for the majority of people and previous attempts to curtail the exponential growth of motorcycles in Vietnam have not been successful. However, one of the reasons for that failure is that most cities have relied almost exclusively on controlling vehicle ownership with little focus on managing vehicle use and the factors that affect the decision to adopt one mode of transport. For example, automobile and motorcycle parking is cheap and plentiful in the majority of urban areas in Vietnam (much of it on the city's sidewalks) and most local governments do not enforce ordinances against the use of public spaces for that. Stronger regulation of parking spaces for motorcycles in core urban areas could nudge a share of users to switch to public transport.

The lack of capacity to coordinate among public entities and private partners could have negative effects on a seamless integration of the different transport modes. The change to multimodal urban passenger transport will initially require institutional strengthening of existing institutions, and later the establishment of a public transport committee or a new multimodal passenger transport authority to ensure coordination across modes and public transport services. When there is no single public transport authority for all modes and operators, the overall public transport system is less convenient for travelers due to unnecessary transfers, long walks, multiple fare payments, and so on.

Vietnam will face strong competition from established players and countries trying to carve a niche as ITS software providers. Multinational companies like Volvo and Siemens already have extensive experience with ITS and advanced telematics system for public transport and some, such as Volvo, have the ability to provide a bundles of buses and software systems for public transport. Further, such countries as Malaysia and Singapore offer better environments to develop technology startups and are already investing in green technologies and smart transport solutions. Vietnam has a short window of opportunity to develop basic capacities needed to compete in this area and position itself as a viable provider of ITS software solutions in the region.

Notes

1. http://www.chaocom.com/vietnam-car-cental/cars-for-hire/vietnam-s-automobile -market-update-2.html.
2. By comparison, the Los Angeles Metro's Bus Operations Control Center, the third largest in the United States with more than 2,200 buses in service on an average weekday, is staffed by 15 to 20 on-duty controllers during regular business hours.

Bibliography

Dahiya, Bharat. 2015. "Shifting Focus to Mobility of People." *China Daily Asia Weekly*. February 6–12. https://www.academia.edu/10556084/Shifting_focus_to_mobility_of _people_China_Daily_-_Asia_Weekly.

Daily Free Press. 2015. "Walsh Announces Partnership with Traffic App, Waze." February 19. http://dailyfreepress.com/2015/02/19/walsh-announces-partnership-with-traffic -app-waze/.

IPSI (Institute for Industrial Policy and Strategy). 2015. "Automotive Manufacturing Value Chain in Vietnam." Mimeo, IPSI, Hanoi.

IPTE (Institute of Planning and Transportation Engineering). 2015. "Demand Forecast of Transportation in Vietnam up to 2020 Vision to 2030." Mimeo, IPTE, National University of Civil Engineering, Hanoi.

KUKA Robotics. 2014. "KUKA KR 1000 Titan Assembles Cylinder Blocks at the FAW Group." KUKA Robotics, Gersthofen, Germany. http://www.kuka-robotics.com/usa /en/solutions/solutions_search/L_2014_FAW.htm.

McKinsey. 2014. "A Road Map to the Future for the Auto Industry." *McKinsey Quarterly* October 2014. http://www.mckinsey.com/insights/manufacturing/a_road_map_to _the_future_for_the_auto_industry.

Pittsburgh Post-Gazette. 2014. "City Expands Use of High-Tech Traffic Signals." May 1. http://www.post-gazette.com/news/transportation/2014/05/02/City-expands-use-of -high-tech-traffic-signals/stories/201405020123.

PwC. 2014. "The New Hire: How a New Generation of Robots Is Transforming Manufacturing." http://www.pwc.com/us/en/industrial-products/assets/industrial-robot -trends-in-manufacturing-report.pdf.

Sturgeon, T. 2015. "Vietnam's Current and Future Role in Information and Communications Technology Global Value Chains." Mimeo.

The Economist. 2013. *The Great Powertrain Race*. Special Report from the April 20 Print Edition. http://www.economist.com/news/special-report/21576219-carmakers-are -hedging-their-bets-powering-cars-great-powertrain-race.

Viet Nam News. 2014. "City Air Pollution Causes Major Health Problems." September 22. http://vietnamnews.vn/environment/260424/city-air-pollution-causes-major-health -problems.html#4lhF7J6OxKJqtwxu.97.

Vietnam Investment Review. 2014. "Air Quality Remains a Headache." October 6. http:// www.vir.com.vn/air-quality-remains-a-headache.html.

World Bank. 2011. *Vietnam Urbanization Review*. Washington, DC: World Bank.

CHAPTER 12

Developing Networked Mobility in Vietnam

Guillermo Arenas

Key Takeaways

Vietnam's auto sector is lacking a vision for the future. The transportation sector is under strain, and has driven the government to consider disinvesting from the auto sector instead of seeking out innovative solutions that can improve transport and boost overall economic competitiveness. Nevertheless, opportunities exist. Over the last few decades, rising per capita incomes and increased urbanization have driven reliance on an individual-use model based primarily on motorcycles. However, with Vietnam's high urban population densities and sparse road networks, the individual-use modality is simply incompatible with an efficient mobility system.

The country should develop an intelligent transportation system (ITS) that is multimodal, networked, and based on shared-use mobility. A comprehensive approach based on the entire spectrum of the transport value chain will not only improve urban mobility but provide opportunities for private sector growth, innovation, expansion into new markets, and positive spillovers in areas including health and services.

Challenges Confronted

Motorcycles dominate Vietnam's motor vehicle market. Motorcycle registrations number nearly 50 million, and domestic sales increased from 2.5 million units in 2009 to 3.3 million in 2013. Because demand is strong and growing, a large share of motorcycles is produced domestically in a handful of large assembly plants (dominated by Honda and Yamaha). Local parts content also is significant.

The passenger vehicle segment has the opposite characteristics. Demand is weak, and though the market is protected enough to dampen imports of new and used vehicles, final assembly is fragmented across many mostly foreign-owned and joint-venture plants. Except for labor-intensive wire harnesses, domestic production of intermediate inputs (auto parts) has failed to develop.

Vietnam has three options:

- Move out of the auto-sector global value chains (GVCs) and target different sectors. This is the current strategy of the government. It views the involvement in auto-sector GVCs as a failed experiment and has identified in its recent development priorities other sectors as targets for participating in GVCs, primarily information and communications technology (ICT), agriculture and agribusiness, and tourism.
- Traditional approaches to GVC development. This approach would recommend a rationalization of the passenger vehicle sector along with increased support for the export of motorcycles, key motorcycle parts, and automotive wire harnesses. Supporting industry development and the attraction of global suppliers would be important elements of these policies.
- Taking a forward perspective that accounts for emerging changes in technology and that shifts the emphasis from the narrow view of the auto sector to a wider view, with it becoming an integral component of a broader mobility value chain. The local capabilities in molding of metals (for motorbikes, for tooling, and for mixed-use vehicles) can be used to upgrade in the sector from assembly of passenger cars to the production of minibuses, a segment underrepresented in the wider region.

Solutions Proposed

Two types of solutions are proposed. One targets upgrading (chapter 11). Disruptive innovation also is possible. This chapter proposes the deployment of an ITS and shared-use mobility to reach a double goal: help Vietnam upgrade its participation in the auto sector GVCs and open opportunities in new target sectors (ICT, tourism); and improve urban mobility in Vietnam, and—by reducing in this way the transit time for the population in urban areas—provide a lever for boosting productivity in the economy and a means for improving quality of life for society as a whole. The proposal leads to upgrading in technology, skills, and the environment, and suggests a shift in emphasis to a different market segment in the auto sector (product upgrading), which also has the potential for fostering functional and intersectoral upgrading.

- *Technology:* The deployment of an ITS and associated technologies for shared-use mobility will require sizable investment, especially in platforms for software and in sensors for real-time data gathering.
- *Skills:* Skills acquired in the conception, development, and implementation of software transport solutions and those possibly originating from new opportunities for ancillary services can be redeployed to provide solutions to other industries too, including logistics, transport, tourism, and health care. The expertise gathered by Vietnam's firms in establishing and managing a modern system of urban mobility can become the basis for exporting services of urban mobility management internationally.

- *Environment:* Inducing a shift in the domestic market from motorcycles to mobility via public transport and shared-use vehicles will reduce greenhouse gases (GHGs) and pollutant emissions.
- *Product, functional, and intersectoral upgrading:* This can be obtained by specializing in the production and export of minibuses equipped with innovative ICT technology for shared use and networked mobility.

Lessons to Be Learned

Disruptive change has important demonstration effects. It shows, for example, the need to expand a traditional GVC analysis of the auto-sector value chain into a mobility value chain. It also shows how leapfrogging (as opposed to incremental innovation and imitative strategies in integrating GVCs) can lead to more successful GVC participation models. The role of services, not only as inputs into the economy but as a means of changing the whole way value is created is also illustrated in this chapter. This is often referred to as servicification of the economy.

The chapter suggests the following role for private firms and for the public sector:

- Private firms in manufacturing and private local services providers are at the center of this approach and can either integrate existing GVCs at higher value-added stages, or become lead firms of new GVCs. Manufacturing firms can specialize in the production of minibuses, a market segment underrepresented in the Association of Southeast Asian Nations (ASEAN) region and hence offering export potential and local demand for Vietnam at higher segments of the auto GVCs than assembly. Private firms will be needed to build the physical infrastructure. Service providers are needed to develop software and applications for operationalizing the model and to manage the system (for example, operating the new bus rapid transit corridors). Local service providers will have new market opportunities for delivering new (consumer and business-to-business) services using the urban mobility software platforms and/or for developing and selling—locally and internationally—advisory services on creating and managing similar models of networked mobility.
- The public sector should take a whole value chain approach and implement regulatory changes and incentive systems fostering adoption of the new model. These changes may include parking restrictions, higher taxes for motorcycles/individual passenger cars (and lower for mixed use cars or for the rental car market), and congestion charges to enter designated zones in urban areas. This approach should eliminate distortions in attracting foreign auto-sector producers for local assembly of cars in Vietnam.
- The proposed urban mobility model will depend on willingness and capacity to enter into private–public partnerships, particularly to develop software solutions and platforms, and to design incentive systems. These can be issues in countries with strong central governments, like Vietnam.

Common Lessons and Potential for Replication in Other Countries

This proposal can be replicated in many developing countries that face the same urban transport issues as Vietnam. Encouraging innovation in technologies and the integration of third-party software into government-run transport services provides opportunities for efficiency, growth, and export. There are also three wider lessons, however, notably:

- Effective industrial policy requires a change of approach. It requires a move from sectors to tasks and competencies of comparative advantage. Next, it requires policymakers to identify specific regulatory barriers that may hinder the full potential in these tasks and activities. It also suggests prioritizing the development of skills and technology that can be redeployed to other sectors, and the financing of public goods in education and infrastructure that are informed by a forward looking approach to development in technology and emerging business models. Finally supporting the creation of local markets, in particular for services, and clustering firms in a well-integrated ecosystem may support upgrading and leapfrogging in GVCs. Such an approach to industrial policy likely will be less expensive than traditional approaches.
- A country's biggest problems can be the biggest source of comparative advantage. Managing the domestic urban mobility problems through innovative solutions that are informed by the latest advances in technology, Vietnam can gather valuable expertise, skills, and infrastructure deployable in any country with similar mobility problems. It can also create a domestic market for goods (the mini-bus) which have favorable export prospects at start and a potential that can be enhanced by designing and exporting a solution package.
- Support for gathering of information and data and use of open source systems can encourage upgrading and leapfrogging. Data and information are important assets, as most industries evolve toward an ever more intensive use of big-data infrastructure and content. Interesting datasets and open source ICT systems allow attracting the best technology, skills, and leading expertise in a sector and in a country identifying problems and simulating effects of alternative remedies. These create innovative solutions can become a source of comparative advantage and support exports of high value-added services, goods, and technology.

Current Conditions and Challenges

Supply-Side Considerations

The auto industry in Vietnam is underdeveloped by regional standards and specializes in assembly and low value-added activities. Although multinational companies in the automotive sector entered the market nearly two decades ago, most companies import the majority of parts and components and only perform final assembly in Vietnam to avoid high import tariffs, which can surpass 50 percent (table 12.1). The added value in the passenger car segment is

Table 12.1 Vietnam's Passenger Vehicle Assembly Plants, 2013

Automaker	Brands assembled	Home country of brand(s)	Region	Capacity	Capacity share (%)
Toyota Motor Vietnam	Toyota	Japan	North	36,500	20
General Motors Vietnam	Chevrolet	United States	North	30,000	16
Vietnam Motors	BMW, Chery, Kia, Nissan	Germany; China; Korea, Rep; Japan	North	24,000	13
Ford Vietnam	Ford	United States	North	14,000	8
Honda Vietnam	Honda	Japan	North	10,000	5
VINAMOTOR	Hyundai	Korea, Rep.	North	5,500	3
Duc Phong	Great Wall	China	North	3,000	2
		North Total	North	123,000	67
Truong Hai Automobile	Kia	Korea, Rep.	Center	20,000	11
Vina Mazda	Mazda	Japan	Center	10,000	5
Vinastar Motors	Mitsubishi	Japan	Center	5,000	3
		Center Total	Center	35,000	19
Vietnam Suzuki	Suzuki	Japan	South	12,000	7
Mercedes Benz Vietnam	Daimler Benz	Germany	South	5,500	3
Mekong Auto	Fiat, SsangYong, PMC	Italy; Korea, Rep.; Korea, Dem. People's Rep.	South	5,000	3
Isuzu Vietnam	Isuzu	Japan	South	2,000	1
		South total	South	24,500	13
		Total capacity 2013		182,500	100
		Total sales 2013		127,000	
		Finished vehicle imports, 2013		16,747	
		Estimated average capacity utilization		40%	

Source: Roland Berger 2014 (plants, sales, capacity); UN Comtrade database (imports); authors' estimate (capacity utilization).

achieved in a number of labor-intensive stages including assembly, welding, painting, and attaching bulky items, or in low value-added parts fit for local sourcing, such as tires, batteries, and wire harnesses. The most valuable parts, such as engines, gearboxes, suspensions, and electronics, are imported from branches of parent companies or from foreign suppliers.

Figure 12.1 shows the average compensation per job in the auto sector in Vietnam and the jobs in which its auto sector has traditionally specialized (bars in green).

Economies of scale and regional integration make it difficult for Vietnam to compete in the personal car segment. Auto production in Vietnam is highly fragmented and, as a consequence, most plants do not reach minimum economies of scale. A typical full-scale auto assembly plant produces 200,000–300,000 cars a year; the largest plant in Vietnam has a capacity of less than 40,000 vehicles a year. Further, because the local market for passenger vehicles is small, Vietnam has been unable to develop a successful local industry of parts and components,

Figure 12.1 Vietnam: Average Compensation per Job in the Auto Sector

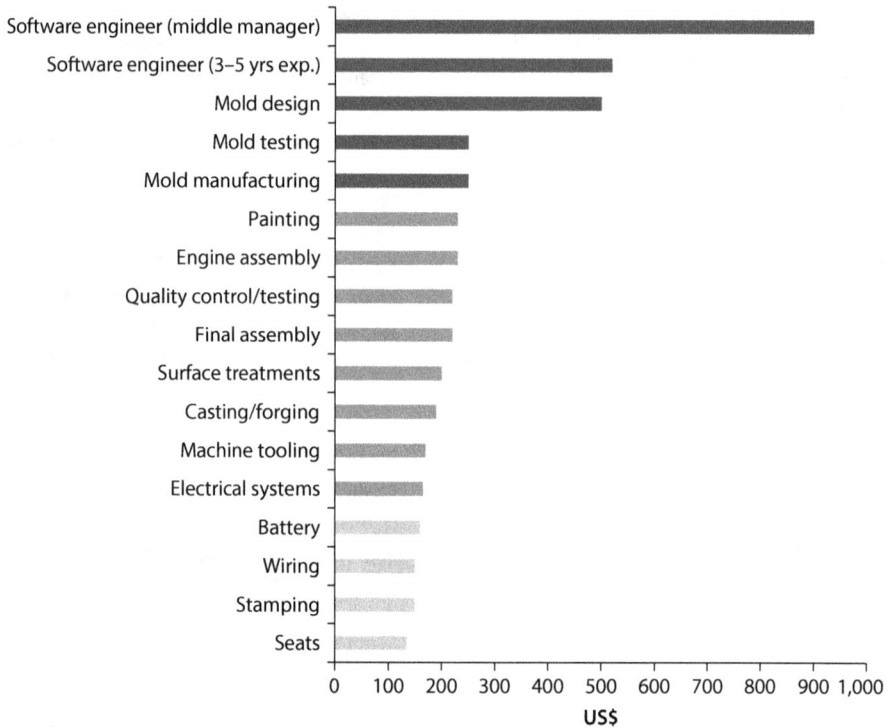

Source: IPSI 2015; Sturgeon 2015.
Note: Jobs in which Vietnam's auto sector has traditionally specialized are shown in green. Other jobs in which some capabilities existing the country are shown in orange. Knowledge-intensive design and tooling jobs and software engineering salaries are shown in blue.

and hence its production costs are estimated at least 20 percent higher than those in neighboring countries. Import tariffs on automobiles between all ASEAN countries will be eliminated by 2018, and Vietnam's auto industry will face fierce competition from more efficient regional auto producers like Indonesia and Thailand.

Vietnam has more opportunities to compete in the commercial vehicle and bus segments in which it has developed some capabilities. The production of medium and heavy commercial vehicles (with a gross vehicle weight over three tons) and buses is much less susceptible to economies of scale. Most major international plants produce 15,000–40,000 medium-size commercial vehicles, and several bus assembly plants remain profitable with production runs of less than 1,000 buses. In contrast to the personal car segment, the local bus and truck industry has developed some capabilities and is manufacturing some parts and components locally with firms expanding into mold design and making the most in-demand parts. Local content in buses and trucks consists of 30 percent engines, gearboxes, and transmission systems and 70 percent of electrical components produced domestically. Truck frames and trunks are produced entirely in Vietnam.

Domestic Demand: Challenges and Needs

Addressing domestic demand is a successful way to build comparative advantage in exports. Vertical specialization within GVCs suggests, for some, that comparative advantage can be won in extremely specialized niches within integrated, globally coordinated value-added chains, overcoming a variety of barriers to network entry, from minimum scale economies in production, to small market size, to underdeveloped national systems of innovation.

We concur with this view, within limits. GVCs open up obvious and profound opportunities for industrial policies that extend beyond openness, institutional reform, and trade facilitation. With fragmentation, peripheral locations have a new ability to integrate more easily with the global core because they can specialize in trade in very specialized tasks (Lanz, Miroudot, and Nordas 2011). They can focus on the export of intermediate goods and services, earning the benefits of trade without the need to develop full-blown domestic industries (Gereffi and Sturgeon 2013). Participation in GVCs also can open conduits for technological learning, process improvements, and product upgrading (Bozorg-Mehri 2015; Humphrey and Schmitz 2002). For evidence we need only to look to the integration of countries like Bangladesh, China, and the Philippines into production networks driven by lead firms based in Europe and the United States (Baldwin 2011). Yet a large and vibrant domestic market is important. It allows countries to reach minimum scale for achieving large-scale production and for building capabilities and skills.

Vietnam has seen rapid motorization due to rising per capita incomes and increased urbanization. Economic reforms have spurred economic growth and quadrupled per capita incomes over the last 15 years. The number of registered motorcycles increased from 1.2 million in 1990 to 37 million in 2013. Motorcycles provide affordable and flexible door-to-door mobility for the majority of Vietnamese citizens and account for close to 80 percent of vehicular trips in the country. With incomes expected to continue rising and an urban population forecast to continue growing, motorization is expected to increase in the short to medium term. Further, Vietnam's per capita income is reaching the threshold after which most countries see a rapid increase in car ownership.

The heavy reliance on motorcycles has negative effects on air quality and traffic safety, so a transition to a different model is necessary. Urban air pollution is a major problem in big cities with deteriorating air quality leading to increased rates of respiratory illness. At peak hours, the concentration level of carbon monoxide in some districts in Hanoi is nine to seven times higher than allowed by Vietnamese standards, and seriously affects health. And because motorcycles offer little protection to drivers, their effects on traffic safety are also grave: in addition to the 6,371 road deaths reported in 2010 (58 percent of which were motorcycle riders), nonfatal road injuries reached the 2 million mark in the same year—a level greater than such larger countries as Nigeria (1.6 million), Russia (1.6 million), and Brazil (1.5 million).

High population densities and sparse road networks in Vietnam's largest cities are, however, incompatible with following the traditional pattern of transitioning from motorcycles to passenger cars as the main mode of transport in urban areas. Urban densities in Vietnam's largest cities are among the world's highest—272 and 150 inhabitants per hectare in Hanoi and Ho Chi Minh City, respectively, compared with 86 in Paris, 62 in London, and 370 in Hong Kong SAR, China. Congestion already is a critical problem as motorcycles, cars, and buses compete for limited road space. At less than 7 percent of the land area in the largest cities, the road network is exceptionally sparse and road expansion is restricted by severely high costs of resettlement (which constitute over 80 percent of the project cost for many city projects). Thus even if a small fraction of current number of trips made by motorcycles were to be replaced by cars, congestion problems would be greatly aggravated.

Concrete Actions

Vietnam needs to switch from focusing on the mobility of vehicles (motorcycles or cars) to mobility of people and adopt a new model that is multimodal and networked if it is to improve urban mobility and create space for GVC upgrading in the automotive sector and in services activities. Mobility should be viewed comprehensively rather than in terms of maximizing the movement of vehicles, and should support the ability of people to make trips by walking, driving, riding a bicycle, using public transit, or any combination of modes of transport. This shift in focus involves placing less emphasis on relieving motorcycle or auto congestion in urban areas and more on expanding and reinforcing mode choice in the same areas. In the former case, the focus is on investing in road and parking infrastructure, in the latter, the focus is on investing in public transport to create a networked and multimodal urban mobility system. Emphasis should be on improving public transport accessibility and connectivity between modes, and on improving coordination with other transport agencies and modal providers.

Vietnam should develop ITSs in its biggest cities. No city in Vietnam has a well-functioning urban transport system, and regular bus services are largely underdeveloped in Hanoi and Ho Chi Minh City. ITSs are a suite of public transport planning, operations management, and customer service applications enabled by advanced ICT. They act to enhance the effectiveness, efficiency, and usability of public transport services. An ITS obtains data from multiple sources—mostly in real time, including sensors, detectors, video cameras, radar, and its own bus fleet—and uses data analytics to enhance day-to-day operations, including service planning and the use of technology to synchronize traffic lights. Several cities around the world are integrating urban passenger transport into ITS.

Shared-use mobility—the shared use of a vehicle, bicycle, or other mode—is an innovative transport solution that should be integrated into the new urban mobility model. It enables users to have short-term access to transport modes on an as-needed basis. Shared-use mobility has had a transformative impact on many global cities by enhancing transport accessibility while reducing ownership of personal automobiles. This can be an important part of multimodal journeys by addressing first- and last-mile connectivity to buses, trains, or other public transit services, fueling the demand for these already established transport modes. The private sector has played a key role in developing shared-use mobility in every country in which it has blossomed: most of the groundbreaking technologies in this field have been developed by entrepreneurs and venture capitalists. Countries that develop such models can benefit from a first-mover advantage and export their solutions internationally.

The key to improving urban mobility is to get the various travel mechanisms to work in a coordinated manner. Multimodal integration is challenging because, due to shifts in trip types and operators, different systems and software must work seamlessly with each other through adding new functionality, or at least to allow for problems to be detected and resolved promptly. As mobility apps continue to improve urban transport, there will be a need for service components to design, operate, and monitor these systems.

The expanded value chain of such an urban mobility model offers greater opportunities for GVC participation at the high value-added end of the chain. Figure 12.2 shows the traditional auto value chain, with the segments in which Vietnam is active in dark blue.

Figure 12.3 maps out the segments that Vietnam could occupy in an expanded mobility value chain, given its capabilities. These include upgrading in manufacturing and post-assembly activities. The average compensation per job (see figure 12.1) for different professions suggests that the gain for Vietnamese workers could be steep, with a software engineer earning almost nine times more than an average worker in the current Vietnamese auto sector.

Figure 12.2 Traditional Auto Value Chain

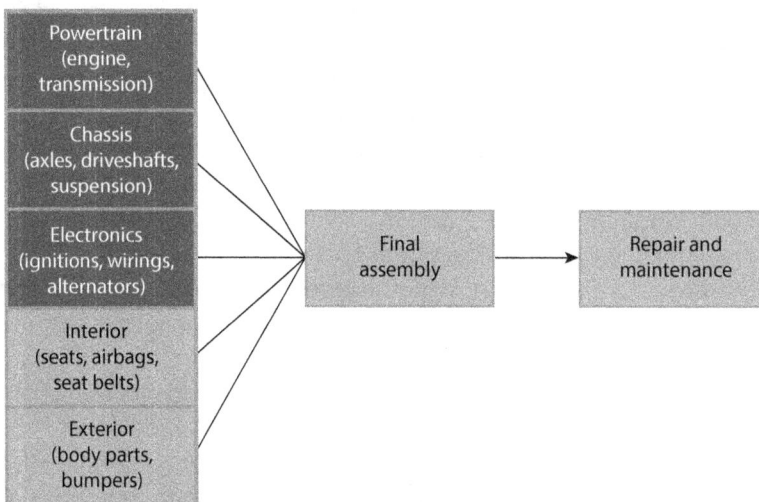

Figure 12.3 Expanded Urban Mobility Value Chain

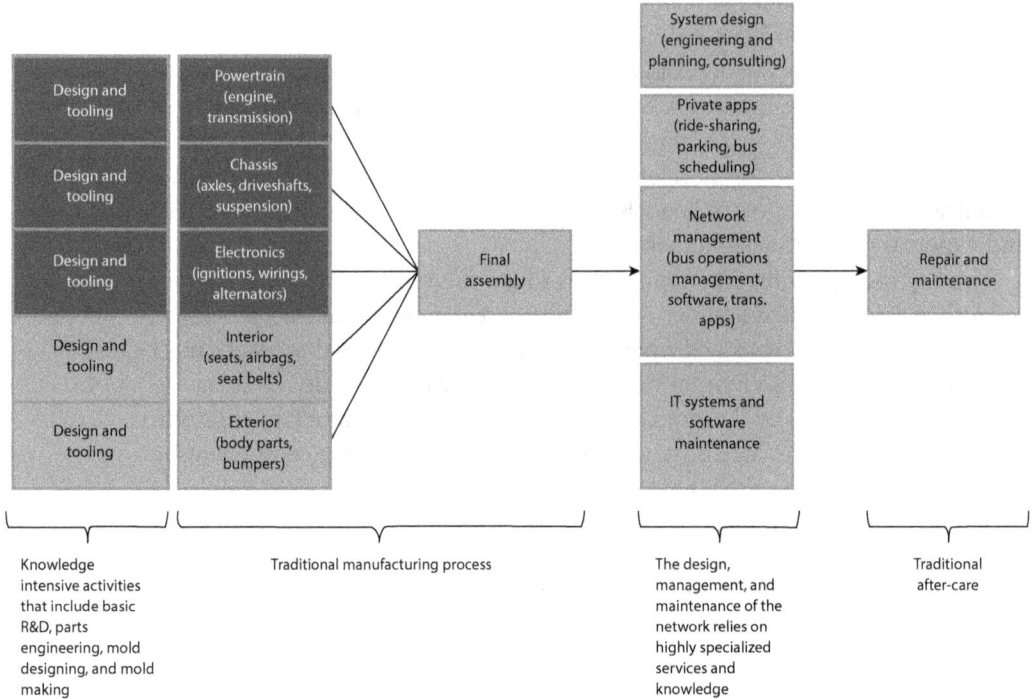

Key Outcomes

The renewed emphasis on public transport as the core of the new mobility model will increase demand for buses, which could create new manufacturing jobs and export opportunities. By 2030, Vietnam will need 38,285 buses in circulation to meet demand, if it were to switch to the proposed model of urban mobility (IPTE 2015). Assuming a standard replacement rate of buses of 12–15 years and that the majority of buses are produced locally, this could translate into between 300 and 500 jobs by 2030. Further, because the local bus industry is in a position to develop more capabilities beyond assembly, the type of jobs created will be better and wages will be higher. For instance, by successfully integrating into mold making and testing, the local bus industry could pay a wage premium of over 25 percent in relation to wages in the basic activities that are currently being undertaken like interior assembly, seats and wiring. On the other hand, the operation of an intelligent bus system in big cities like Hanoi and Ho Chi Minh City will also create an additional—although modest—number of jobs. A bus operations control center with typical responsibilities (coordinating bus operations, responding to mechanical breakdowns, managing on-time performance, among others) could provide an additional 30–40 jobs per major city in which it is implemented.

The biggest potential benefit of switching to a multimodal system will be on the software development side. An ITS system like the one proposed provides plenty of opportunities for local engineers to develop software for bus scheduling, maintenance scheduling, integrated ticketing systems, and Real-Time Passenger Information (RTPI) for smart phones, in addition to services needed to integrate third-party software into the public transport system. Further, an ITS always needs adjustment, enhancements, and upgrades and provides opportunities for long-term maintenance services contracts for local firms. In the United States, three occupations with higher-than-average wages (software developer, hardware developer, and engineer) account for 32 percent of the jobs needed in the ITS industry.

Vietnam could also see the digital transport services ecosystem expand through the development of transport applications. Besides developing software directly linked to transport intelligent systems, local developers will find opportunities to develop smart phone applications that respond to locality-specific transport issues. For instance, if a significant percentage of traffic congestion is directly linked to searching for a parking space, this will provide incentives to develop applications that, relying on sensors installed at each parking space, allow users to use GPS to find empty parking spaces in the city. Again, these skills—and the hardware/infrastructure investments needed to bring these solutions to market—could be transferred to develop services and solutions for other advanced industries like logistics, transport, and health care.

Besides the potential benefits for value added, export, and upgrading in GVCs, the shift from motorcycles and other private vehicles to public transport will help the environment too. It will likely reduce road congestion and pollution in urban areas. Public transport has the potential to transport more people than individual cars for a given amount of road space (articulated buses can replace around 100 cars and occupy only 5 percent of the road space needed by the latter) reducing congestion and emissions at the same time. The renewed emphasis on public transport systems will also help reduce travel time and improve accessibility to commercial areas. For instance, it is estimated that the new bus rapid transit system in Ho Chi Minh City will reduce travel time for public transport along the project corridor by a third and increase by 13 percent the number of users that can access the Thu Thiem development area within 45 minutes—creating more opportunities for economic development along the corridor. Additionally, Ho Chi Minh City's bus rapid transit project will reduce GHG emissions by 23,000 tons/year compared to a business as usual case and reduce pollution in the affected areas. This is an important outcome after a recent report from the Ministry of Transport revealed that 8.1 million patients spend an estimated $137.7 million each year on examinations and treatment for respiratory diseases in Hanoi and Ho Chi Minh City alone.

Drivers and Enablers

The deployment of an ITS and associated technologies will require heavy investment to acquire the necessary software and hardware needed to put the system into place. Although a significant investment in hardware (cameras, sensors, radar, and so on) must be done before the operational phase, the real new solutions to urban traffic problems will demand even more complex software platforms.

For example, the city of Pittsburgh is piloting a new initiative to install a network of smart traffic signals that use radar sensors and cameras to monitor traffic, and sophisticated algorithms to instantly adjust signals based on real-time conditions without human assistance to minimize wait time for drivers. Each intersection is fitted with a computer that formulates a plan based on traffic observations and communicates it to neighboring intersections and it can instantly adjust to accommodate surges caused by disabled vehicles, crashes, street closures, or event traffic.

The availability of advanced local cloud computing infrastructure and programming capabilities will be key to the functioning of a modern ITS. The pilot described for the city of Pittsburgh operates in real-time, as each control box re-computes its traffic allocation plan and re-communicates projected outflows as frequently as once per second in rolling horizon fashion. This enables both effective operation and responsiveness to sudden changes in traffic conditions but demands a significant technological resources. Vietnam should use this opportunity to improve its cloud computing and other ICT infrastructure and invest heavily in the development of workforce programming skills. The deployment of a modern ITS should be used as a catalyst to create positive spillovers of skills and capabilities into other sectors of the economy.

The multimodal nature of the new mobility model will demand close collaboration between the public and private sectors and academia. Realizing that most local governments do not have the resources or skills to solve the urban mobility problems by themselves, a growing number of cities are entering into partnerships with the private sector to address these issues. For instance, the city of Boston is using real-time data from Waze, the world's largest community-based traffic and navigation app, to improve traffic signal timing and ease congestion. It is expected that this partnership will help diminish traffic jams and allow reported incident data to go straight to city officials who can deal with such occurrences. In similar fashion, the pilot undertaken by the city of Pittsburgh to deploy a network of high-tech traffic signals was a result of collaboration with Carnegie Mellon University, and this collaboration will likely expand in the future.

The government of Vietnam should create an enabling environment for startup firms that encourages private-public collaboration. There are significant barriers to starting and growing ICT companies in Vietnam, including limited access to finance, limited access to internationally effective managerial talent, limited infrastructure (that is, incubators and accelerators), and a general lack of support and encouragement for private entrepreneurship. By removing barriers to innovation and developing an e-commerce framework harmonized with global platforms, Vietnam could create regionally and globally competitive firms that can expand to other markets.

Barriers, Threats, and Challenges

The main challenge facing this new model of urban mobility is to convince motorcycle users to switch to public transport as their main mode of transport. Motorcycles provide affordable and flexible door-to-door mobility for the majority of people, and previous attempts to curtail the exponential growth of motorcycles in Vietnam have not been successful. However, one of the reasons for that failure is that most cities have relied almost exclusively on controlling vehicle ownership with little focus on managing vehicle use and the factors that affect the decision to adopt one mode of transport over the other. For example, automobile and motorcycle parking is cheap and plentiful in the majority of urban areas in Vietnam (much of it on the city's sidewalks) and most local governments do not enforce ordinances against the use of public spaces for those purposes. Stronger regulation of parking spaces for motorcycles in core urban areas could nudge a significant share of users to switch to public transport as their main transport modality.

The lack of capacity and ability to coordinate between several public entities and private partners could have negative effects on a seamless integration of the different transport modes. The change to multimodal urban passenger transport will require institutional strengthening of existing institutions and the establishment of a public transport committee or a new multimodal passenger transport authority to ensure the coordination across modes and public transport services. When no single public transport authority for all modes and operators is available, the overall public transport system is less convenient for travelers as a result of unnecessary transfers, long walks, multiple fare payments using different mediums, and so on.

Vietnam will face strong competition from established players and countries trying to carve a niche as ITS software providers. Multinational companies like Volvo and Siemens already have extensive experience with ITS and advanced telematics system for public transport and some, like Volvo, have the ability to provide a bundles of buses and software systems for public transport. Further, countries like Malaysia and Singapore offer better environments to develop technology startups and are already investing in green technologies and smart transport solutions. Vietnam has a short window of opportunity to develop basic capacities needed to compete in this area and position itself as a viable provider of ITS software solutions.

Bibliography

Baldwin, Richard. 2011. "Trade and Industrialisation after Globalisation's 2nd Unbundling: How Building and Joining a Supply Chain Are Different and Why It Matters." Working Paper 17716, National Bureau of Economic Research, Cambridge, MA. http://www.nber.org/papers/w17716.

Bozorg-Mehri, Darius. 2015. "The Role of Engineering Consultancies as Network-Centred Actors to Develop Indigenous, Technical Capacity: The Case of Iran's Automotive Industry." *Socio-Economic Review* 13 (4): 747–69.

Gereffi, G., and T. Sturgeon. 2013. "Global Value Chains and Industrial Policy: The Role of Emerging Economies." In *Global Value Chains in a Changing World*, edited by Deborah K. Elms and Patrick Low. Geneva: World Trade Organization.

Humphrey, J., and H. Schmitz. 2002. "How Does Insertion in Global Value Chains Affect Upgrading in Industrial Clusters?" *Regional Studies* 36 (9): 1017–27.

IPSI (Institute for Industrial Policy and Strategy). 2015. "Automotive Manufacturing Value Chain in Vietnam." Mimeo, IPSI, Hanoi.

IPTE (Institute of Planning and Transportation Engineering). 2015. "Demand Forecast of Transportation in Vietnam up to 2020 Vision to 2030." Mimeo, IPTE, National University of Civil Engineering, Hanoi.

Lanz, R., S. Miroudot, and H. Nordas. 2011. "Trade in Tasks." OECD Policy Working Papers 117, Organisation for Economic Co-operation and Development, Paris.

Roland Berger. 2015. "Automotive Value Chain Global Outlook: Study on Future Automotive Growth Markets." Mimeo.

Sturgeon, T. 2015. "Vietnam's Current and Future Role in Information and Communications Technology Global Value Chains." Mimeo.

United Nations. 2016. "UN Comtrade (database)." http://comtrade.un.org/.

PART 3

Operationalizing the GVC Agenda in Vietnam

CHAPTER 13

Operationalizing the GVC Agenda in Vietnam

Richard Record and Daria Taglioni

This volume presents a large amount of information and analysis of the current state of Vietnam's participation in global value chains (GVCs). Some chapters aim to quantify the costs and benefits of Vietnam's participation in GVCs, unpack the key supply-side constraints to better integration, and dig deeper into some of the key GVCs where Vietnam is active and has ambitions to capture a larger share of value added.

Vietnam has benefited from engagement in GVCs that have provided significant investment and lifted economic growth and job numbers. This process has been one of the key drivers of the country's success in sustaining high growth over close to 30 years. More remarkable perhaps, Vietnam has achieved growth with equity rather than at the cost of it, unlike many other fast-growing developing economies. In that time, the living standards of Vietnam's youthful population have been transformed. Steep reductions in the poverty rate have been achieved, and the country has graduated from low-income to lower-middle–income country status.

Yet questions remain as to whether the current growth model can be sustained in the years ahead:

- Are there diminishing returns from the current labor-intensive mode of GVC participation?
- Might the environment and social costs of active GVC participation begin to weigh unfavorably against the benefits of investment and job creation?
- Are there risks from a heavy reliance on trading in tasks with foreign players, with limited value addition generated by domestic firms?
- Might a different approach be necessary to take Vietnam to the next, and more challenging, stage of its development pathway as the country looks to middle-income status by 2035?
- How can Vietnam avoid falling into some of the development traps into which other countries have slipped?
- What role do the myriad trade agreements that Vietnam has signed play in this process?

This chapter builds on the earlier chapters of the volume and presents five key reform and investment priorities for Vietnam, in cooperation with its development partners, as the country looks to its future engagement with GVCs. It also provides suggestions for concrete policy actions that can constitute a starting point for operationalizing the GVC agenda in Vietnam.

Five Key Reform and Investment Priorities

Five key priorities are identified for Vietnam's future engagement in GVCs.

Foster the Domestic Private Sector in GVCs by Improving the Drivers of Investment and by Leveling the Playing Field

Development traps are invariably about productivity stagnation, and productivity is precisely where Vietnam's performance is mixed. The rate of growth in labor productivity (output per worker) has been declining since the late 1990s, explained by a sharp decline in total factor productivity growth. The decline in labor productivity growth has been seen across most sectors, but mainly in mining, construction, public utilities, finance, and real estate, where state-owned enterprises (SOEs) have retained their dominant role. Thus far it has been easy to overlook these trends due to rapid labor force growth and capital accumulation. But in the next development phase, each of these factors is expected to weaken sufficiently to expose economic growth to weaknesses in underlying productivity trends.

The main reason for the drop in productivity growth is especially worrisome. Steady erosion in the productivity growth of the domestic private sector—universally viewed as the main engine of future growth—has ensured that it is now just as inefficient on average as the state sector. Why? Domestic private firms are overwhelmingly small, which prevents productivity gains from scale economies, specialization, and innovation—ingredients for sustained long-term growth. Moreover, small firms have become increasingly capital intensive, which—without scale economies—has led to a sharp decline in their capital productivity. The few large domestic firms are even more unproductive than the smaller ones. This reflects their short-term view on investment and profits and their rising concentration of land and capital assets in construction, real estate, and banking and finance, for example. Such sectors show some of the country's lowest levels and growth rates of productivity.

Foreign-invested firms have expanded their presence and led rapid growth in exports. Recently signed trade agreements will further enhance Vietnam's attractiveness as a foreign direct investment (FDI) destination. FDI inflows are welcome as they create additional employment opportunities for Vietnam's young and growing population. But links to domestic firms have been lacking in key sectors, impeding productivity-enhancing transfers of technology and management practices. This suggests that domestic companies are unable to compete in the current business environment and provide inputs at a quality and quantity demanded by multinational companies.

Reviving productivity growth is imperative if Vietnam is to meet its ambitious income objectives for 2035. The reform agenda will be demanding, given that the productivity-growth decline is widespread. Focus is needed in three areas.

First, Vietnam needs to create an enabling environment for a more productive and competitive domestic private sector. This will require the microeconomic foundations of the market economy to be strengthened, mainly property rights protection and competition policy enforcement. Correcting distortions in the factor markets—capital and land markets primarily—also will be important. For the most part, factor markets are restrictive, underdeveloped, overly controlled, and managed by the state.

Second is the need for a comprehensive overhaul of the SOE sector to level the playing field. Increased attention is needed to reduce the number of enterprises under majority state control. The government should issue a clear SOE ownership policy that focuses on raising the value of state capital (barring exceptional cases). It should be enforced by obligating the SOEs to face direct market-competition pressures and hard budget constraints. SOEs should also uphold global standards on reporting requirements and be insulated from bureaucratic interference. The policy should also delineate and streamline ownership and regulatory responsibilities within the government. Staffing the SOEs with competent professional managers and board members is needed as well.

Third, it is necessary to enable domestic firms to increase productivity and profitably participate in GVCs in key sectors. Addressing the cross-cutting issues of strengthening the modern services sector—an important input for manufacturing production—should be a key focus of the reforms. It should encompass improving the connection of supply-chain centers within Vietnam and between the country and its trading partners.

Strengthen Vietnam's GVC Integration and Economic Upgrading by Promoting Servicification, and by Shifting the Goals of Industrial Policy Toward a Focus on Higher-Value Specialization within GVCs

Economic upgrading is at the heart of Vietnam's efforts to capture a greater share of domestic value added along key GVCs in which the country participates. However, the issue is not one of picking the right firms or industries for the next 20 years, but rather putting in place structures, institutions, and infrastructure that create a vibrant private sector economy in which resources can flow quickly toward efficient and competitive firms.

In the past, Vietnam successfully leveraged external trade agreements to motivate and lock in difficult reforms. In its earlier reform phases, the bilateral trade agreement with the United States, followed by accession to the World Trade Organization (WTO), were key to the process of transition from state to market. The desire to benefit from improved market access, attract increased FDI, along with the rigor of precommitted obligations, helped add discipline and push through challenging reforms, particularly on the scope of activities by SOEs and on services restrictions.

Vietnam at a Crossroads · http://dx.doi.org/10.1596/978-1-4648-0996-5

Thus Vietnam's participation in large preferential trade agreements such as the European Union–Vietnam Free Trade Agreement (EVFTA), the Regional Comprehensive Economic Partnership (RCEP), and the Trans-Pacific Partnership (TPP) is timely (box 13.1), potentially offering new external drivers of reforms in new and more challenging areas, and helping the country set the next phase of

---

**Box 13.1 Vietnam's Participation in the Trans-Pacific Partnership:
What Happens Next?**

After more than five years of negotiations, the Trans-Pacific Partnership (TPP) was concluded in October 2015. The TPP brings together 12 prospective members, including Australia, Brunei Darussalam, Canada, Chile, Japan, Malaysia, Mexico, New Zealand, Peru, Singapore, and the United States, along with Vietnam itself. The combined GDP of the TPP market is equal to about 40 percent of world GDP and 30 percent of world trade. Vietnam has strong trade and investment links with TPP members, which accounts for 38.8 percent of exports, 22.2 percent of imports, and 38.3 percent of the FDI stock.

The TPP was expected to generate considerable benefits for Vietnam in terms of trade, investment, growth, and job creation. Among the current TPP signatories, Vietnam—as the economy with the lowest per-capita GDP—has unique comparative advantages, in particular in labor-intensive manufacturing and in sectors that are currently subject to high tariffs, such as textiles and garments (where the workforce is also highly feminized). Estimates suggested that the TPP could add as much as 8 percent to Vietnam's GDP, 17 percent to its real exports, and 12 percent to its capital stock over twenty years.

However, entry into force requires ratification by the United States, which—with the election of a new administration and subsequent withdrawl from the TPP in January 2017—now looks to be highly unlikely. But, even without ratification, much of the reform agenda set out in the TPP will still need to be implemented by Vietnam. This is because of both the over-lapping nature of Vietnam's trade commitments (particularly EVFTA and RCEP) as well as the clear need for second-generation reforms to boost domestic productivity and competitive-ness. In addition, the process of negotiating the TPP has improved understanding among Vietnam's policymakers on the need to reduce barriers to services trade, simplify nontariff measures, improve enforcement of intellectual property rights, and address the role of state-owned enterprises in markets. While improved market access would have provided an addi-tional impetus to these reforms, they remain both beneficial and necessary in their own right.

And the TPP has set a new standard in FTAs that will almost certainly be emulated in future agreements. Regardless of the prospects for the TPP, Vietnam will continue to engage with the multilateral trading system and seek to enter into new FTAs to both improve market access and stimulate reforms. The TPP is recognized as a "21st century" agreement, and it is expected that future FTAs will similarly include broad commitments beyond tariffs in areas such as NTMs, labor and environmental standards, reform of SOEs, and transparency of government procure-ment, to name a few.

---

reforms to liberalize factor markets. Vietnam was expected to benefit significantly from the TPP in terms of improved market access. A new administration in the United States now means that it is unlikely that the TPP will enter into force in its current form. However, much of the TPP agenda remains relevant, and reforms in areas such as intellectual property rights, worker rights, and environmental protection, that would have been necessary for the TPP, have value of their own, even in the absence of the TPP. Furthermore, similar commitments will need to be made as other FTAs are expected to follow a pattern similar to the TPP in terms of standard and comprehensiveness.

While the use of preferential trade agreements can play a driving role, it is not a guarantee for upgrading and strengthening GVC performance. In particular, complex standards and complicated rules of origin can make it hard for domestic firms to make use of preferential market access. Whether the agreements lock in the status quo—that is, foster Vietnam's current comparative advantage in low value-added processes—or promote a dynamic transition to more sophisticated tasks will depend on the accompanying policy initiatives at the domestic level.

The policies and programs of countries and multilateral and domestic institutions set the context for corporate decision-making, and we have seen an evolution in the form and effects of industrial policy along with the evolution of the business networks that make up GVCs. While sectors are different and must be analyzed individually, as they are in depth in part 2, there are cross-cutting issues, parallel trends, and shared policy dilemmas that can be usefully drawn out. While the Đổi Mới reforms to create a socialist-oriented market economy initiated in 1986 were aimed at reducing barriers to internal trade, successful upgrading will very likely consist of some combination of foreign and domestic technological, managerial, and financial resources, with new opportunities opened and constrained by the interplay of information and communications technology (ICT) and GVCs. Full-blown, vertically integrated, and nationally bounded industrial sectors belong to a developmental era that passed some time ago. Shifting the goals of industrial policy toward upgrading in GVCs will now be key.

Facilitate GVC Participation in Sustainable Development by Promoting Social Upgrading and Cohesion through Skills Development

Much of Vietnam's GVCs engagement has been around labor-intensive manufacturing, especially garments and footwear. Achieving higher levels of productivity and growing the level of domestic value added in these GVCs will require greater upgrading and investment in workforce skills. This is essential both from a productivity and equity perspective. In fact, effective protection of labor standards increasingly is a prerequisite for accessing premium buyers in GVCs. Participation in programs such as Better Work Vietnam can help domestic suppliers demonstrate compliance with basic labor standards with external verification. But although Vietnam has labor regulations in place, it must uprate implementation and enforcement.

While Vietnam performs well on cross-country measures of basic educational performance such as foundational numeracy and literacy, the education system is in general poorly suited to a modern international business environment that places an increasingly large premium on higher skills, especially in services. Further efforts are needed therefore to target supply-side factors, including not only human capital, technical skills, and soft skills, but also the infrastructure for providing modern services.

In manufacturing, it is similarly important for Vietnam to develop skills that will enable greater participation in higher value-added segments of GVCs. Workforce and educational needs, particularly related to functional upgrading strategies, will need improvement. Vietnam also will need to invest in educational programs that train future industry workers to adapt to global sectoral trends.

To develop software and ICT-enabled services, skills-based capacity building will also need to be prioritized. Foreign language skills, managerial skills, and technical training programs will need to be enhanced.

Focus on Building Domestic Capacity, Supported by Quality Regulations and Institutions

Vietnam needs a robust modern services sector for continued success in leveraging external opportunities. This is an area where the country lags behind competitors. Modern services such as finance, insurance, telecommunications, and transport and logistics are critical inputs for manufacturing exports. Also, direct service exports offer the opportunity to diversify exports. If Vietnam can develop its human capital with its ICT infrastructure and connectivity, it can become competitive in information technology–enabled sectors. These include design services, software and programming, and business and professional services. Finance is another sector that needs attention. Lack of access to early-stage funding—and of financing (loans or equity)—is a crucial constraint in any dynamic entrepreneurial startup ecosystem.

Vietnam's foreign investment regime recognizes three categories of sectors. Some are prohibited, while others are conditional—meaning screening procedures are in place—either for all investors or just for foreign investors. A raft of services sector investments fall under the conditional category. It will be important to rationalize this list to provide a level playing field for all investors, domestic and foreign. Similarly, persistent foreign ownership limitations could be reconsidered. FDI has been a major growth engine in Vietnam. As development intensifies in the next two decades, the country will experience a critical need for capital deepening. Because local capital markets are small and underdeveloped, they will continue relying on foreign capital.

Similarly, dispute resolution is an important issue. Investors, wary of the legal system, often specify dispute settlement by arbitration in other jurisdictions such as Singapore. The increasing complexity of services sector transactions and linkages to manufacturing make it important to reinforce the rule of law and contract enforcement. GVCs rely on complex webs of contracts among participating firms, so contract enforcement is important for joining—and especially moving up—higher value-added chains.

ICT-enabled services in such sectors as business and professional services (and information technology services, such as programming) represent future potential. Market players, including India and the Philippines, have demonstrated that business process outsourcing, which relies on a strong ICT framework, can be a major source of employment and economic activity. ICT will have an increasingly transformative role in countries' development. ICT, ICT-enabled technologies and services, and ICT-powered products will play a key role in nearly every industry in the coming years.

The innovative power of ICT already is visible, but the potential of this technology is still emerging. ICT-transformed processes and products are networked and autonomous so that connected factories, connected vehicles, and connected inputs increasingly will interact in systems where robotic control is taking over decision-making. This leads to manufacturing, agricultural production systems, transport systems, products, and producer and consumer services that are not only intelligent but far more efficient than traditional versions.

This gain is because of the networked nature of ICT-driven systems, processes, and products and the tendency to create a strong gravitational effect around few dominant de facto global standards and few global actors (brands, suppliers, platform leaders, and buyers). The increasing ubiquity and global coverage that digital technologies afford generate new disruptive business models that can be deployed globally and controlled remotely from single locations. Smaller, non-integrated players are sidelined more easily while networked players can leverage the production network for new product development, systems integration, and provision of value-added services, which has three implications.

First, digital systems, processes, and products will increasingly transcend individual factories, firms, and national boundaries, and will require unprecedented levels of international cooperation and regulation. Second, they will require capabilities distributed across the world. Finally, as such systems, processes, and products increasingly are networked and connected to cloud computing–based big data processes for real-time and continuous analysis, feedback, and improvement, and as the scale of operations is so large, and their functioning enhanced so much by agglomeration effects, their effective deployment must have global scale.

For enhancing competitiveness in GVCs and in the ICT-powered economy, Vietnam will need to develop its firms' capabilities and its human capital through technical skill acquisition and strong soft skills (managerial, foreign-language skills, and so on).

The country has already made progress in reducing barriers to establishing skilled personnel and individual services. Once implemented, the already ratified ASEAN Mutual Recognition Arrangements for professional services, for example, will help facilitate the movement of talent into the country, which will be instrumental in strengthening firms' capabilities. As in goods sectors, services are outsourced based on sophisticated contractual arrangements. This means that areas such as contract enforcement and the rule of law are again important foundational areas.

The deep trade agreements with the European Union, Japan, and the United States are another welcome step. Such agreements will allow faster access to innovation from their knowledge clusters. New technologies, processes, and product areas require a fair amount of de-codification and (re)-codification (of new processes), and so most arise from existing knowledge clusters where the pool of skills and support functions is deep and broad. This requirement also implies that such clusters are natural standard-setting bodies. Hence preferential access to the large pools of knowledge clusters in North America, Europe, and Japan can be a source of competitiveness for Vietnamese firms.

Deeper efforts to reform Vietnam's business environment will also be required. These include the streamlining of border procedures and making them more transparent and predictable. Similarly important will be efforts to limit barriers to an effective startup ecosystem by improving access to capital, accelerators, and incubators, and the ability to do business either as diaspora returnees or resident nationals. Reducing corruption by improving vendor selection transparency for government contracts, streamlining the procurement processes, equalizing incentives between local and foreign-invested bidders, and strengthening intellectual property rights should also be areas of focus.

Close the Connectivity Gap with Peer Countries in Hard and Soft Infrastructure

As Vietnam integrates more fully and profitably with GVCs, it must also boost its connectivity. Firms in value chains need to be able to move goods within Vietnam and across its borders cost-effectively and reliably, so as to keep inventory carrying costs low and to comply with the strict requirements of lead firms for on-time delivery. Connectivity has three key attributes, all requiring policy attention.

First, efforts will be required to improve institutional connectivity. This is the software side of things and includes trade facilitation, structural and regulatory reforms, and transport and logistics facilitation. Key bottlenecks include the hundreds of complicated non-customs regulations permitting across-the-border trade activities. These are granted and managed by a raft of state management agencies. The overall regulatory approach is piecemeal, at times overlapping and contradictory. Vietnam's local logistics service suppliers, while numerous, do not always have the capacity to handle complex multimodal transactions. Health, sanitary, and phytosanitary regulations also are rated below those of peers.

Second, further investments are needed in physical connectivity to upgrade the hardware, such as ports, airports, road and rail links, and ICT infrastructure. A well-connected country is one with abundant and high-quality physical infrastructure, especially international gateways and multimodal interfaces. Hardware also includes energy, which is vital to the continued success of manufacturing firms and can be traded among neighboring countries. Current transport modes are overloaded in and around the major economic clusters and do not connect well to each other or to major trade gateways. This reflects lack of coordination to develop economic zones and transport corridors. Key issues include poor road conditions and greatly underdeveloped freight-rail and inland-waterway infrastructure. Another key issue includes supply–demand mismatches in deepwater maritime port infrastructure. Lingering shortcomings in connective infrastructure explain why the country faces elevated logistics costs and poor reliability. From a trade competitiveness angle, freight and logistics are not yet key drivers of direct investment, foreign or domestic.

Third, it is necessary to facilitate greater people-to-people connectivity. This attribute refers to ease of movement of people across borders for service provision, education, and tourism. Vietnam has abolished caps on the number of foreign workers that foreign firms can hire. It also has introduced new procedures for obtaining work permits for them. Managers, executives, and specialists who enter the country as intracorporate transferees are allowed to stay for an initial three years, with the possibility of extension, subject to receiving a work permit. But there is wide scope to better meet global businesses' needs to bring in specialist international staff, as any restrictions affect Vietnam's attractiveness as a production destination.

When building infrastructure for better connectivity (physical, digital, and institutional), it is vital to ensure that the digital revolution does not create a wedge between the better networked (countries, individuals, firms) and the non-networked. Such infrastructure connects Vietnam with global hubs of technology and larger cities with smaller centers and rural areas, opens opportunities, and ensures that the development potential of GVCs reaches the largest share of Vietnam's population. Without it, the matching of Vietnamese technologies, services, and talents with global teams may lead to negative distributional effects domestically, including income shifts from nonparticipants and increasing wedges between the remuneration of production functions and those of services, innovation, and core R&D functions.

Concrete Policy Actions: An Agenda for Making the Most of Vietnam's Engagement in GVCs

Operationalizing the GVC agenda for Vietnam will require determined efforts by the government, working closely with its development partners, including the World Bank Group. Jointly, this requires linking Vietnam's GVC priorities with instrumental policies, understanding and addressing horizontal bottlenecks and impediments within and among sectors, ensuring an enabling domestic regulatory environment particularly for services, leveraging regional trade agreements, appropriately sequencing reforms corresponding to agenda priorities, and identifying opportunities for innovative change within sectors of concern, policy, and international agreements.

The government of Vietnam is best positioned to set the direction, objectives, targets, and timeframes of actions, establish and enforce necessary regulations, facilitate inter- and intragovernmental relationships, and provide resource capacity to activate the GVC agenda including public sector investments.

Development partners such as the World Bank Group can support Vietnam in its efforts to upgrade the country's participation in GVCs. This can include facilitating access by policymakers and private sector stakeholders to global knowledge on GVC approaches, opportunities, and comparative experiences of other countries at different levels of development. Technical assistance can be deployed to provide the necessary handholding in guiding stakeholders through an upgrading process and in undertaking reforms. There is also scope for investment lending to finance hard or soft infrastructure. Where policy and institutional bottlenecks are the binding constraints, policy-based lending can help build a consensus on difficult but beneficial reform initiatives.

Such an ambitious endeavor requires a solid package of horizontal reforms and vertical initiatives in specific sectors. Moreover, actions are not to be implemented in isolation. Success can be achieved only by a comprehensive agenda that cuts across the many dimensions discussed in the action tables at the end of chapter 1.

Environmental Benefits Statement

The World Bank Group is committed to reducing its environmental footprint. In support of this commitment, we leverage electronic publishing options and print-on-demand technology, which is located in regional hubs worldwide. Together, these initiatives enable print runs to be lowered and shipping distances decreased, resulting in reduced paper consumption, chemical use, greenhouse gas emissions, and waste.

We follow the recommended standards for paper use set by the Green Press Initiative. The majority of our books are printed on Forest Stewardship Council (FSC)–certified paper, with nearly all containing 50–100 percent recycled content. The recycled fiber in our book paper is either unbleached or bleached using totally chlorine-free (TCF), processed chlorine-free (PCF), or enhanced elemental chlorine-free (EECF) processes.

More information about the Bank's environmental philosophy can be found at http://www.worldbank.org/corporateresponsibility.

green
press
INITIATIVE

www.ingramcontent.com/pod-product-compliance
Lightning Source LLC
Chambersburg PA
CBHW071957220326
41599CB00032BA/6268